ZBrush® Professional Tips and Techniques

ZBrush® Professional Tips and Techniques

Paul Gaboury

WILEY

John Wiley & Sons, Inc.

Acquisitions Editor: Mariann Barsolo
Development Editor: Stephanie Barton
Technical Editor: Eric Keller
Production Editor: Christine O'Connor
Copy Editor: Sharon Wilkey
Editorial Manager: Pete Gaughan
Production Manager: Tim Tate
Vice President and Executive Group Publisher: Richard Swadley
Vice President and Publisher: Neil Edde
Media Producing Supervisor: Rich Graves
Media Associate Producer: Doug Kuhn
Media Quality Assurance: Josh Frank
Book Designer: Mark Ong, Side by Side Solutions
Compositor: Chris Gillespie, Happenstance Type-O-Rama
Proofreader: Louise Watson, Word One New York
Indexer: Robert Swanson
Project Coordinator, Cover: Katherine Crocker
Cover Designer: Ryan Sneed
Cover Image: Paul Gaboury

Copyright © 2012 by John Wiley & Sons, Inc., Indianapolis, Indiana

Published simultaneously in Canada

ISBN: 978-1-118-06680-5
ISBN: 978-1-118-22238-6 (ebk.)
ISBN: 978-1-118-23633-8 (ebk.)
ISBN: 978-1-118-26102-6 (ebk.)

For general information on our other products and services or to obtain technical support, please contact our Customer Care Department within the U.S. at (877) 762-2974, outside the U.S. at (317) 572-3993 or fax (317) 572-4002.

Wiley publishes in a variety of print and electronic formats and by print-on-demand. Some material included with standard print versions of this book may not be included in e-books or in print-on-demand. If this book refers to media such as a CD or DVD that is not included in the version you purchased, you may download this material at http://booksupport.wiley.com. For more information about Wiley products, visit www.wiley.com.

Library of Congress Control Number: 2012936811

10 9 8 7 6 5 4 3 2 1

Dear Reader,

Thank you for choosing *ZBrush® Professional Tips and Techniques*. This book is part of a family of premium-quality Sybex books, all of which are written by outstanding authors who combine practical experience with a gift for teaching.

Sybex was founded in 1976. More than 30 years later, we're still committed to producing consistently exceptional books. With each of our titles, we're working hard to set a new standard for the industry. From the paper we print on to the authors we work with, our goal is to bring you the best books available.

I hope you see all that reflected in these pages. I'd be very interested to hear your comments and get your feedback on how we're doing. Feel free to let me know what you think about this or any other Sybex book by sending me an email at nedde@wiley.com. If you think you've found a technical error in this book, please visit http://sybex.custhelp.com. Customer feedback is critical to our efforts at Sybex.

Best regards,

Neil Edde
Vice President and Publisher
Sybex, an Imprint of Wiley

This book is dedicated to Jim and Helen Cook. Without your support, I would never have had the opportunity to write this book; thank you so much.

Acknowledgments

I'm so excited to provide this book to all who enjoy creating art in ZBrush. This book would never have been possible without the amazing ZBrush community. Thank you for always inspiring me and pushing me to keep experimenting to improve my artistic journey. I would also like to thank all the ZBrush artists I have met over the years for their willingness to share their work, thoughts, and techniques with me.

Thank you to my colleagues at Pixologic for all the support you have given me over the years. I could not imagine developing ZBrush without you. I would especially like to thank Jaime Labelle and Ofer Alon for the continued support during the writing of this book. Thank you to all the artists who contributed to this book, burning the midnight oil to create the amazing tips for all of us to learn from. I can't thank you enough for taking your free time to help contribute to this book: Magdalena Dadela, Joe Lee, Zack Petroc, Morgan Morey, Tomas Wittelsbach, Sebastien Legrain, Michael Defeo, Rudy Massar, Mike Jensen, Marco Menco, Joseph Drust, Vitaly Bulgarov, Steve Warner, Bryan Wynia, Geert Melis, Christopher Brändström, Mark Dedecker, and Julian Kenning.

Thank you to the all the editors and the Sybex team for making this book possible and for helping to put this book together: Mariann Barsolo, Stephanie Barton, Christine O'Connor, and Pete Gaughan. I cannot give enough appreciation to the technical editor, Eric Keller, for being so honest throughout the process. This book would not be what it is without your advice.

To all my family in the areas of Stevensville, Ontario, Canada, and Buffalo, New York, thanks for allowing me to be that loud and crazy kid growing up. I would not be the person I am today without all of you. To my mother, Mindy, my father, David, my step-mother, Janette, and my sister, Tammy: thank you for all the support you gave me to realize my dreams and accomplish my goals, some of which are still to come. I cannot tell you how much the four of you have influenced my life.

To the love of my life, Cali, there is no way this book would have happened without you. Thank you for being there to advise me, push me, and continue providing that loving support. I enjoyed working those long nights together. You will always keep me inspired to discover art.

About the Author

Paul Gaboury is the lead application engineer for Pixologic, the makers of ZBrush. Paul is involved with the development of ZBrush and works with artists around the world offering support on ZBrush and Sculptris. Paul has been working with CG software since 2001. He has worked with several studios such as Legacy Effects, Walt Disney Animation Studios, Pixar Animation Studios, Industrial Light & Magic, and many more, enhancing their ZBrush sculpting pipeline and providing training and development, and giving demos and support to all the artists in the studio. As part of the Pixologic team, Paul also travels to various schools giving demos on ZBrush and works with the institutions' instructors to build and establish a ZBrush curriculum.

Paul graduated with a BFA from Bowling Green State University and was an extension student at Gnomon School of Visual Effects.

A fantastic group of ZBrush artists contributed their expertise to this book. Please see the Artist Spotlight features in each chapter for the individual biographies of these extremely creative people.

Contents

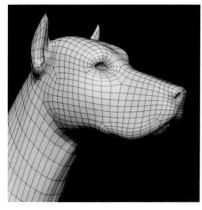

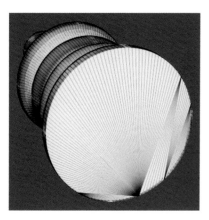

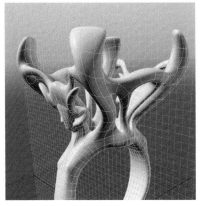

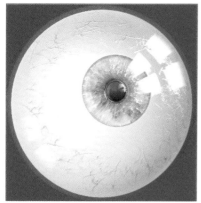

Chapter 6   Working with Scan Data   193

**Chapter 7   Posing—Bringing Movement
to Your Work   221**

Foreword

My name is Rick Baker, and I am a ZBrushaholic. That's right—I am addicted to ZBrush.

If you don't want to be addicted to ZBrush, you must put this book down immediately and run away. If you don't take my advice and you read Paul's *ZBrush® Professional Tips and Techniques* book, I would be willing to bet that you, too, will become addicted.

My life just hasn't been the same since I became a ZBrush addict. I am constantly enjoying sculpting crazy creatures on my computer.

I didn't think it could happen to me. When computer modeling first started, I thought that I would give it a try, but modeling with points and polygons just wasn't for me. It was so foreign—I couldn't make anything organic-looking. No way I was going to get hooked on this computer stuff; nope, I'll stick with my real-world sculpting. But then along came ZBrush. I have been hooked ever since. It was so much like real-world sculpting—only better, faster, and way more fun.

So take my advice: if you, too, want the ZBrush addiction, this book will definitely give you what you're looking for. It's filled with dozens of tips and insights to feed your addiction, including how to create a Subsurface Scattering SSS material in Chapter 9 and a cool walk-through of creating hair with FiberMesh in Chapter 6. You will spend every free moment on your computer sculpting, painting, and having a blast making all sorts of amazing things.

You were warned.

Sincerely,
Rick Baker

As a teen, Rick Baker began creating artificial body parts in his own kitchen. One of the earlier films Rick worked on was as an assistant to Dick Smith on The Exorcist. *He received the inaugural Academy Award for Best Makeup for his work on* An American Werewolf in London. *He also created the "werecat" creature Michael Jackson transforms into in the music video* Thriller. *Subsequently, Baker was nominated for the Best Makeup Oscar ten more times, winning on seven occasions, both records in his field. Baker claims that his work on* Harry and the Hendersons *is one of his proudest achievements. On October 3, 2009, he received the Jack Pierce Lifetime Achievement Award at the Chiller-Eyegore Awards. Rick's most recent Oscar in 2011 was for the makeup effects he created in* The Wolfman. *Baker's most recent work can be seen in MIB3.*

Introduction

Welcome to *ZBrush® Professional Tips and Techniques* and the world of digital sculpting. During my years of traveling in and out of studios, schools, medical institutions, conferences, and many other industries, I found myself speaking with artists about various techniques and how certain features of ZBrush work to improve pipelines. I discovered that there was always more than one way to create something in ZBrush, but there was not one good location to learn all the techniques.

I wrote this book with the hope of sharing the many tips and techniques I gathered from these presentations with the community, to inspire you to discover new ideas on how to use ZBrush.

Because ZBrush is so powerful, it can be hard to figure out the necessary steps to accomplish specific sculpts. In this book, you will find various techniques that can be applied to several industries. Artist Spotlights feature ZBrush specialists from various markets, including film, games, jewelry, and education. You will also find chapters dedicated to sculpting, texturing, rendering, and much more. The book also contains Special Projects, which provide a final image of a sculpt and share a step-by-step tutorial on how parts of the image were accomplished.

Finally, my hope is that these techniques will get you to start thinking about how you can change your workflow in ZBrush and give you a great base to expand from to continue your journey in digital sculpting.

Who Should Read This Book

This book is meant primarily for artists who have been using ZBrush for a while and have a basic knowledge of the program. However, there are definitely techniques in here that will be invaluable to beginners. At least, I wish I'd known some of this stuff when I started using ZBrush more than six years ago.

In addition, this book is great to accompany any curriculum at any institution as a resource for ZBrush workflows. This is also a great resource for any self-taught artist trying to learn more about how ZBrush can be used in different industries. Finally, this book is great for artists making the transition from clay sculpting to digital, from Photoshop to 3D, from traditional 3D packages to digital sculpting, and for artists who are just looking to use the computer as a new medium.

What You Will Learn

In *ZBrush® Professional Tips and Techniques*, I will show you how you can use ZBrush to create several workflows by combining various tools to accomplish a final image or sculpt that will be rapid-prototyped out. This book is full of step-by-step tutorials and completed images in ZBrush.

You will learn several tips that extend beyond the basics of ZBrush: sculpting techniques, texturing, rendering, posing, hard-edge sculpting, creating hair, and so much more. This book is also chock-full of tips from ZBrush artists sharing workflows that they use every day at their studios.

After you finish this book, you will have an arsenal of knowledge for ZBrush, giving you a solid foundation to expand your art in creating more realistic CG images and animations.

The goal of this book is to provide you with tips and techniques to make you more familiar with all the parts of ZBrush and combine those elements into your own workflow.

Hardware and Software Requirements

Computers are always changing, and ZBrush has grown with these changes. It can run on two operating systems (Windows XP/Vista/7 and Mac OS X 10.5 or newer), but figuring out your hardware can be more involved. This book also includes a DVD full of assets that will require you to have at least ZBrush 4R2b to open all tools and projects found on the DVD. You will also need to have QuickTime or VLC player to play all videos found on the DVD.

For hardware, ZBrush really relies only on your RAM and processor. Because it's not an OpenGL application, the video card has no real effect on performance. ZBrush doesn't need much to run, but I recommend a minimum of 4 GB of RAM and a dual-core processor. For best results in ZBrush, you should install 8 GB of RAM and get the best processor you can afford or even two processors. ZBrush is currently a 32-bit application, but Pixologic has announced that future versions of ZBrush will be 64-bit; I would install 12 GB of RAM or more to take full advantage of this version when it arrives.

Even though at the time of this book's release, ZBrush 4R2b was still a 32-bit application, I still recommend having a 64-bit operating system so that ZBrush can use up to 4 GB of RAM on the Windows side and at least 3.5 GB of RAM on the Mac side.

ZBrush offers a free upgrade to all registered users; therefore, this book was written primarily with ZBrush 4R2b but also includes tips for ZBrush4R3. For many of these tips and techniques, you will need at least ZBrush 4R2b. To learn more about the most current ZBrush system requirements, visit the Pixologic website:

www.pixologic.com/zbrush/system/

How to Use This Book

This book was designed with a particular workflow. This book is set up so that each odd-numbered chapter focuses on a specific area of ZBrush and includes Artist Spotlights offering tips from two artists representing different industries. Each even-numbered chapter presents a Special Project of one of my sculpts and includes two more Artist Spotlights.

Chapter 1, "Understanding the Basics," gives you some basic tips on sculpting, painting, creating base meshes, and much more. This chapter is not only great for beginners but also has some great tips for any level of ZBrush user. This chapter includes Artist Spotlights from Magdalena Dadela and Joe Lee.

Chapter 2, "Special Project—Creating Accessories for a Bust," will give you four tips from my sculpt of a bust I created to be tested for a rapid-prototype. There are tips on creating a logo, creating a zipper, creating a base of the chess piece, and sculpting skin. This chapter includes Artist Spotlights from Zack Petroc and Morgan Morey.

Chapter 3, "Sculpting—Developing Your Next Piece," covers some really cool techniques for improving your sculpting in ZBrush. These include hard-edge techniques, creating a brush, using ZSpheres and ShadowBox, and using a morph target. This chapter includes Artist Spotlights from Tomas Wittelsbach and Vitaly Bulgarov.

Chapter 4, "Sculpting Hard-Surface Details," guides you through several steps on how to create hard-edge components and use the NoiseMaker for patterns. This chapter includes Artist Spotlights from Sebastien Legrain and Steve Warner.

Chapter 5, "Adding a Splash of Color," covers how you can use ZBrush to paint your sculpts, including the basics of polypainting, Projection Master, and SpotLight; using Photoshop with ZBrush; combining painting with UV Master; and using various masking techniques for painting. This chapter includes Artist Spotlights from Michael Defeo and Rudy Massar.

Chapter 6, "Working with Scan Data," covers how to use scan data in ZBrush as a great start. This technique is used in several industries including film, games, toys, and collectibles. You'll learn the basics of scan data manipulation, creating a ball cap for the data, and creating hair with FiberMesh. This chapter includes Artist Spotlights from Mike Jensen and Bryan Wynia.

Chapter 7, "Posing—Bringing Movement to Your Work," covers how you can use ZSpheres to rig your models, whether you have one subtool or several subtools, and how to take ZBrush layers to Maya as blend shapes. This chapter includes Artist Spotlights from Geert Melis and Marco Menco.

Chapter 8, "Special Project—Creating Hockey Skates," takes you through two specific techniques on how to create laces, how to create a custom stitch brush, and how to use Decimation Master to maintain a logo. This chapter includes Artist Spotlights from Joseph Drust and Christopher Brändström.

Chapter 9, "Rendering—Bring Life to Your Image," covers how you can use the BPR render in ZBrush to create more realistic rendered images. You will learn how to create a multiple shaded material for a Subsurface Scattering SSS render, render out a realistic eye, use the filter system, and understand the shadow controls of the BRP settings. This chapter includes Artist Spotlights from Mark Dedecker and Julian Kenning.

How to Contact the Author

I would love to hear your thoughts about the book, or if you have any questions, please email me at paul.gaboury@gmail.com. In the subject line, please just let me know you are contacting me about the book by putting something like, "I read your book and have a question." Thank you for picking up this book and for all the support. Above all else, enjoy the reading—and happy ZBrushing.

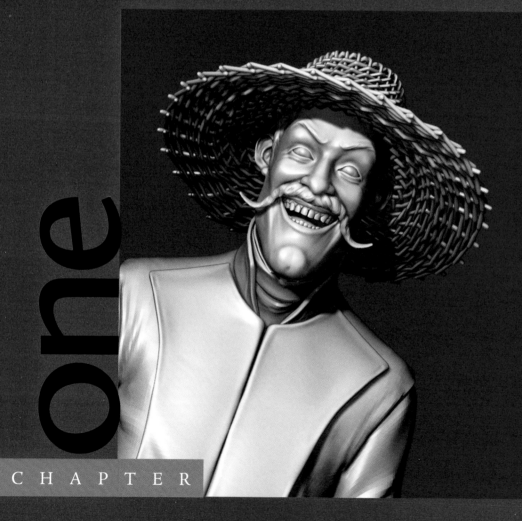

Image by Magdalena Dadela

one

Understanding the Basics

This first chapter introduces you *to tools and features of ZBrush that you will use constantly throughout your journey. Understanding the powerful core of ZBrush is essential before you dive into more complex procedures. I often notice that the simplest ZBrush features serve as a foundation for the more complex tricks along my workflow.*

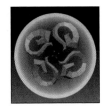

People often ask me how to become a great sculptor in ZBrush, and my answer is always "Time and effort." You must put in the time to learn the new art form. However, the effort you expend as you learn is crucial. Use your time to the fullest. ¨

My goal in this book is to encourage you to use new workflows by helping you understand more of ZBrush. This chapter introduces a wave of new features that you can build upon to get better and faster results. I encourage you to open your mind to new techniques and, above all, to have fun doing it.

- Customizing your ZBrush
- Recovering your subdivision levels
- Using Reproject Higher Subdivision
- Using Relax deformation
- Using local subdivision
- Creating a custom tileable alpha with 2.5D
- Using alphas to create meshes
- Creating wallpaper
- Creating your own palette

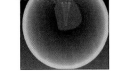

Customizing Your ZBrush

Before artists can create, they must first understand their tools. ZBrush is constantly changing the way I sculpt, but before I can get to the cool features, I need to set up a comfortable work area. Just like a painter, a ZBrush artist needs to get all his tools in the right locations. Some users prefer the default user interface (UI), but these next few tips will give you the necessary information to set up your very own ZBrush UI.

Customizing Your 3D Brush Fly-Out Window

As a ZBrush artist, you will visit the Brush palette often to switch brushes. The brush fly-out window in Figure 1.1 can be overwhelming. However, you can easily customize it.

Press B on your keyboard to call up the 3D brush fly-out window. Note that the 3D brushes in Figure 1.1 are available only when a tool is in Edit mode. The brush fly-out appears at the current position of the brush icon. Pressing B is the same as clicking the large brush icon in the Brush palette at the top of the interface or clicking the large brush icon on the left of the default ZBrush interface, as shown in Figure 1.2. You can find a list of ZBrush hot keys on the ZBrush wiki at `www.pixologic.com/docs/index.php/ZBrush_4_Shortcuts`.

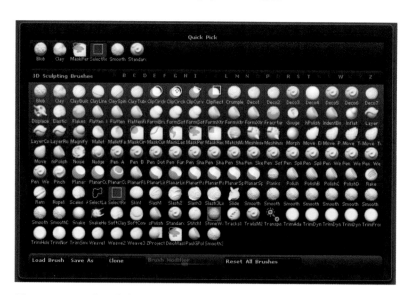

Figure 1.1 *3D brush fly-out window*

Figure 1.2 *3D brush icon at the top of the icons*

To customize the 3D brush fly-out, follow these steps:

1. Open your Windows Explorer or Mac Finder. Go to the following directory:

Windows = `Program Files(x86)\ZBrush4R2b ZBrush4\ZData\BrushPresets`

Mac = `Applications\ZBrushOSX ZBrush4R2b 4.0\ZData\BrushPresets`

These directories contain all the 3D brushes in the fly-out window. Any brushes you remove will no longer appear in the 3D brush fly-out window. I do *not* recommend deleting these brushes completely from your system.

2. Move the brushes you do not want to be in the fly-out window into the following directory:

> Windows = Program Files(x86)\ZBrush4R2b\ZBrushes
>
> Mac = Applications\ZBrushOSX 4.0R2b\ZBrushes

This moves the brushes into LightBox, under the Brush tab.

3. After you remove the brushes from the fly-out window folder, you must restart ZBrush to apply the changes.

Be careful not to delete certain brushes such as the Transpose.ZBP, any brush that starts with Clip, any brush that starts with Mask, SelectLasso.ZBP, SelectRect.ZBP, Smooth.ZBP, or any of the ZSketch brushes, because this will render certain features unusable. If you are unsure, never delete a 3D brush. You can watch the DVD video in the Chapter 1 Assets folder called *Customize Brush Fly-Out* for more details.

Customizing Your LightBox Tabs

LightBox is an internal ZBrush browser that makes it easy to access assets such as 3D brushes, tools, projects, textures, and alphas. Figure 1.3 shows an open LightBox with the Project tab highlighted. This tab displays all projects saved in the ZProjects folder.

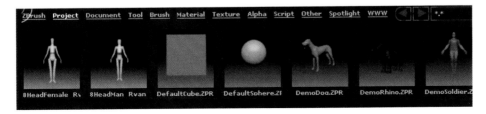

Figure 1.3 Default open LightBox with projects highlighted

All LightBox tabs can host several brushes, alphas, textures, and so on. Because you just learned how to remove brushes from the 3D brush fly-out, let's move Deco1.ZBP into LightBox. The following example can be applied to any brush:

1. Open two Windows Explorer or Mac Finder windows.

2. In one of the Explorer/Finder windows, go to the following directory:

> Windows = Program Files(x86)\ZBrush4R2b\ZData\BrushPresets
>
> Mac = Applications\ZBrushOSX 4.0R2b\ZData\BrushPresets

3. Search for the brush called Deco1.ZBP.

4. In the other Explorer/Finder window, go to the following directory:

> Windows = Program Files(x86)\ZBrush4R2b\ZBrushes
>
> Mac = Applications\ZBrushOSX 4.0R2b\ZBrushes

5. Move Deco1.ZBP into the ZBrushes folder. This folder relates to the Brush tab at the top of the LightBox interface.

6. If ZBrush is still open, you will see the Deco1 Brush in LightBox when you click the Brush tab. To remove the brush from the 3D brush fly-out window, you must restart ZBrush. However, when you add any brush to LightBox, that brush immediately appears even if you do not restart ZBrush.

7. To add more content into LightBox, visit the following folders:

   Windows = Program Files(x86)\ZBrush4R2b

   Mac = Applications\ZBrushOSX 4.0R2b

Each relates to the same titled tab in LightBox, as shown in Table 1.1.

Table 1.1: ZBrush and LightBox matchup

ZBrush Folder	LightBox Tab
ZAlphas	Alpha tab
ZBrushes	Brush tab
ZDocs	Document tab
ZMaterials	Material tab
ZProjects	Project tab
ZScripts	Script tab
ZSpotlights	Spotlight tab
ZTextures	Texture tab
ZTools	Tool tab

Adding a Folder Shortcut to LightBox

As a digital artist, I have already saved up several gigabytes of textures and alphas on my external hard drive. If I wanted to just move all of my textures and alphas into the ZTextures and ZAlphas folders, I could then access the textures and alphas in LightBox.

However, if I prefer not to take up more space on my hard drive or I just want to keep these files on my external hard drive, I can add a shortcut in LightBox to my external hard drive. This also works for any folder on your computer. This is currently possible only on a Windows machine. Here are the steps:

1. Create a shortcut to the folder or hard drive you want LightBox to access.

2. Move the shortcut into the following directory:

   Windows = Program Files(x86)\ZBrush4R2b\ZProjects

Figure 1.4 shows that I have placed the shortcut in the ZProjects folder.

3. If ZBrush is not already open, launch it. As you can see, LightBox opens by default to the Project tab. That is why I have placed my shortcut to the external hard drive in the ZProjects folder.

I can now search my texture and alpha files as well as anything on my external hard drive from this shortcut.

Adding a Texture or Alpha to a 3D Brush from LightBox

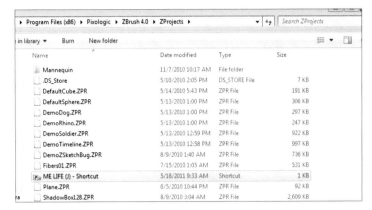

Figure 1.4 *Shortcut in the LightBox* ZProjects *folder*

As you become a crafty veteran of ZBrush, you will start to add various features to your 3D brushes for texturing and/or sculpting. LightBox is a perfect source to browse through resources and add elements to your selected brush. You can add a texture and an alpha by following these steps:

1. Load a project from LightBox so you have a tool in Edit mode. Select the Project tab in LightBox, as shown in Figure 1.5, and then double-click the DefaultSphere.ZPR project to load a polysphere into ZBrush. Also make sure the Standard brush is selected.

2. If you already have a tool in Edit mode, ZBrush asks whether you want to save changes to the current open project. Save the project to this point.

3. Navigate to the Texture tab in LightBox and select bark17.jpg. Figure 1.6 shows the selected texture file.

4. Double-click the bark17.jpg image. The bark texture is added to the Standard brush.

5. Now navigate to the Alpha tab in LightBox, and find the alpha called Leathery_skin13.psd (see Figure 1.7).

Figure 1.5 *LightBox Project tab with* DefaultSphere.ZPR *selected*

Figure 1.6 *LightBox Texture tab with* bark17.jpg *selected*

Figure 1.7 *Alpha called* Leathery_skin13.psd *in LightBox*

6. Double-click the Leathery_skin13 alpha. As you can see in right image of Figure 1.8, the leathery skin alpha has been added to the Standard brush.

You can use this technique with any 3D brush and at any time in your creative process.

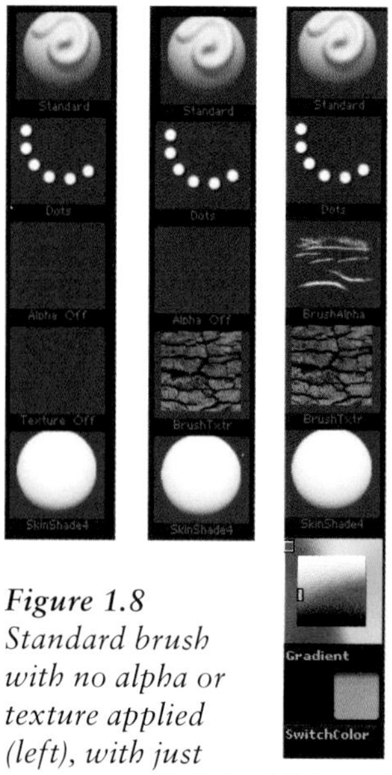

Recovering Your Subdivision Levels

Reconstruct Subdiv has saved me many times, and this button is my solution when I encounter an issue with a tool file and I still have a high-resolution OBJ of the same Tool; I can import the OBJ and get back my subdivision levels.

The Reconstruct Subdiv button will reconstruct your subdivision levels back to the lowest level if you have a tool that only has the highest level. As shown in Figure 1.9, the Reconstruct Subdiv button is in the Tool palette → Geometry subpalette.

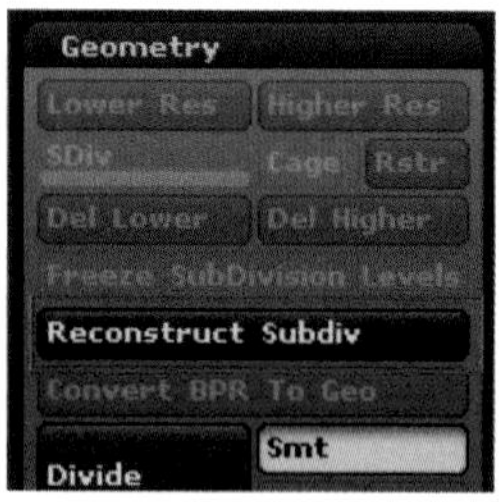

Figure 1.10 shows that my dog tool clearly has a high polygon count. However, it has no subdivision levels. ZBrush is a multiresolution subdivision-level application, so I want to take advantage of this.

Figure 1.8 Standard brush with no alpha or texture applied (left), with just texture applied (middle), and then with texture and alpha applied (right)

Figure 1.9 Reconstruct Subdiv button in the Geometry subpalette

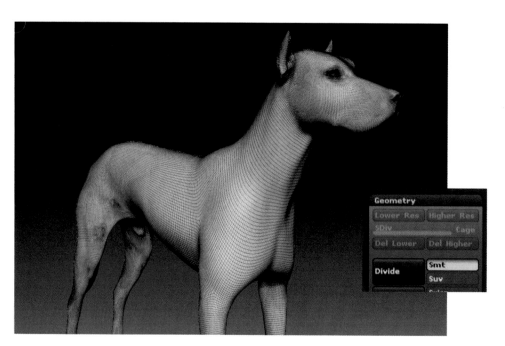

Figure 1.10 ZBrush Dog with high poly count and no subdivision levels

By clicking Reconstruct Subdiv once, I gain back one subdivision level (see Figure 1.11).

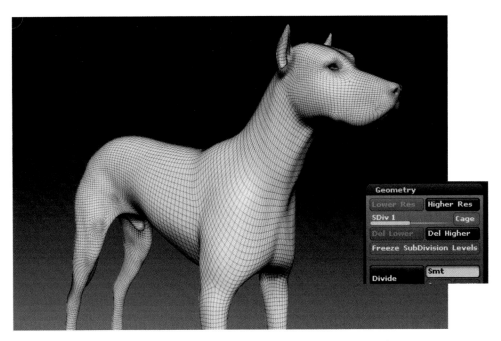

Figure 1.11 *ZBrush Dog with fewer polygons and two subdivision levels*

Figure 1.12 shows that when I click Reconstruct Subdiv again, I get another level of subdivisions.

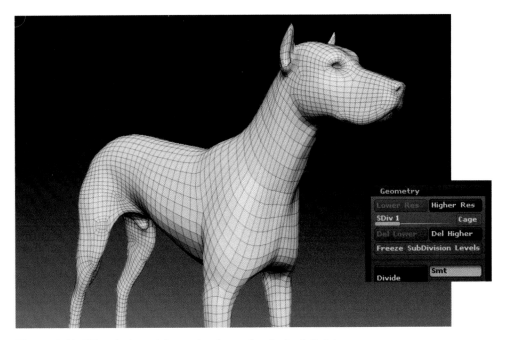

Figure 1.12 *ZBrush dog with another lower level of subdivision*

When ZBrush has no more subdivision levels to reconstruct. A warning will pop up right below all of the palettes, starting at the Alpha palette.

Using Reconstruct Subdiv is a cool trick, but it will not work on every tool. Tools created from ZSketch, Unified Skin, Extractions, and ShadowBox will not work with Reconstruct Subdiv. Don't worry if you don't know what these mesh creation methods are. By the end of this book, you will have a better understanding.

Using Reproject Higher Subdivision

I cannot tell you how often I get caught up in my sculpt and then realize how much I have damaged the topology of my creation. I will have overlapping geometry or geometry that is so close together that I cannot continue to sculpt on the mesh.

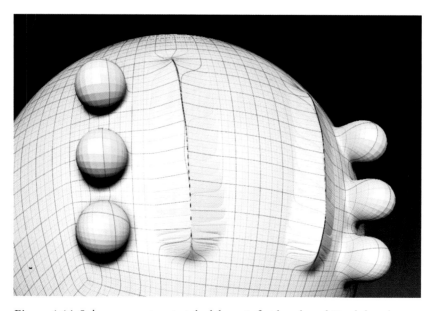

Figure 1.13
Reproject Higher
Subdiv button

The Reproject Higher Subdiv button is near the bottom of the SubTool subpalette (see Figure 1.13).

In the example shown in Figure 1.14, the geometry has been stretched and pinched pretty heavily on a sphere. The bubblelike parts were created with the Inflat brush, and the crisp edges were created with the Pinch brush.

I set the tool to the highest subdivision level and I walk down to a lower subdivision level. I usually go at least two to three levels lower than the highest. I will smooth out the mesh by using the Smooth brush, as you can see in Figure 1.15, to the point where my geometry looks more relaxed.

Do not walk back up your subdivision levels after you have smoothed out the mesh. ZBrush will update the mesh as you walk up, and your high-level detail will be lost.

Figure 1.14 Sphere geometry stretched from Inflat brush and Pinch brush

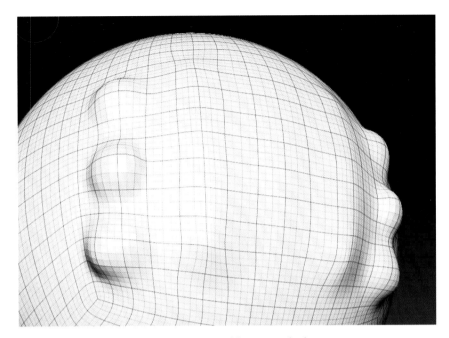

Figure 1.15 *Sphere on lower subdiv level but smoothed out*

When I click the Reproject Higher Subdiv button, ZBrush will recall the highest-level details and project those details into the mesh with a more relaxed geometry flow. Figure 1.16 shows that my sphere still has an inflated and pinched surface, but my geometry has been redistributed so I can continue to sculpt.

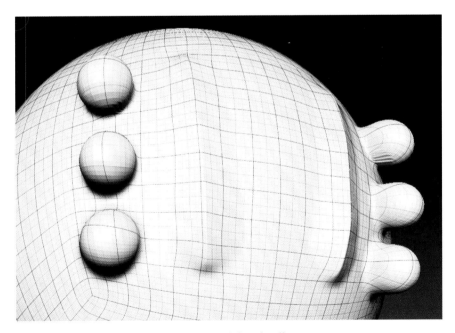

Figure 1.16 *New geometry with sculpted detail still intact*

Using Relax Deformation

The next tool to add to your toolbox is the Relax deformation. This is a great tool to use with the clipping brushes or if you have really stretched out any geometry. As you can see in Figure 1.17, the model has quite a bit of overlapping and stretched geometry.

In the Tool → Deformation subpalette, I slide the Relax feature all the way over, as shown in Figure 1.18.

Sometimes you must use the Relax slider more than once. I also recommend duplicating the subtool before using Relax. Relax will give a slight polish to your model. After you apply Relax, you can use Project All to get your mesh back to its original state with the new relaxed geometry.

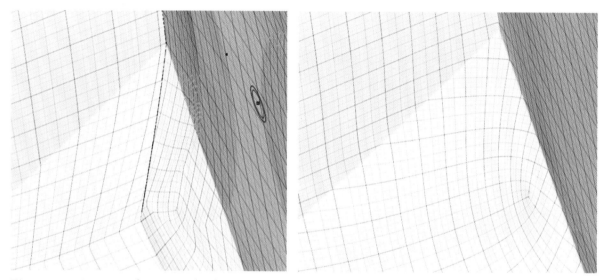

Figure 1.17 *Geometry that is completely overlapped*   **Figure 1.18** *Geometry after the Relax deformation*

Using Local Subdivision

Often you will need more geometry in a certain section of your model; this is where you can locally subdivide the mesh by using masking. You do this most commonly in environments, but I have used this technique on some of my characters too.

I would like to add a walkway around the middle of the cliff in Figure 1.19. I do not want to just add another subdivision level because I don't need the whole mesh to be divided, or the computer system may not be able to give me another subdivision level.

As you can see in Figure 1.20, my geometry is pretty evenly distributed, but I need to add more geometry to create a walkway on the cliff.

Figure 1.19 *Adding a walkway around the cliff*

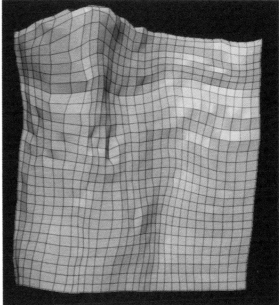

Figure 1.20 *Rock wall in Polyframe mode*

To add the walkway, follow these steps:

1. Mask out the section you want to subdivide locally on the highest subdivision, as shown in Figure 1.21.

2. Invert the mask on the mesh, as shown in Figure 1.22. Do this by holding Ctrl and clicking anywhere in an empty space on the ZBrush document.

Figure 1.21 *Mask out the section you want to subdivide.*

Figure 1.22 *Invert your mask.*

3. Now walk down to the lowest subdivision level of your tool, as shown in Figure 1.23.

4. Click Divide in the Tool → Geometry subpalette or use the shortcut Ctrl+D to divide the mesh. The result looks like Figure 1.24. ZBrush will divide the mesh only where no masking is applied.

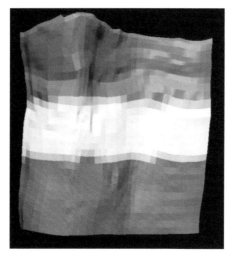

Figure 1.23 Lowest level with mask still applied

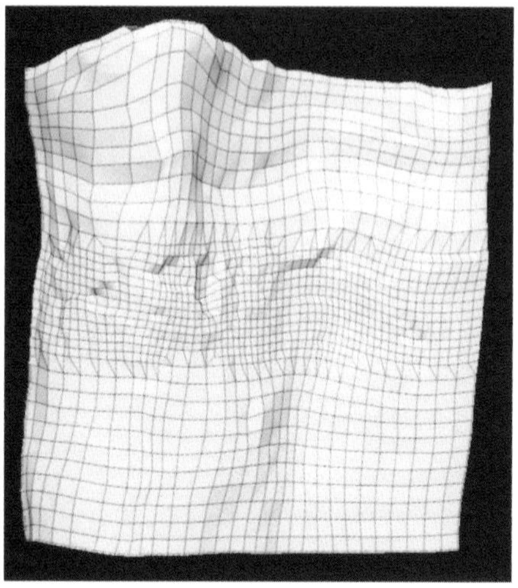

Figure 1.24 Local subdivision

5. You may have noticed some triangles in the mesh. Hold the Alt key as you click the Divide button to get a result like that shown in Figure 1.25. In this technique, ZBrush will make sure that the mesh contains only quads.

However, this action creates a mesh that becomes two separate pieces. If I sculpted across the geometry where the local subdivision took place, the geometry would begin to separate.

As you can see in Figure 1.26, I have also sculpted on the extra geometry to make the walkway blend in with the rest of the cliff.

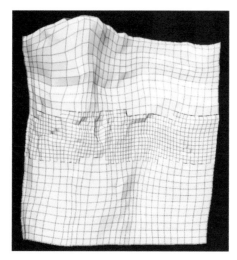

Figure 1.25 Local subdivision while holding the Alt key

Figure 1.26 Finished cliff with walkway

Creating a Custom Tileable Alpha with 2.5D

When ZBrush was first released, you could have a document with Z-depth. This capability is still in ZBrush today. However, because of advances in 3D mesh in Edit mode, you can freely move, scale, or rotate; so the ZBrush 2.5D document is used less and less. But you should not overlook the 2.5D feature. In this section, you will see how powerful 2.5D technology can be by creating a tileable alpha.

For this technique, you can make a brick wall by using only a brick like the one in Figure 1.27. Make sure you are out of Perspective mode when you use this technique.

Follow these steps to create a tileable brick wall.

1. Change the document size to something squared, such as 512×512. (From the Document palette, change the resolution and click Resize, as shown in Figure 1.28.) If the Pro button is on, turn it off. During this first step, a brick may still be on the document. If so, you will need to clear it by clicking Clear in the Color palette (accessed with the shortcut Ctrl+N).

Figure 1.27 Generic brick used to create a brick wall

2. After you resize and clear the document, redraw the brick onto the document and put it in Edit mode.

3. Move the brick to the top of the document (see Figure 1.29). It's important to stay away from the edges of the document. If your model is cut off by the canvas at all, it will not be tileable.

Figure 1.28 Changing the document size

Figure 1.29 Brick moved to the top of the document

4. Go to the Marker palette and click the M+ icon (see Figure 1.30). ZBrush makes an exact copy of the brick in the same position.

5. Take the brick out of Edit mode, making the switch to 2.5D mode. Hold the ~ key to make the document tile-able at the top (see Figure 1.31).

Figure 1.30 Marker palette

6. Move your cursor over the little gray square at the top of the document. You can see an example in Figure 1.32. This is the marker from step 4.

7. Click that marker. ZBrush drops the original brick but will not have it in Edit mode (see Figure 1.33).

8. Activate the Gyro by clicking the Move button at the top of the interface. Then move the brick down to the bottom of the document (see Figure 1.34).

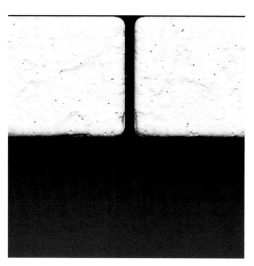

Figure 1.32 Marker point

Figure 1.31 Brick moved to make the top tileable

Figure 1.33 Brick dropped to the document in the original position

Figure 1.34 Brick moved to the bottom of the document with Gyro

9. Switch to the MRGBZGrabber tool (see Figure 1.35). When ZBrush asks whether you would like to switch to this tool, click Yes. Now draw on the document with MRGBZGrabber. You will notice that the tool will not draw outside the document borders. After you complete the drag, ZBrush will send the document as an alpha to the Alpha palette and also send the document color to the Texture palette (see Figure 1.36).

10. You now have a plane in Edit mode on the document. The Standard brush with a DragRect stroke, and the brick alpha are selected (see Figure 1.37).

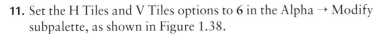

I created the plane by clicking Plane3D. I converted it to a polymesh by clicking the Make Polymesh3D button in the Tool palette.

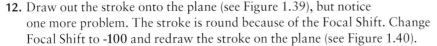

Figure 1.35
MRGBZGrabber
tool

Figure 1.36
Document sent
to Alpha and
Texture palettes

11. Set the H Tiles and V Tiles options to **6** in the Alpha → Modify subpalette, as shown in Figure 1.38.

12. Draw out the stroke onto the plane (see Figure 1.39), but notice one more problem. The stroke is round because of the Focal Shift. Change Focal Shift to **-100** and redraw the stroke on the plane (see Figure 1.40).

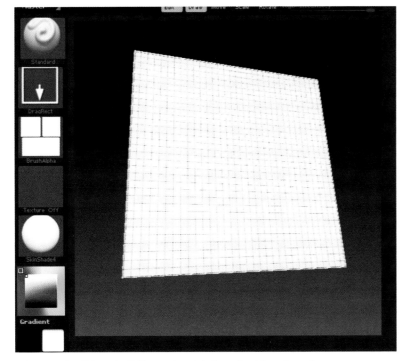

Figure 1.37 Plane in Edit mode with Standard brush and alpha selected

Figure 1.38 H Tiles and V Tiles options in the Alpha palette

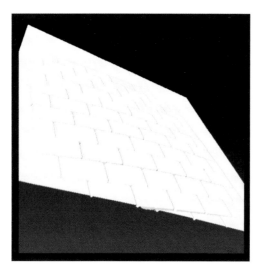

Figure 1.39 *Brick wall drawn out with an obvious curve*

Figure 1.40 *Brick wall with Focal Shift set to -100*

13. Finally, let's give the brick more of a broken-up look by using Surface Noise in the Tool palette. Edit the curve and sliders of Surface Noise, as shown in Figure 1.41. Set Noise Scale to **217** and Strength to **-0.0025** to get the results you see in Figure 1.42. Noise will not be applied until you click the Apply To Mesh button in the Surface subpalette.

I encourage you to try a couple of your own curves and see the results. The noise used in Figure 1.41 can be found on the DVD in `Chapter 1 Assets` folder.

If you want to add a different noise to the mesh, repeat the process or use masking to specify where to apply the noise, as shown in Figure 1.43.

Figure 1.44 displays the finished result of the wall after both Surface Noises have been applied.

Figure 1.41 *Surface Noise edit*

Figure 1.42 *Result of brick when applying Surface Noise*

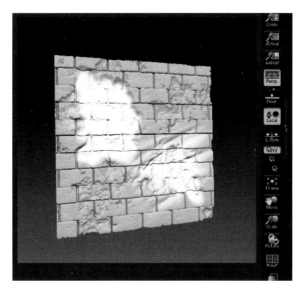

Figure 1.43 *Surface Noise with masking applied*

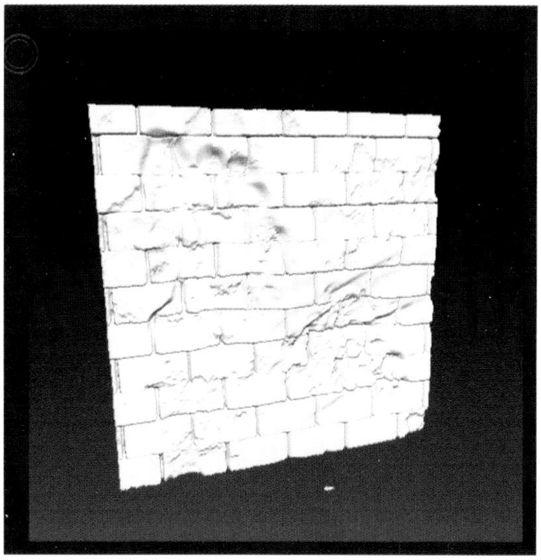

Figure 1.44 *Finished brick wall*

Using Alphas to Create Meshes

We are always looking for ways to finish projects faster. With this next technique, you can create meshes extremely quickly. For this example, I use only a small section in the Alpha palette, the Make 3D From Alpha controls (see Figure 1.45).

Figure 1.45
Make 3D From Alpha submenu

This is a simple technique that can be used in so many ways; let's begin.

1. Import the Flower_Alpha.PSD in the `Chapter 1 Asset` folder that you see in Figure 1.46 into the Alpha palette.

2. Click the Make 3D button to create something similar to the image in Figure 1.47.

3. You might want to adjust some of the settings for the Make 3D button. Table 1.2 details these settings.

Figure 1.47
Flower mesh created from the alpha

Figure 1.46
Import an alpha.

Table 1.2: Settings for the Make 3D button

MRes	Controls the number of polygons when the mesh is created. The higher the number, the more accurate the alpha but the higher the polygon count.
MDep	Controls the depth, or thickness, of the mesh.
MSm	Controls the mesh smoothness around the edges.
DblS	Controls the water-tightness of the mesh. If this is off, the mesh will be completely open on the back.

Try the following settings to create the flower in the figure:

- MRes = 350
- MDep = 15
- MSm = 10
- DblS = On

Here are a few more examples of how to use Make 3D.

Figure 1.48 shows the flower with a gray gradient applied. If you add grayscale to your alpha, you create height difference. Try the following settings:

- MRes = 350
- MDep = 15
- MSm = 10
- DblS = On

The file is saved on the DVD in Chapter 1 Assets as Flower_Alpha_Grey.PSD.

Figure 1.48 *Gray-tone flower*

Figure 1.49 shows a brick alpha with a value of 2 for the H and V Tiles. The settings are as follows:

- MRes = 500
- MDep = 5
- MSm = 2
- DblS = On

The file is saved on the DVD in Chapter 1 Assets as Brick_Alpha.PSD.

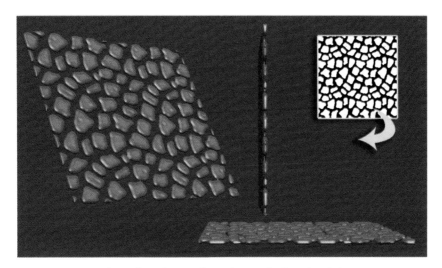

Figure 1.49 *Brick mesh with H and V Tiles applied to the alpha*

Figure 1.50 shows an alpha with the word *ZBrush*. The settings for this one are as follows:

- MRes = 1000
- MDep = 20
- MSm = 3
- DblS = On

The file is saved on the DVD in Chapter 1 Assets as ZBrush_Text_Alpha.psd.

There are so many options with this technique that I will leave the rest to you. Play with these settings often to learn them and to really see how far you can take an alpha.

Figure 1.50 *Mesh from ZBrush word*

Creating Wallpaper

Despite the 70s stigma, I think wallpaper is really cool. You can use it in so many ways, such as for walls in a video-game level to keep the polygon count low or for a pattern on a flat surface such as a cafeteria floor. Follow these steps to create wallpaper:

1. Create a plane with UVs that fits perfectly in the 0-to-1 space. I have included the Tool plane that I used in this demo. This file is called `Wallpaper.ZTL` in the `Chapter 1 Assets` folder.

2. Subdivide the plane to create some polygons. First turn the Smt button off next to the Divide button (in the Tool → Geometry subpalette). I subdivided my plane to nine subdivision levels with Smt off (see Figure 1.51). Turning Smt off will maintain the corners of the plane. If Smt is on, the corners will become round.

3. Select the Standard brush with the DragRect stroke. Now import the file named `Wallpaper.PSD` by clicking Import at the top of the Alpha palette, as shown in Figure 1.52. `Wallpaper.PSD` is in the `Chapter 1 Assets` folder.

4. Make sure that RGB is the only button on at the top of the interface (see Figure 1.53). This is the first time we have used only RGB. Chapter 5, "Adding a Splash of Color," covers painting with ZBrush, but for now tell ZBrush to use only color information. Also make sure the RGB Intensity is set to **100**.

Figure 1.51 Subdivisions of the plane with Smt off

Figure 1.52 `Wallpaper.PSD` *file imported*

Figure 1.53 With only RGB on, ZBrush will only paint when using the brush.

5. Turn your brush Focal Shift all the way to -100 to avoid a soft roll-off to the stroke.

6. Pick a base color for your wall. Click the Color palette and then click the FillObject button, as shown Figure 1.54, to fill the object with the selected color.

7. Now pick a color for `Wallpaper.PSD`. I chose red. In the Brush → Curve subpalette, set the WrapMode slider to 2 (it is shown with the default 0 setting in Figure 1.55).

8. Activate DragRect and Deactivate ZAdd. Pick a spot on the plane to draw your stroke. WrapMode should make another three instances of the same stroke. However, with WrapMode turned on, the stroke is perfectly tileable (see Figure 1.56).

   With WrapMode on, I do not have to worry about the plane edges because the stroke will carry over.

9. Let's add one more element in the middle of the stroke. Drop the Saturation of red a little and select Alpha 06, which ships with ZBrush.

10. Draw out a lighter circle between the flowers (see Figure 1.57). Also notice how perfectly the circles are being cut for tiling purposes.

11. Switch back to the first red by clicking within the color picker and dragging the cursor out to that color. Your cursor should turn into a little cross with the word *Pick* below it. This is telling ZBrush to pick the color below the cursor. Then draw out the stroke again to get results similar to Figure 1.58.

Figure 1.54 *Color FillObject button*

Figure 1.55 *WrapMode in the Curve subpalette of the Brush palette*

Figure 1.56 *WrapMode result on the plane*

Figure 1.57 *Stroke 2 drawn with Alpha 06 applied*

12. In the Tool → Texture Map subpalette, click the New From Polypaint button. This converts all polypaint information into a texture that you apply to the mesh. You should see no difference in your mesh, but you should see a texture applied in the Texture Map subpalette, as shown in Figure 1.59.

Figure 1.58 *Drawn-out stroke. Wallpaper is now complete.*

Figure 1.59 *Texture created from New From Polypaint button*

13. You can see a Clone Txtr button near the top of the Texture Map subpalette. Click this button. ZBrush sends the new texture to the Texture palette at the far left of the interface, as shown in Figure 1.60.

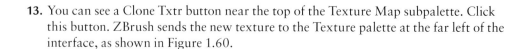

What's the difference between the Texture palette and the Texture Map subpalette?
- A Texture palette texture is applied to the brush itself.
- A Texture Map subpalette texture is applied to the selected tool.

14. Make sure WrapMode is off in the Brush → Curve subpalette. Now turn the AlphaTile button in the Brush → Alpha and Texture subpalette to 8. You can see this setting in Figure 1.61.

15. Turn off the texture in the Texture Map subpalette by clicking the texture and changing the selection to Texture Off (see Figure 1.62). Also turn off the cloned texture in the Texture palette.

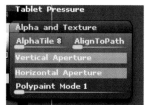

Now select your base color again and click Color → FillObject so you get the result shown in Figure 1.62.

Figure 1.60 *Texture applied to the brush*

Figure 1.61 *AlphaTile set to 8*

16. Turn the Texture you made back on in the Texture palette. Click and drag anywhere on the plane. Your finished wallpaper should look like Figure 1.63.

17. You are not done yet. Undo the color information you just applied so you have a single-colored plane. You can convert any texture into an alpha by clicking the MakeAlpha button at the bottom of the Texture palette pop-out. Find this button at the bottom right of Figure 1.64.

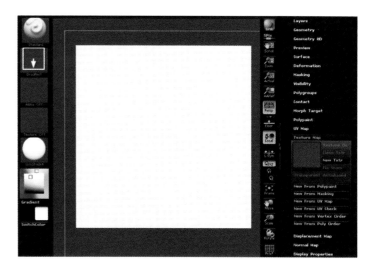

Figure 1.62 Fill the plane with a base color by clicking Fill Object.

Figure 1.63 Finished wallpaper

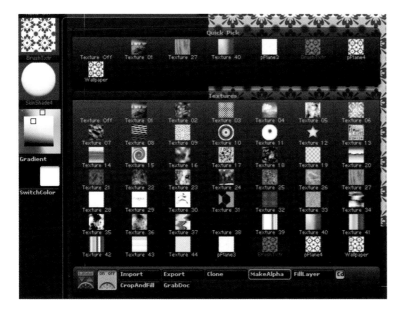

Figure 1.64 MakeAlpha button

18. ZBrush automatically makes an alpha of your texture file. Turn off RGB at the top of the interface and turn on ZAdd. Now draw anywhere on the plane. Your results should look like those in Figure 1.65.

Figure 1.66 shows the wallpaper applied with only RGB on, and Figure 1.67 shows the wallpaper applied with RGB and ZAdd on at the same time.

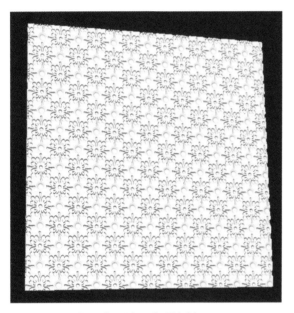

Figure 1.65 *Result with only ZAdd on*

Figure 1.66 *Wallpaper applied with only RGB on*

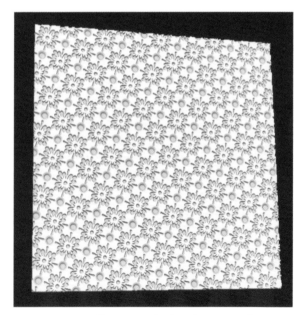

Figure 1.67 *Wallpaper applied with RGB and ZAdd on at the same time of the stroke*

Creating Your Own Palette

As you become comfortable with ZBrush, you will find yourself using certain tools frequently. You can completely customize your ZBrush user interface and build your own palette filled with your preferred tools by following these steps. You can also watch the video called Create a Custom Palette in the Chapter 1 Assets folder.

1. Choose Preferences → Config subpalette. Turn on the Enable Customize button (see Figure 1.68), so you can completely move any slider or button wherever you want.

2. Click the Create New Menu button in the Preferences → Custom UI subpalette. A pop-up window asks you to name the new palette. I named mine *Paul* and I docked it in the right tray of ZBrush, ready to begin my customization.

Figure 1.68 Turn on the Enable Customize button.

Remember to dock any palette in a ZBrush tray—found on the left and right sides of the interface. You must click and drag the palette into the tray, or you can click the little circle icon with an arrow, at the top left of every palette in ZBrush.

The palette that you created is automatically placed in alphabetical order along the top after you click it for the first time.

---

3. Let's place the brushes that we use constantly. To move any icon or slider in Enable Customize mode, hold Ctrl+Alt as you click the icon or slider (see Figure 1.69).

Figure 1.69 Make sure to always move the smaller icon in palettes to select the specific brush, alpha, and so on.

When you move something like a brush, stroke, alpha, texture, or material into any location in the new palette or ZBrush, you must not move the large icons; you must move the little icons. The little icon indicates the actual brush, whereas the larger icon is a link to the palette itself. The large icon is highlighted in blue. The actual brush that you want to move when holding Ctrl+Alt is highlighted in red.

As you can see in Figure 1.70, I have added several brushes and sliders that I use constantly into my custom Paul palette.

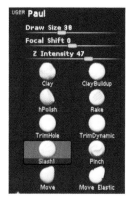

Figure 1.70 Custom Paul palette with brushes and sliders

It's important to add icons and sliders from the palettes, not from the current UI open in ZBrush. That is, to add the Draw Size slider to the custom palette, hold Ctrl+Alt and drag it from the Draw palette; *do not* drag it from the top of the interface, or it will disappear.

Figure 1.71
Custom subpalette
labeled Strokes

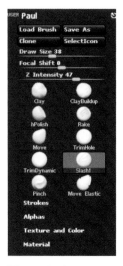

Figure 1.72
Completed Paul
palette with all the
subpalettes

After you get the hang of working with the palette, you can start to add your own subpalettes into the custom palette:

4. Open the Preferences → Custom UI subpalette. Hold Ctrl+Alt as you click the Custom Subpalette button and drag it into the custom palette being created. This action adds a new custom subpalette. You cannot name this subpalette until you add some part of the UI in the subpalette.

Figure 1.71 shows a new subpalette labeled Strokes. Now I can open and close my preferences for strokes within my palette. You can name a subpalette by holding Ctrl+Alt and then clicking the word *Untitled* after you add something to the subpalette.

Continue to build the custom palette so you can access your most used tools. If you use many of ZBrush's built-in shortcuts, you don't need to move everything into a palette. You can see my completed Paul palette with all of its subpalettes in Figure 1.72.

Now that you have created a custom palette, let's call up this palette wherever your cursor is as you work:

5. Turn off the Enable Customize button in the Preferences → Config subpalette. Then create a shortcut to the custom palette by holding Ctrl+Alt and clicking the name of the palette. In my case, the name is Paul. I called up my Paul palette by applying the number 4 as my hot key.

6. The last big step is remembering to save your UI so the custom palette you just slaved over is not lost forever. Go to Preferences → Config → Store Config subpalette.

If you want to save this UI for another machine, you will need to click the Save UI button. A dialog box opens so you can save it anywhere on your machine. To load this UI into your other machine, click the Load UI button and select the UI that was created. Remember to click Store Config after loading.

Remember that you can completely customize the ZBrush UI to your artistic interest. Any palette, icon, or slider can have its own shortcut.

What's Next

This was a great start to some basics of ZBrush. The next chapter will be the first of the Special Projects where I break down items of my work to share with you the techniques that were used in creating the piece.

Through the chapters you will also have several Artist Spotlights from various talented artists from multiple industries sharing more great tips and techniques.

ARTIST SPOTLIGHT: JOE LEE
EMBOSSING AND ENGRAVING WITH ZSPHERES

IN ADDITION TO USING THE POWER of sculpting brushes, you can also shape your sculpt by using ZSpheres. In this cool technique, you combine ZSpheres and adaptive skinning with the Project All feature. The result is a type embossing that is clean, precise, and looks engraved.

The following image shows results using this technique as a positive and negative value on a sphere. The DVD that accompanies this book presents a short video, with no audio, of me performing this process, in the Joe Lee Assets folder.

You will find a ZBrush project in the Joe Lee Assets folder on the DVD that is called tutorialFiles.ZPR that will allow you to load my tool used in this tutorial into your own ZBrush session (see Figure 1.73).

1. Begin by loading PolySphere.ztl from LightBox in the Tool menu; this will ensure that the polysphere is in Edit mode on the document.

2. Insert a ZSphere through the SubTool subpalette by clicking the Insert button and then select the ZSphere subtool.

3. Activate Transparency in the Transform palette by clicking the Transp button so the relationship between the ZSphere and the polysphere is easier to see. This Transp button is also found on the right side of the default UI of ZBrush. Figure 1.74 shows the results of having the Transparency button on.

EMBOSSING AND ENGRAVING WITH ZSPHERES

Figure 1.73 *Completed image of this tip*

Figure 1.74 *Turn on the transparency button to see through the sphere.*

Figure 1.75 *What the SubTool subpalette will look like at this point.*

The next image shows how your SubTool subpalette should look at this time.

4. Adjust and activate Symmetry in the Transform palette. Deactivate >X< and select >Z<, >M<, and (R). Set RadialCount to 4, as shown in the Figure 1.76.

Now you're all set up to draw ZSpheres on top of the surface of the polysphere. To do this, disable the Transparency button so that the polysphere appears solid and then start clicking on the surface of the polysphere. It's important to make sure that the ZSphere is still the active subtool.

EMBOSSING AND ENGRAVING WITH ZSPHERES

Figure 1.76 *Activate Z-symmetry with radial on and set to 4.*

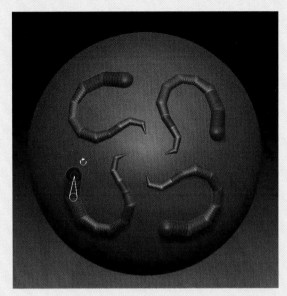

Figure 1.77 *ZSpheres drawn onto the sphere.*

5. Draw the ZSphere chains onto the surface of the polysphere in any pattern of your choice. Figure 1.77 shows an example of a pattern.

   Note that it may help to polypaint a guide onto the polysphere beforehand.

6. Before activating the Tool → Adaptive Skin subpalette, move the Density slider to 1 and click the Use Classic Skinning button before going into Preview mode. Figure 1.78 shows the results with these settings.

   Before converting PolyMesh3D based on the ZSphere's Adaptive Skin preview into a new PolyMesh tool, it's important to break the connection between the root ZSphere and the ZSphere chains that rest on the polysphere surface.

7. While still in the Tool → Adaptive Skin subpalette, deactivate the Preview button or press the hot key A so ZSpheres are visible again.

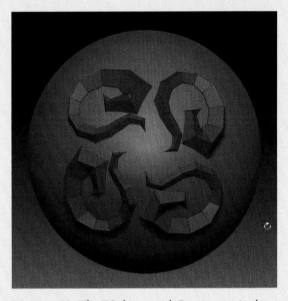

Figure 1.78 *The ZSpheres with Preview on in the Tool→Adaptive Skin subpalette.*

EMBOSSING AND ENGRAVING WITH ZSPHERES

8. Activate Transparency again in the Transform palette.

9. The four ZSphere connectors leaving the root are now visible, as shown in Figure 1.79. Click the Draw button (Q hot key) and create a new ZSphere in the middle of the ZSphere connectors.

10. Next, you have to make sure that Classic Skinning is activated in the Tool → Adaptive Skin subpalette. Otherwise, you won't see the separation of the mesh when you create the poly-mesh from the ZSpheres.

If you toggle to Preview mode to view the new adaptive skin, you can see that the break is clean with no twisting on the ends (see Figure 1.80).

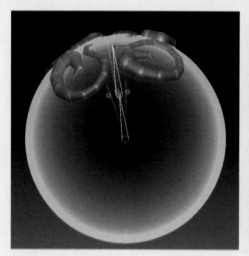

Figure 1.79 *Create new ZSpheres in the middle of the sphere.*

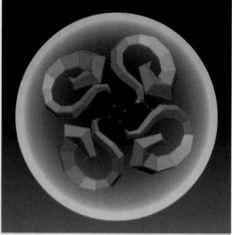

Figure 1.80 *Preview mode with the ZSpheres drawn in the middle of the sphere.*

It's important to note that even though the ZSphere chains on the surface of the polysphere are now detached from the ZSpheres at the center of the polysphere, you can use those ZSpheres you added in step 10 to adjust any twisting problems that may appear when the chains are converted into a mesh.

By holding Alt while rotating a selected ZSphere, you get the desired angle when you enter Preview mode. It is important to remove the twisting in the adaptive skin, because when the mesh of the adaptive skin is flush against the surface of the polysphere, the projection will be nice and clean, and the result will be more precise.

11. To rotate an Adaptive Skin mesh with the ZSphere chain, select the ZSphere preceding the rest of the chain. The ZSphere is ready for rotation when the dark and light split on the selected ZSphere and it is highlighted red. Figure 1.81 shows ZSpheres before rotation.

To prevent yourself from accidentally moving ZSpheres while you select them, switch to Scale mode (hot key = E). Then, after you have selected the ZSphere by clicking it, switch back to Rotate mode (hot key = R) and make the necessary adjustment.

EMBOSSING AND ENGRAVING WITH ZSPHERES

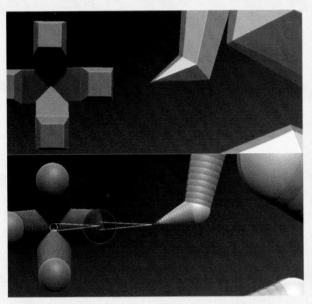

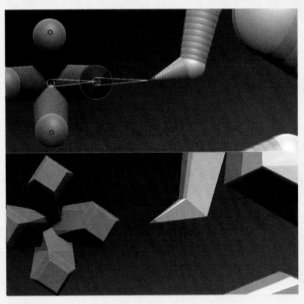

Figure 1.81 *Rotate the ZSpheres to make some adjustments.*

Figure 1.82 *Preview mode after ZSpheres have been rotated.*

12. With the ZSphere selected, click the Rotate button (R hot key) and hold the Alt key while clicking the ZSphere, sliding either left or right. The light and dark edges on the ZSphere will be the only indicator of rotation progress. Figure 1.82 shows the result after rotation.

13. After you achieve the desired Adaptive Skin rotation, press Ctrl+Shift and click the Current Brush icon at the left of the interface to open the pop-up library of selection brushes. Then click the SelectLasso brush icon.

14. Use the Lasso Select brush to hide the parts of the adaptive skin at the center of the polysphere. To do this, press Ctrl+Shift+Alt together and draw a lasso around the part you want to hide. The red color of the lasso selection indicates that the brush is in Hide mode. When you release the brush, the parts of the adaptive skin will be hidden (see Figure 1.83).

15. With the remaining adaptive skin visible, click the Make PolyMesh3D button in the Tool palette. The new polymesh should be instantly replaced as the active tool now, with no hidden geometry.

Next we want to apply creasing to the edges that run the length of the design forms. We can isolate the edges by using a technique that uses the SelectLasso tool.

16. Set the brush Draw Size to 3 (the smallest size that still enables you to see a red circle for the brush).

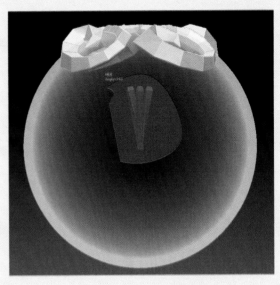

Figure 1.83 *Hide the center of the mesh that is inside the sphere with the SelectLasso tool.*

EMBOSSING AND ENGRAVING WITH ZSPHERES

17. Because we used a Symmetry mode to create the original Adaptive Skin tool, we need to set up the same settings for the newly made PolyMesh3D tool. As you did in step 4, from the Transform palette deactivate >X< and select >Z<, >M<, and (R). Set RadialCount to 4 again.

18. Switch to Polyframe mode under the Transform palette by clicking the PolyF button, or use the shortcut Shift+F.

19. Now we will hide a strip of polygon faces by using Shift+Ctrl and the Lasso tool, by hovering the brush cursor over a vertex until the red dot magnetically catches on it.

20. Click an edge that runs perpendicular to the edge you want to crease, while the red dot is still caught on the vertex. The strip should now be hidden and ready to apply a crease. Figure 1.84 shows the edge selected to hide a row of polygons.

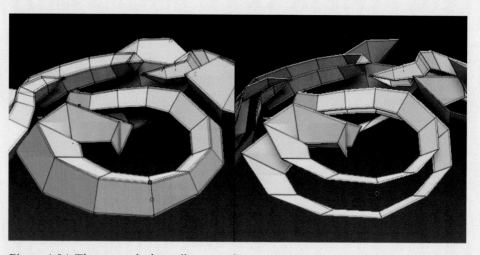

Figure 1.84 The exposed edge will receive the creasing.

21. To create nice sharp edges in ZBrush, you can use the Crease button in the Geometry sub-palette of the Tool palette. This adds a dashed line along the edges that border the hidden polygons. After you click the Crease button, you'll see the hidden polygons reappear and the dashed line indicating the creasing.

22. Now repeat the same process and crease the unselected strip of faces. You get a crease for the endcaps that will prohibit rounding of the end edges when subdivided. This tip is more apparent when the endpoints are not scaled to a point.

23. Divide the newly creased SubTool until you get adequate smoothness, as shown in Figure 1.85.

Figure 1.85 Subdivide the new SubTool to a smooth result with crisp edges.

EMBOSSING AND ENGRAVING WITH ZSPHERES

24. You can increase the complexity of the design by mirroring it across the Y axis. The easiest way to do this is to use the Mirror function in the SubTool Master ZPlugin in the ZPlugin palette, as shown in Figure 1.86. Use the following settings:

- Append as new SubTool
- Y Axis

As you can see in Figure 1.87, after mirroring on the Y axis, the two subtools make for a unique shape, which we can now either Emboss or Engrave into our polysphere.

Figure 1.86 Turn on the Y axis in SubTool Master and Append as new SubTool.

Preparing for the Embossing Effect

Now that we have the mesh ready let's use this to create the embossing on the sphere.

1. Bring the polysphere into the subtool list by using the Insert button in the Tool → SubTool subpalette.

2. Subdivide the polysphere to about six subdivisions.

3. We are now almost ready for projection, but first we need to activate the Farthest and Outer buttons so ZBrush projects only outward to the farthest vertex in the Tool → SubTool subpalette, just under the ProjectAll button.

4. Go ahead and click the ProjectAll button now.

5. Activate Solo mode at the bottom of the icons on the right side of the interface to inspect the projection on the polysphere by itself (see Figure 1.88).

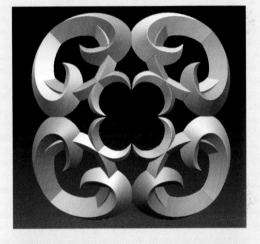

Figure 1.87 You can see that when the SubTool is mirrored you get a very cool result.

Preparing for the Engraving Effect

To create the Engraving effect, we'll repeat some of the preceding steps, but we'll also need to make some preparations to the creased design subtools:

1. Bring the polysphere into the subtool list by using the Insert button in the Tool → SubTool subpalette.

2. Subdivide the polysphere to about six subdivisions.

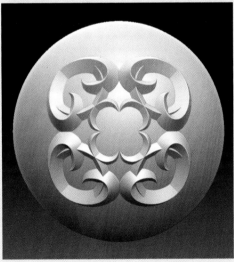

Figure 1.88 The result of the emboss on the sphere

EMBOSSING AND ENGRAVING WITH ZSPHERES

3. Now select the first design PolyMesh3D subtool.

4. With the slider set to the highest setting, delete the lower subdivisions by clicking Del Lower in the Tool → Geometry subpalette.

5. To get the engraving effect, we'll need to reverse the direction of the polygons by clicking the Flip button under Display Properties in the Tool → Display Properties subpalette. Figure 1.89 shows the results after clicking the button. If Double is on in Display Properties, you will be able to see both sides of the mesh regardless of the flipped normals.

6. Repeat steps 4 and 5 for the second creased design subtool.

7. Return to the polysphere's subtool settings and this time select Farthest and Inner in the Tool → SubTool subpalette.

8. Click ProjectAll and toggle Solo mode to inspect the engraving (see Figure 1.90).

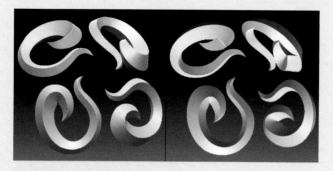

Figure: 1.89 Click on Flip in the Tool → Display Properties subpalette to flip the normals.

HOPING TO ONE DAY *be an architect, Joe Lee studied environmental design at Texas A&M University, only to find that the only structures he would enjoy building for a living would be virtual. With the help and encouragement of a high school friend who was already in the video game industry, he joined Iguana Entertainment (now Acclaim Studios Austin) as a journeyman. There he contributed to the Nintendo 64 Turok sequel before helping with in-game cinematics for the studio's various in-house projects in a dedicated department.*

Joe took some time off to pursue traditional sculpting and painting in a studio environment, and during this time he found ZBrush and saw potential for exploring the ZTool as a way to sculpt and paint with clean hands. His new enthusiasm for the medium brought him back to the industry, where he joined the team at Edge of Reality to contribute to such console games as Pitfall: The Lost Expedition, Shark Tale, *and* The Incredible Hulk *(2008), before eventually landing at Disney Interactive Studios/Junction Point Studios.*

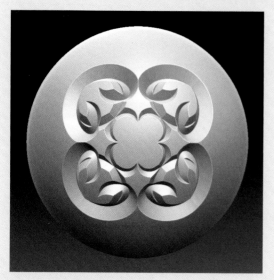

Figure 1.90 Result when the mesh is used to cut into the sphere

ARTIST SPOTLIGHT: MAGDALENA DADELA
USING 2.5D BRUSHES TO CREATE HAIR AND FUR ALPHAS

CREATING HAIR AND FUR for video game characters can be a tedious process that relies heavily on one's abilities to paint a good alpha texture.

ZBrush's default brushes are a fast and easy way to create alphas that work beautifully in the game engine or 3D software and require no painting skills or complex brush setups.

1. Select Plane3D from the Tool palette.
2. Change the plane into a 3D polymesh by clicking the Make PolyMesh3D button, and then draw it onto your canvas.
3. Press T to put the plane in Edit mode, as shown in Figure 1.91.

USING 2.5D BRUSHES TO CREATE HAIR AND FUR ALPHAS

Figure 1.91 *Select the Plane3D in the Tool Palette.*

4. Select the SkinShade4 material that you see in Figure 1.92.

5. Select a black color in the Color palette on the left side, with Mrgb activated at the top of the interface. Click FillObject in the Color palette to fill the plane with black, as shown in Figure 1.93.

6. Press G, or choose Zplugin → Projection Master to enter the Projection Master dialog box.

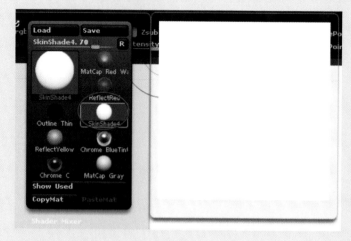

Figure 1.92 *Select the SkinShade4 material.*

Figure 1.93 *Click on the FillObject in the Color palette.*

USING 2.5D BRUSHES TO CREATE HAIR AND FUR ALPHAS

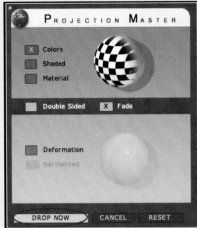

Figure 1.94 *Click on Drop Now in the Projection Master.*

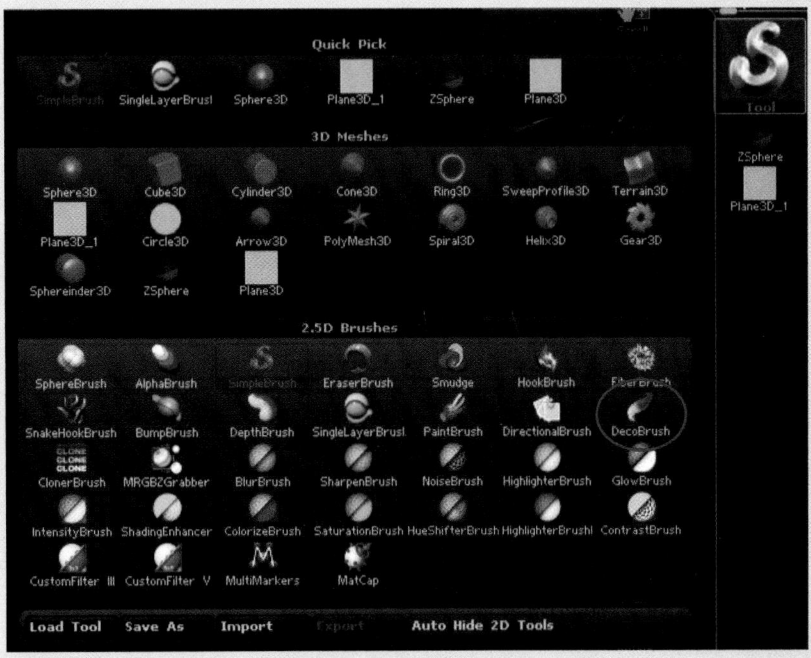

7. Select only the Colors option in the dialog box and click Drop Now, as shown in Figure 1.94.
8. From the Tool menu, select DecoBrush, as shown in Figure 1.95.
9. Make sure you set the Texture to Off, as shown in Figure 1.96. By default, the Deco brush is set up with a colorful gradient texture, which we don't want in our case.

Figure 1.95 *Select the Deco brush from the 2.5D brushes.*

Figure 1.96 *Turn off the texture on the Deco brush.*

USING 2.5D BRUSHES TO CREATE HAIR AND FUR ALPHAS

10. Start drawing your hair out. You can play around with different alphas as well to vary the brush intensity and Focal Shift, as shown in Figure 1.97.

11. After you're happy with the result, open the Texture panel on your left and select GrabDoc, as shown in Figure 1.98, to export your alpha and use it on a brush.

Figure 1.97 Examples of hair alphas made with the Deco brush

Figure 1.98 Click on the GrabDoc button to capture the document.

Weaving Some Magic with ZSpheres

ZSpheres are a great tool to create a base mesh for a character or to create an object very quickly. But they're also a fantastic way to achieve complex shapes very fast that would otherwise be a real headache when using traditional modeling. Let's use a straw hat as a simple example of how easy ZSpheres make creating objects.

1. Select a ZSphere from the Tool palette, as shown in Figure 1.99, and make sure you are in Edit mode (click T if you are not already in Edit mode).

USING 2.5D BRUSHES TO CREATE HAIR AND FUR ALPHAS

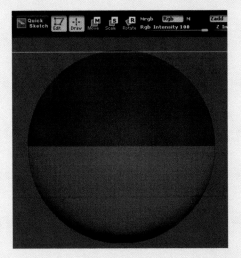

Figure 1.99 *Select a ZSphere in Edit Mode.*

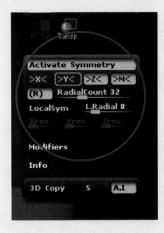

Figure 1.100 *Turn Z-axis and Radial button on in the Transform palette*

2. Now let's set up the symmetry. To make a nice weave, we need to work in Radial symmetry in the Z axis; make sure to activate Z and R in the Transform palette, as shown in Figure 1.100.

3. We also have to choose the radial count; this controls the number of times that the ZSpheres are repeated around the first ZSphere. Set this to about 32 for a tight weave.

4. This is where the fun begins. With your brush set to a relatively small size, draw a new ZSphere and then enter Move mode by pressing W so you can create something similar to Figure 1.101.

5. After moving the new ZSphere out a little away from the original ZSphere, go back into Draw mode by pressing Q and create another ZSphere.

6. Repeat the drawing and moving actions as long as you want to and in a pattern you like until you're happy with the design. Figure 1.102 shows an example. To retain a consistent size with the newly created ZSpheres, I like to draw them in the middle of the extended arm instead of at the end of the branch. That way, the first ZSphere I've drawn remains the one that dictates the size.

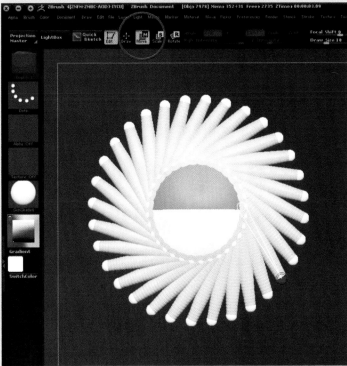

Figure 1.101 *Switch to Move mode to move the ZSpheres out from the center ZSphere.*

USING 2.5D BRUSHES TO CREATE HAIR AND FUR ALPHAS

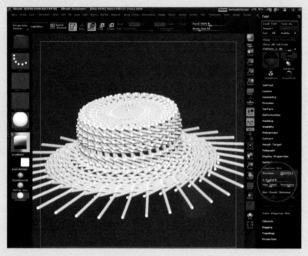

Figure 1.102 *Finished design of the hat.*

7. To preview your geometry, use the Preview button in the Adaptive Skin subpalette of the Tool palette, as shown in Figure 1.103.

8. After you're satisfied with your new creation, use the same Adaptive Skin subpalette to create a final 3D mesh out of the ZSpheres by clicking the Make Adaptive Skin button (see Figure 1.104).

9. You can play with the Density settings, but I feel it's best to leave them at the default setting. You can always subdivide the new mesh later.

10. Your new hat will now appear as a separate tool in the Tools menu. You can sculpt it and shape it further to your heart's content. Figure 1.105 shows the final result as a subtool to my main character.

Have fun. I look forward to your creations. A straw hat is only one use of this technique. It lends itself very well to making baskets, braids, wrought-iron gates, and many other patterns that are hard and time-consuming to create with a traditional modeling package. The best thing about this technique, of course, is that it allows you to create excellent normal and occlusion maps for texturing.

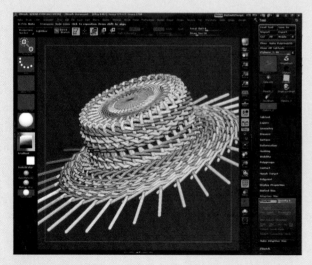

Figure 1.103 *Click on Preview in the Tool → Adaptive Skin subpalette.*

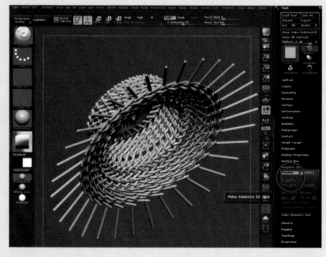

Figure 1.104 *Click the Make Adaptive Skin button to create a new SubTool.*

USING 2.5D BRUSHES TO CREATE HAIR AND FUR ALPHAS

Figure 1.105 Final result of the hat on my character

MAGDALENA DADELA *is a senior character artist and digital sculptor with five years of experience in games and film. After graduating from Jagiellonian University in Poland with a degree in English literature, Magdalena discovered her true passion—3D. She entered a 3D animation and visual effects course at Vancouver Film School to pursue a career in the industry. After a short period at Realtime Worlds in Scotland, she became a character modeler for Ubisoft Montreal, where she has worked on projects such as* Assassin's Creed: Revelations, Assassin's Creed: Lineage, Far Cry 2, *and* Predators, *the movie.*

www.mdadela.com

SPECIAL PROJECT | HOODY

CREATE SKIN DET

CREATE ZMan LO

CREATE A ZIPPE

CREATE A STAN

Special Project—Creating Accessories for a Bust

I used several techniques to *create the bust for this exercise to have him come alive. Before diving into ZBrush, though, I took a step back and thought about how to create each SubTool for this bust. I looked for simple approaches to create some common accessories.*

This chapter takes you through the process of creating pieces for the character in my bust, beginning with how I created the ZMan logo that is stitched into the fabric of the hoody.

- Creating the ZMan logo
- Creating the zipper
- Creating the stand
- Creating a skin texture

Creating the ZMan Logo

First, you need to find a black-and-white image of the Pixologic ZMan logo. Follow along with creating the ZMan logo by downloading the texture named ZMan.psd off the DVD in the assets folder of Chapter 2. You can see the ZMan.psd image in Figure 2.1.

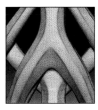

Off we go. Follow these steps to import your ZMan logo into ZBrush:

1. Click the Import button in the Texture palette to import the logo as a texture. The texture appears on the left side of the interface, in the texture slot. ZBrush has assigned the logo to your current brush, and any strokes you create will use the shape of the texture.

2. Select Plane3D in the Tool palette.

Figure 2.1 ZMan logo as a texture

3. By default, the Plane3D tool is a parametric 3D object: the sculpting brushes do not affect it. To convert it into a 3D mesh that you can sculpt on, click the Make PolyMesh3D button at the top of your Tool palette.

4. Now let's subdivide the polygons of the plane so that the brush strokes appear smooth on the surface of the plane. Choose Tool → Geometry, deactivate the Smt button next to Divide, and divide the mesh to level 5 (see Figure 2.2).

   The Smt button activates smoothness when you divide in ZBrush. With Smt off, the corners of the plane will not become rounded. This is a great way to subdivide a mesh without affecting the overall shape of the object.

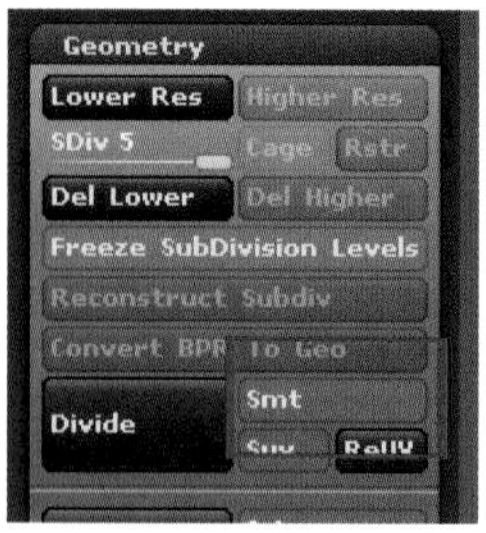

5. Click the large icon under the Tool → Texture Map subpalette and select the ZMan logo, as shown in Figure 2.3. This action applies the logo as a texture to the plane.

6. Under the Tool → Masking subpalette, click the Mask by Intensity button. At first, nothing seems to happen.

7. Turn off the ZMan logo in the Texture Map subpalette. Your result should be the same as Figure 2.4. The logo has been applied to the plane as a mask, as indicated by the gray color on the plane.

8. At the bottom of the SubTool subpalette, change E Smt and S Smt to 1 and the Thick slider to 0.4. Click Extract, and you get something similar to Figure 2.5. Click the Accept button so ZBrush will create the logo.

Figure 2.2 Turn off Smt in the Geometry subpalette to disable smoothness when dividing.

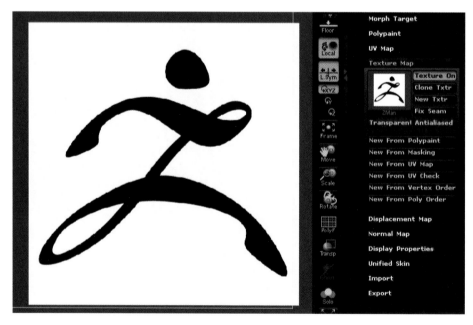

Figure 2.3 Applying the ZMan logo to the plane

Figure 2.4 The ZMan logo is applied as a mask to the plane.

Figure 2.5 Extracting the mask to create the logo

Notice that when you complete an extraction, ZBrush assigns a polygroup to the back, middle, and front portions of the mesh (see Figure 2.6).

9. To activate your polygroups, click the PolyF icon (or press Shift+F to activate Polyframe mode).

10. Display only the middle section by Ctrl+Shift-clicking the middle section to isolate the visibility, as shown in Figure 2.7.

11. Click the Edge Loop button in the Tool → Geometry subpalette to add an edge loop of polygons on either side of the visible section, as shown in the left image of Figure 2.8.

12. In the Tool → Visibility subpalette, use the Shrink button (or Ctrl+Shift+S) to reduce the selection so that only the inner polygroup is visible.

Figure 2.6 Notice the back, middle, and front of the logo have different polygroups.

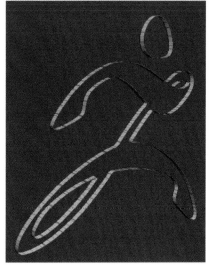

Figure 2.7 Inner polygroup selected

13. With just the inner polygroup visible, mask the whole mesh off by clicking the MaskAll button in the Tool → Masking subpalette (or by holding Ctrl while clicking anywhere in the empty space), as shown in the middle image of Figure 2.8.

14. Make the whole mesh visible by holding Ctrl+Shift while clicking on an open space, as shown on the right in Figure 2.9.

15. Hold Ctrl and click anywhere on the document to invert the masking (see Figure 2.9).

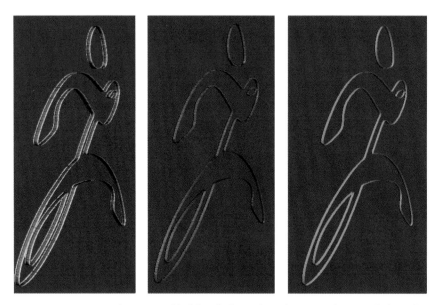

Figure 2.8 *Inner polygroup added by clicking the Edge Loop button (left), selection reduced to the innermost polygroup (middle), and inner polygroup masked (right)*

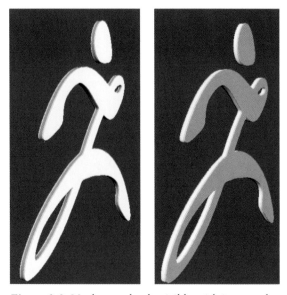

Figure 2.9 *Mesh completely visible with inner polygroup masked (left), and mask inverted after the whole mesh is visible (right)*

16. You can now bevel the surface by inflating the unmasked portion. To do this, expand the Tool → Deformation subpalette and move the Inflate slider to the right. Figure 2.10 shows a nice bevel along the logo.

17. Repeat the process with the new inner polygroup to create another edge loop, as shown in Figure 2.11.

18. Mask off the new inner polygroup and then invert it as you did in the previous steps (see Figure 2.12) to repeat the inflating of the border.

19. Finally, inflate the mesh again with the Deformation Inflate slider.

The final result for the logo is shown in Figure 2.13.

With this simple technique, you can create a base mesh. You can find a perfect example of another way to use this technique at www.zbrushcentral.com/showthread.php?t=095181. When you have a moment, watch the videos on how the motorcycle was constructed.

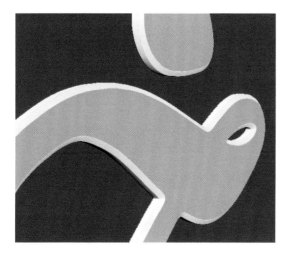

Figure 2.10 Bevel along the mesh

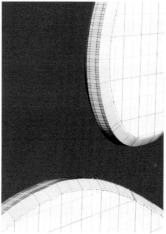

Figure 2.11 New edge loop

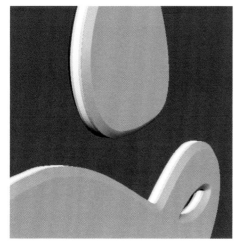

Figure 2.12 The second inner polygroup exposed with the rest of the mesh masked off

Figure 2.13 Finished ZMan logo

Placing the ZMan Logo on the Hoody

Now you need to position the ZMan logo tool to match the curve of the hoody. The MatchMaker brush makes this task easy. With one quick stroke, the logo can match the shape of any surface behind it. Load the Hoody.ZTL from the Chapter 2 Assets folder. Make sure to have the hoody in Edit mode. This hoody was sculpted from the PolySphere that is shipped with ZBrush.

1. Append the logo as a SubTool to the hoody and then position the logo in place (see Figure 2.14).

2. The logo is too large, so you must adjust the size by clicking the Scale Mode button (hot key = R) above the canvas. Now you can use the Transpose tool to make the logo fit as shown in Figure 2.15.

   You want to make the logo match the surface of the hoody so it looks more like a patch sewn on the fabric (see Figure 2.16). This is where the magic happens with the MatchMaker brush: it uses the Z-depth information of the canvas to deform the surface.

3. Turn off the Persp button on the right shelf to disable perspective so it does not affect the deformation created by the brush.

4. Position the camera to look straight ahead at the logo in front of the hoody (see Figure 2.17).

5. In this position, you can switch to the MatchMaker brush quickly by pressing B, M, and then M again. With one stroke, the logo will match the hoody (see Figure 2.18).

Figure 2.14 Logo positioned in place after appending it

Figure 2.15 Scale of ZMan logo changed to fit in position

Figure 2.16 Logo flatness compared to the curve of the hoody

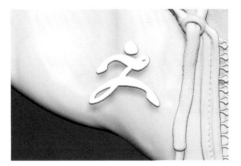

Figure 2.17 Position the camera to look straight ahead.

Figure 2.18 ZMan logo matched to the shape of the hoody

6. Now you must move the logo closer to the hoody. The camera must not move after using MatchMaker, or the logo will become misaligned with the hoody. You must switch to Move mode at the top of the interface to move the logo freely.

7. Hold the Alt key while Move mode is active. Move mode lets you move any subtool without drawing out the Transpose line if you click the subtool while holding the Alt key.

8. To move the logo right up next to the hoody, hold the Alt key in Move mode, click the logo, and then let go of Alt without letting go of the Left Mouse button or taking the Wacom pen off the tablet or Cintiq. Now you can move your mouse or pen up and down, which will move the logo in Z-depth. You can see my result in Figure 2.19.

MatchMaker will match any geometry lying behind the target mesh even if it's a separate subtool. Be sure to keep the geometry mesh (for example, the ZMan logo) smaller than any other mesh you wish to match behind it.

Creating the Zipper

The powerful ShadowBox tool makes the zipper the easiest piece to create. With practice, you will find that ShadowBox offers a great solution for creating a simple base mesh. The easiest way to create a ShadowBox mesh is to use the Shadowbox128.ZTL preset found in the Tool section of LightBox.

Making the Zipper Shape

1. Deactivate the Persp button on the right shelf. Then rotate the view of the ShadowBox tool so the back side faces you, as shown in Figure 2.20.

2. Mask out a design of one zipper to create a basic shape, as shown in Figure 2.21. A great tool to use is the BackTrack feature in the Stroke → LazyMouse menu; select Line and Path on the MaskPen brush (see Figure 2.22). Hold Ctrl as you activate these options. Otherwise, the options will not activate on the MaskPen brush but rather on your selected

Figure 2.19 ZMan logo in position on the hoody

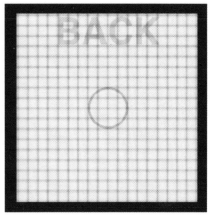
Figure 2.20 Shadowbox in Edit mode with back facing the camera

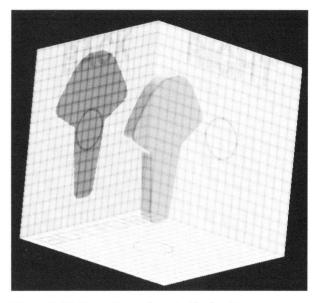
Figure 2.21 *Basic zipper shape in ShadowBox*

Figure 2.22 *Hold the Ctrl key when turning on the BackTrack options you see here.*

sculpting brush. BackTrack lets you draw out a line first before the stroke is applied. Once you have the zipper click the ShadowBox button in the Tool → Geometry sub-palette to convert the mask into geometry.

Making the Zipper Mask

The MaskCurve brush is a great tool for creating lines with harsh or soft angles in the mask because of its ability to draw smooth curves as well as sharp curves. Follow these steps to make the zipper mask:

1. Divide the mesh to about 700,000 polygons. Use the MaskCurve brush to mask out the center of the zipper, as shown on the left in Figure 2.23.

2. Create the mask. Click X to enable X-symmetry. With the MaskCurve brush selected, hold the Ctrl key and mask out the top half first. Tap the Alt key when you get close to the top of the zipper to create a curve in the mask (see the image on the right in Figure 2.23).

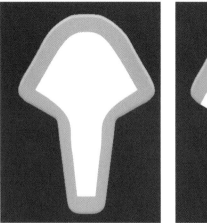

Figure 2.23 *The final masked-out edges of the zipper to sculpt the middle section (left). The MaskCurve brush creates a precise mask on the zipper (right).*

3. Add the first mask by drawing the second mask along the side of the zipper, as shown on the left in Figure 2.24. You can keep adding to any mask in ZBrush by holding the Ctrl key and drawing out a new mask.

4. The last mask is the easiest. Just mask off the bottom of the zipper by drawing a straight line across (see the right image in Figure 2.24).

5. To create the bevel in the zipper, add a blur to the mask by holding the Ctrl key and clicking the mask. Do this about six times. Each time you click the mask, the edges blur a little more. Hold Shift and rotate the zipper to snap it to a side ortho-graphic view. Then hold Ctrl+Shift and select ClipCurve in the Brush palette. Use the ClipCurve brush to push back the geometry (see the image on the left in Figure 2.25).

6. To create a stronger crease in the form, expand the Deformations subpalette of the Tool palette and move the Inflate slider to the left a few times. This creates a negative inflation of the unmasked area (see the image on the right of Figure 2.25).

Figure 2.24 Second mask completed along zipper edge (left), and last mask applied to zipper (right)

Figure 2.25 The result of using the ClipCurve brush (left), and a stronger crease using the Deformation Inflate slider negatively (right)

7. Create the inner bevel by repeating the preceding three-step masking process. Then place the Transpose Line tool in the center of the mesh so you can use the Scale mode to create the bevel. Switch to Move mode to push the geometry back, as shown in Figure 2.26.

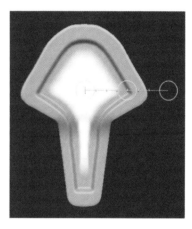

Figure 2.26 Tranpose line positioned to create the inner bevel

8. Use the ClipCurve brush to refine the shape of the zipper, as shown in Figure 2.27.

   All that is left to do is to create the string of zippers. The duplicate option with the Transpose Line tool when in Move mode will become your best friend for this kind of task.

9. Switch to Move mode and draw out an action line just as you see in Figure 2.28. Hold the Ctrl key while you click and move the middle circle to duplicate the zipper. I also like to hold the Shift key here so that the zipper I am duplicating will stay along the line of the Transpose line.

Figure 2.27 ClipCurve brush used to refine the edges of the zipper

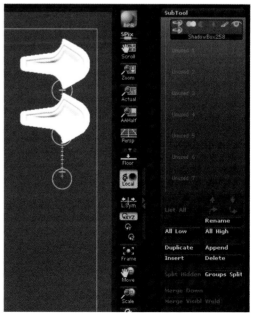

Figure 2.28 Double the zipper subtool

10. To create the rest of the zippers, click the ReplayLast button in the Stroke Palette to continue to move and duplicate the zippers until you get something as shown in Figure 2.29.

With this workflow, you could create a variety of zipper shapes to add style for your next character model. Don't forget that each zipper can be polygrouped so that you can move each individual piece of the zipper.

Creating the Stand

*Figure 2.29
String of
zippers for the
hoody*

What would a bust be without a stand? To create the stand, I used an old-school tool that is perfect for this job. ZBrush ships with various ZTools, including the primitive meshes. I would like to introduce you to the SweepProfile3D primitive, which is a great way to start a model for the stand for the bust.

1. Select the SweepProfile3D tool from the library in the Tool palette. Normally you would convert this tool into a polymesh to sculpt it, but this time you'll use the sliders in the Initialize subpalette to shape the tool before sculpting. These sliders are toward the bottom of the Tool palette when a 3D primitive is selected; you will see a subpalette called Initialize (see Figure 2.30).

2. Move the points on the S Profile curve so the primitive has a point at the top and is open at the bottom (see Figure 2.31). Don't worry about the holes at the top and bottom of the mesh. You will take care of that later.

*Figure 2.30 Initialize
subpalette*

3. Give the point in the middle a sharp edge (see Figure 2.31) by clicking the dot in the graph, dragging it out of the graph and then back into the graph.

4. Play around with the S Profile curve to make something like Figure 2.32. This is the start of a stand.

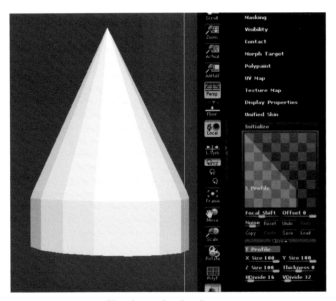

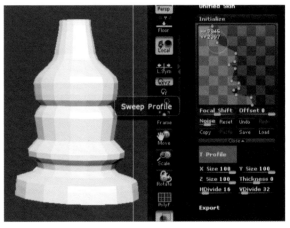

Figure 2.32 S Profile edit to match the model

Figure 2.31 S Profile edit with a hard point

After you establish the basic shape by using the Initialize settings, it's time to convert it into a polymesh.

5. To convert your shape into a polymesh, click the Make PolyMesh3D button at the top of the Tool palette.

Now the primitive is a mesh, and the faces are contained within a single polygroup. Polygrouping is key for creating interesting details in the mesh.

6. Subdivide the mesh and use the result as a test to see where you can crease certain edges. Figure 2.33 shows how the mesh is subdivided and smoothed.

   You don't want the whole stand to be smoothed; you want some sharper edges, which you can easily make with the Crease feature in ZBrush.

7. Set the SDiv slider in the Geometry subpalette back to **1** and delete higher subdivisions. Then with the SelectRect brush, hold Ctrl+Shift to hide the parts of the mesh. Figure 2.34 shows the middle section of the stand with a sharper edge.

8. You can now crease the open edge by clicking the Crease button in the Tool → Geometry subpalette, as shown in Figure 2.35. The creased edge appears dotted, as shown in Figure 2.36.

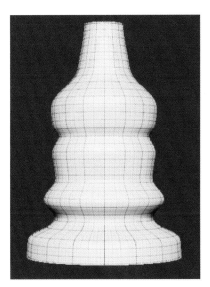

Figure 2.33 *The stand mesh has been subdivided.*

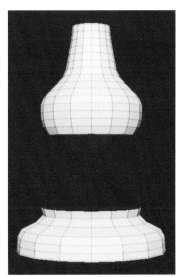

Figure 2.34 *Hide parts of the mesh to expose the edges that need to be creased.*

Figure 2.35 *The Crease button creases the edges exposed.*

Figure 2.36 *A creased edge is indicated by a dotted edge.*

9. Continue to hide parts of the mesh and crease the edges. Next, use the Edge Loop button to add polygons to certain areas. When you click Edge Loop, ZBrush adds a new row of polygons around the exposed edges. Just as you did for the ZMan logo, hide the geometry you want to add an edge loop to. In Figure 2.37, you can see the sections where I added an edge loop.

10. Now shrink the polygroups again by clicking Ctrl+Shift+S so you can mask off only the purple polygroup. (Your polygroup may be a different color because ZBrush assigns polygroup colors randomly.) After masking off the purple polygroup, unhide the whole mesh back so you can invert the mask to achieve what you see in Figure 2.38.

11. Now add a little volume: expand the Deformations subpalette of the Tool palette and push the slider to the right a little. The result is shown in Figure 2.39.

12. Clear the mask by Ctrl-dragging on any open part of the canvas. Now when you subdivide the mesh four times, you get results similar to Figure 2.40.

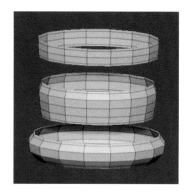

Figure 2.37 Parts of the mesh are hidden, and edge loops are added to the visible polygons.

Figure 2.38 Purple polygroups masked off (your model may use a different color).

Figure 2.39 Inflating the unmasked areas of the stand

Figure 2.40 The subdivided stand after the inflation

I created a metal ring around the stand, but you don't have to do this step. Just as we used Extract for the ZMan logo, I added a subtool by masking out an area with the MaskRect brush. Then I extracted out the mask by using the Extract button in the SubTool subpalette to create a ring around the stand. This way, I can add a different material to this ring. Figure 2.41 shows this process.

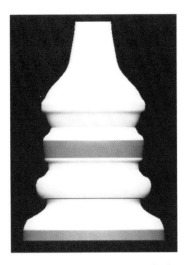

Figure 2.41 *The mesh masked out (left), and the result of using the Subtool Extract (right)*

Completing the Stand

Finally, you will close up the holes on the top and bottom of the stand so it looks like a solid object:

1. While the stand is at the highest subdivision level delete all the lowest subdivisions by clicking the Del Lower button in the Tool → Geometry subpalette.

2. Click the Close Holes button, shown in Figure 2.42, in the Tool → Geometry subpalette. This button is available only if the mesh does not have higher levels of subdivision.

   After you do this, all holes of the selected subtool will be closed. However, if you turn on PolyFrame, you will see that the hole is closed by some large triangles (see Figure 2.43). Even though ZBrush can sculpt on triangles, these triangles are very large in scale and have no uniform geometry flow to them. These triangles are not good for sculpting in ZBrush, especially if you want to subdivide this up to higher polygon counts.

3. Because of the simplicity of this mesh, fixing the large irregular triangles is easy. Activate the eye for only the stand in the SubTool subpalette, as shown in Figure 2.44. For the next

Figure 2.42 *The Close Holes button in the Geometry subpalette*

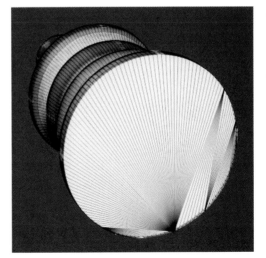

Figure 2.43 *The Close Holes button creates triangular polygons that fill the open holes in the mesh.*

Figure 2.44 The eye that is on in the SubTool palette will be remeshed.

Figure 2.45 The ReMesh All button with X-symmetry off

Figure 2.47 The bottom subtool is the remeshed version of the original triangle mesh.

Figure 2.48 Project All button in the Subtool subpalette

step, the stand must be the only subtool used, so we must turn off the eyes for the other subtools. Next click the X in the ReMesh All button off (see Figure 2.45) so that ZBrush does not use the X-symmetry when you remesh the stand.

4. Click the ReMesh All button. ZBrush creates a new Subtool by skinning a new mesh from the original stand subtool, as shown in Figure 2.46. ReMesh All creates a new subtool of quad polygons with no irregular triangles.

5. You need to transfer the detail of the original stand to the remeshed version. First select the new remeshed subtool in the SubTool subpalette.

   Think of the remeshed version as the target mesh, and the original stand with the triangles subtool as the source mesh. Make sure the eye is on for the original stand. To transfer the detail, use the Project All button in the Tool → SubTool subpalette. When you use Project All, ZBrush projects the detail from all visible subtools onto the selected subtool. The correct arrangement is shown in Figure 2.47.

Figure 2.46 New SubTool created from ReMesh All

6. Click the magic Project All button in the Tool → SubTool subpalette (see Figure 2.48).

7. When using Project All to transfer detail from one subtool to another, you may get the best results by projecting detail on each subdivision level. Start from the lowest Sdiv on the target mesh (remesh stand) when the source mesh is set to the highest-level (original triangle stand) setting and Project All at each subdivision level, working up to the highest level. As shown in Figure 2.49, Project All is used on level 1 of the target mesh in the left image, and then subdivided up to Project All again in the middle image, and the same process is used in the third image.

Figure 2.49 The Project All completed on three levels

In Figure 2.50, the stand is now a completely quad mesh with the same detail of the original stand. This is a desirable mesh for sculpting because of the evenly disrupted polygons.

Project All is a powerful tool to create a new base mesh when you need to get your sculpted detail back from the original sculpture.

Figure 2.50 Finished remeshed stand with details projected from the original stand mesh

Creating a Skin Texture

The approach that I describe here for creating skin detail is extremely simple. This technique is about building up the skin in layers. For the sake of understanding the various ways to use this technique, I will demonstrate it on a sphere:

1. Load a polysphere from LightBox, draw it on the canvas, and activate Edit mode (hot key = T). Subdivide the polysphere to level 6, which will give you 1.572 million polygons.

2. Start the base of skin by using the Surface feature, which is a subpalette of the Tool palette. Activate the Noise button. Figure 2.51 shows what happens to the surface of the mesh.

3. Adjust the Scale and Strength sliders as well as the Noise curve to produce the result shown in Figure 2.51. Just get your setting close to those below:

   • Noise Scale = 4

   • Strength = -0.014

   • Focal Shift = 86

4. Move the SNormal slider at the bottom of the palette all the way to **100**. This limits the amount of inflation that can occur when you apply the noise to the mesh.

5. Apply the Surface Noise by clicking the Apply To Mesh button to give you what I have in Figure 2.52. You can also apply a slight smooth to this in the Tool → Deformation subpalette.

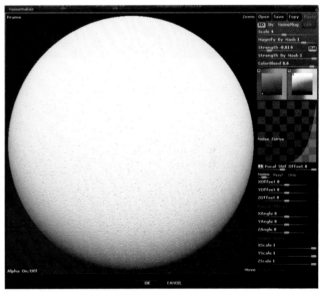

Figure 2.51 Surface Noise settings

When I turn up the specularity on the SkinShade4 material you can see this first pass will help to break up the specularity on a model (see Figure 2.53). Therefore, the light that passes over a face will be less harsh in areas of high light concentration. A *specular* area is an area where more light concentrates and that has a shiny look.

The next step is to create creases in the skin texture. The Skin brush is the perfect tool for creating this type of detail.

6. Go to the LightBox → Brush → Patterns folder. Double-click the Skin1 brush to select it. Alternate the brush size and move closer to the polysphere to see what the Skin brush does when applied (see Figure 2.54).

Figure 2.53 Surface Noise will break up the specular reflections of the mesh, increasing the realism of the skin texture.

Figure 2.52 Surface Noise results

Figure 2.54 Skin brush applied up close to the polysphere (left), and the skin brush applied to the polysphere further away from the camera (right)

Figure 2.55 A customized version of the Standard brush used for imperfections

7. Finally, apply the kind of organic imperfections you usually see on skin. Select the Standard brush and set the Stroke type to DragRect. Select Alpha 04 from the Alpha library (see Figure 2.55). Use the brush to add blemishes, as shown in Figure 2.56. You can always save these brushes to use on any model by clicking Save As in the Brush palette.

8. Use the Clay brush with DragRect stroke and Alpha 04 applied. Set the Z Intensity slider to **32**.

Continue to apply different alphas to these brushes to add more imperfections, as shown in Figure 2.57.

Figure 2.56 The results of the Standard imperfection brush

Figure 2.57 More imperfections added

Let's see how we can add alphas from LightBox to any brush.

9. On the DVD, you will find the file SW_Pores_05.psd in the Chapter 2 Assets folder. Load this file into the following directory of ZBrush so that you can load it from LightBox:

> Windows = C:/ProgramFiles(x86)/Pixologic/ZBrush4r2b/ZAlphas
>
> Mac = Applications/ZBrushOSX4r2b/ZAlphas

10. Back in ZBrush, open the LightBox Alpha menu. You will see a texture called SW_Pores_05.psd. Double-click this alpha twice. The alpha is loaded as a texture to the select brush, which should be the Standard brush, as shown in Figure 2.58.

11. To apply this texture to the Alpha palette, click the MakeAlpha button at the bottom of the fly-out window (see Figure 2.59). This button converts the selected texture into a grayscale image and places it in the Alpha library. You can then apply the alpha to your Sculpting brush.

12. Now that you have created an alpha from the texture SW_Pores_05.psd, select the alpha on the Clay brush so you can use it on the mesh to create skin pores as I did.

Figure 2.58
SW_Pores_05.psd
added to the
selected brush

You can see how amazing the result is when you use a custom detailing brush on your mesh. Continue to experiment with these techniques.

Figure 2.59 *The MakeAlpha button at the bottom of the Texture fly-out window*

What's Next

The brush system in ZBrush is pretty incredible. The next chapter will take you through some really great tips for sculpting in ZBrush.

ARTIST SPOTLIGHT: MORGAN MOREY

USING QUICKSKETCH TO HASH OUT JEWELRY IDEAS

I'VE BEEN USING ZBRUSH for a long time to design jewelry, and I only recently realized how useful a tool QuickSketch is. QuickSketch is found at the top left of the interface. When you couple the initial tool with the Lazy brush, it can be powerful.

After you click the QuickSketch button, ZBrush will switch to a PenShadow brush and fill the document with a 3D plane. Turn on LazyMouse in the Stroke palette, as shown in Figure 2.60.

With X symmetry on with these settings, you can draw superb curves and the most elegant shapes in a few strokes of a brush, as you can see in Figure 2.61.

Figure 2.60 Turn on LazyMouse in the Stroke palette.

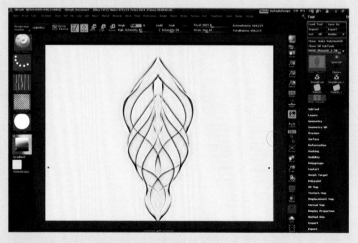

Figure 2.61 With x-symmetry on you can get smooth lines.

USING QUICKSKETCH TO HASH OUT JEWELRY IDEAS

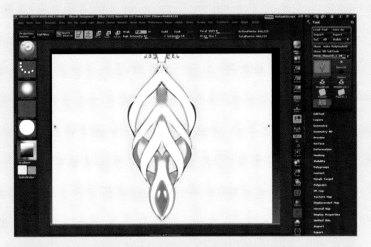

Figure 2.62 Finished reference image to sculpt from

Figure 2.63 Along with x-symmetry turn on y-symmetry in the Transform palette.

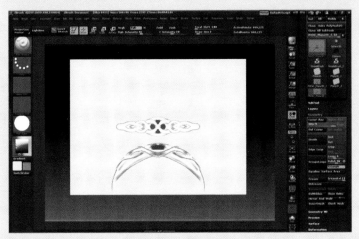

Figure 2.64 Draw out the side of the ring.

After you establish your line work, you can then add color to create loose paint-ups; just turn off the texture of the brush and set the alpha to 28 or any other of your preference. Make a few more strokes, and you have a great reference to begin your sculpt, as shown in Figure 2.62.

When designing a ring, QuickSketch enables you to use symmetry to your advantage. Choose Transform → Active Symmetry → Y and you will have two axes of symmetry for your brush (see Figure 2.63).

With both X and Y symmetry on, you can draw a four-way symmetric ring with ease. I generally start by drawing the stone shape I'll be working around and the setting, and then I draw the shoulders and shank as I see fit. Next I turn off the Y symmetry and draw the side view of the ring so I can see how each element interacts, as shown in Figure 2.64.

USING QUICKSKETCH TO HASH OUT JEWELRY IDEAS

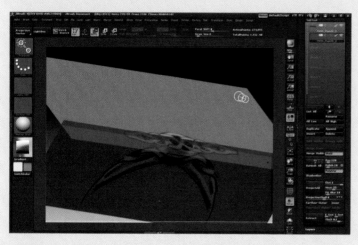

If I'm working on a very complex design, I create a cross viewport with two images so I can design in 3D space. This way, I can see both 2D designs. I do this by duplicating the plane and using the Transpose tools to rotate and position as necessary, just as in Figure 2.65.

Figure 2.65 Duplicate the plane and rotate it..

Using ShadowBox with My QuickSketch Design

ShadowBox is one of the greatest tools Pixologic has come up with in recent years. It allows you to draw geometry in simple brush strokes by using the Masking brush to define the form from two or three planes.

With this in mind, you can combine masking brushes with symmetry and Lazy Mouse to generate fantastic intricate lattices and easily define natural form.

This next part is optional but still useful. If you have an image you want to use as a reference, follow these steps to assign your 2D design to a 3D plane:

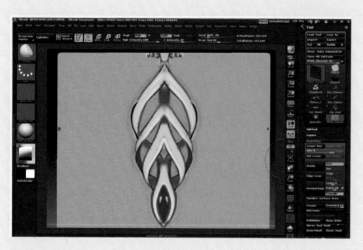

1. Create a 3D plane in the Tool palette.
2. Make the 3D plane a polymesh by clicking the Make PolyMesh3D button at the top of the Tool palette.
3. Import the image you want into the Texture palette.
4. In the Tool → Texture Map subpalette, select your imported texture so it is assigned to the plane.
5. Adjust the plane by using Transpose Line as necessary and using Move mode to stretch it.

Figure 2.66 is my QuickSketch design assigned to a plane by using the preceding steps.

Figure 2.66 QuickSketch design assigned to the plane

USING QUICKSKETCH TO HASH OUT JEWELRY IDEAS

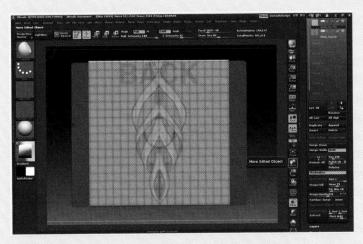

Figure 2.67 *Make sure Ghost is off when Transparency is on.*

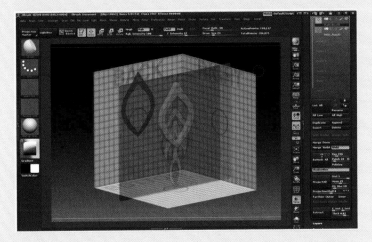

Figure 2.68 *Based on the design, mask out the back face of ShadowBox.*

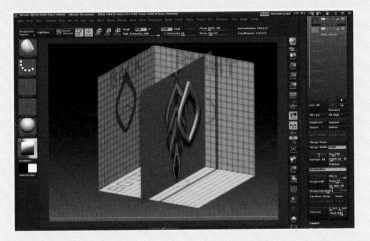

Figure 2.69 *Masked out all three panels of ShadowBox*

6. Open LightBox. Under the Tool menu, slide across to ShadowBox256.ZTL. Double-click this tool to load it into the Tool palette. Then append your image plane to the ShadowBox. Use Transparency without Ghost on to line up your design to the ShadowBox, just as I did in Figure 2.67. Remember that Transparency and Ghost are on the right side of your interface.

7. If you hold Ctrl and mask out the back panel based on the design, you will see the geometry created immediately, as shown in Figure 2.68.

8. If you want to change the thickness of the mask, the other two panels need to be introduced: Ctrl-click and drag a box with MaskRect over the other two panels. You can draw a design on the other two axes. However, I find it easier to draw the parts flat and change their shape with conventional methods by using Move mode. Figure 2.69 shows the masking of the other two panels to adjust the thickness.

USING QUICKSKETCH TO HASH OUT JEWELRY IDEAS

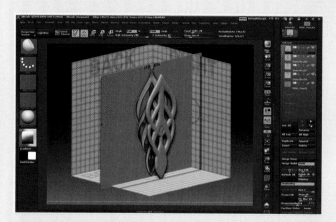

Figure 2.70 Results from the mask

9. It is important to note that you can put too much detail into masks when using ShadowBox. I tend to draw one element per ShadowBox, so duplicate the element in the SubTool subpalette by clicking the Duplicate button and then erase the mask on the back plane without erasing the other two planes. If you do it right, you will use just the mask on the side and bottom planes, and you'll have a giant square in the way of your panel. So generally I leave a little of the previous design behind, which I erase later to give me the result you see in Figure 2.70.

You can repeat this process of duplicating and redrawing the mask as many times as you want; the advantage of starting a new ShadowBox is that the thicknesses will be uniform. When you are happy with your design, go back down the SubTool stack and turn off the ShadowBox button. Enjoy your finished work. My finished piece appears in Figure 2.71.

The best way to layer and interlace your pieces is to use the Move brush while holding the Alt key. This will push or pull the mesh along the normals. After you use the Move brush a little, you should get something similar to Figures 2.72 and 2.73 below.

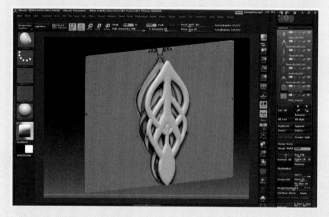

Figure 2.71 Finished piece from ShadowBox

Figure 2.72 Finished piece with adjustments using the Move brush

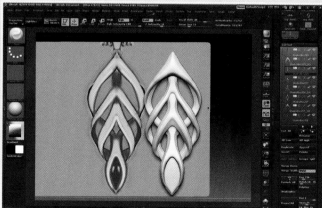

Figure 2.73 Another view of the finished piece

USING QUICKSKETCH TO HASH OUT JEWELRY IDEAS

Exporting for Printing

So you've finished a fantastic piece of jewelry that will be the envy of all your friends, but you need to bring it into reality.

You need to ask yourself some questions to determine whether your design is feasible:

- Are there floating parts?
- Is everything well intersected?
- Are there holes in the geometry?

You learn these things with practice, so I can't give you all the questions and solutions. But I will do my best. After your piece passes this initial inspection, you can move forward:

1. Save your piece separately and save it somewhere safe. I cannot stress this enough, because if the file corrupts or something else happens, you will be devastated, especially if you plan to use your design in your business. So be sure to back up your project.

2. Merge your visible subtools and select the tool you created. Now the model needs to be decimated, because when you send it to your printers, you must send a file that is about 15–20 MB, depending on your printer preferences. Open ZPlugin → Decimation Master, as shown in Figure 2.74. If you haven't installed Decimation Master, you can find it on the Pixologic website: www.pixologic.com/zbrush/downloadcenter/zplugins/.

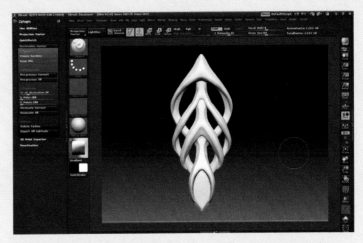

Figure 2.74 Use the Decimation Master plug-in to reduce the polygons.

3. In Decimation Master, select Pre-Process Current. Now go make a cup of tea, because depending on the power of your computer and the total poly count of your model, the processing can take a while. You'll know when the job is finished, because you can rotate the model again.

   In Figure 2.75, you can see that the mesh is high in poly count and is completely quaded.

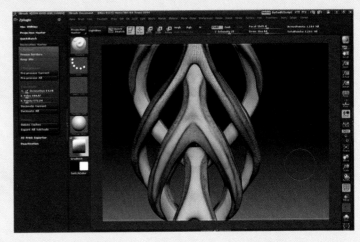

Figure 2.75 The mesh is high in poly count and all quads.

USING QUICKSKETCH TO HASH OUT JEWELRY IDEAS

4. Next move the % Of Decimation slider until the K poly is around the 330–380 mark to make the file size something reasonable for the printers. You can also move the K poly slider to your desired poly count. Then select Decimate Current. After you do this, you won't really see any difference, but the poly count of the model will have changed, as you can see in Figure 2.76.

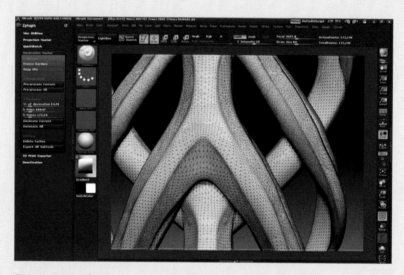

Figure 2.76 The mesh with less polygons and all triangles.

5. Save your file with DECIMATED appended to the end of the filename. Save the tool. I also like to save an OBJ version by clicking Export in the Tool palette so I can render it later.

6. Open the plug-in 3D Print Exporter in the ZPlugin palette. Once again, if you do not have this installed, you can get it from the Pixologic website at `www.pixologic.com/zbrush/downloadcenter/zplugins/`.

7. In the 3D Print Exporter, select Update Size Ratios. I generally like to work in millimeters (mm). Choose your sizes and click STL Binary. Most printers I use prefer STL Binary, but if your printer uses one of the other file extensions, use those. Save your file, and that's your model ready to print. If you are not sure about sizes, get a ruler and measure the model onscreen to see what it will look like.

You will know that your file has been saved as an STL file when you see the following dialog box (Figure 2.77).

Figure 2.77 Menu indicating that the file was successfully saved as an STL.

USING QUICKSKETCH TO HASH OUT JEWELRY IDEAS

I generally like to check my STLs before I send them off, so I can find volumes, check thicknesses, and see whether there are any problems in the mesh. For this, I use MiniMagics 2.0, which is a free program. Here is a quick rundown of checks you should make:

- Check the volume in MM3. From this, you can work out weights in metal.
- Run diagnostics.
- Inversed normals and bad edges usually occur when geometry is collapsed. This is generally bad but can be fixed by the printers.
- Mesh Shells – When there are separate SubTools the printers will fix this with a push of the button.
- You can also measure areas to check thicknesses if needed.

In Figure 2.78, you can see how I used MiniMagics to measure the piece.

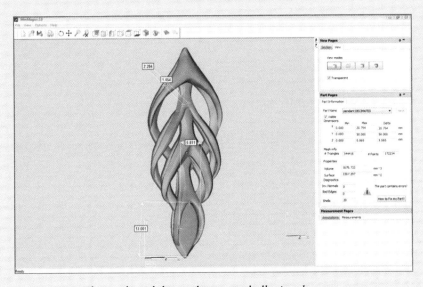

Figure 2.78 *The mesh with less polygons and all triangles.*

MORGAN MOREY *grew up in a family of artists, so he initially studied 3D animation as a way of doing something artistic while at the same time something different from his parents' jewelry work. However, after graduating and spending a year sitting around emailing places for work, to no avail, he took up the craft of jewelry making after being inspired by a visit to the International Jewellery London trade show. Sounds like something from Star Wars: "It is inevitable" that you will follow in your parents' footsteps.*

But how often in life do you get the chance to do something very few people are doing or have even considered? So now he creates jewelry by using ZBrush to design levels of detail impossible to achieve by hand. He is currently working on building up a business from scratch to sell ZBrush jewelry on commission and for retail. He also advises on ZBrush CAD workflow.

www.mousejeweller.co.uk

ARTIST SPOTLIGHT: ZACK PETROC
CREATING MESH THICKNESS WITHOUT LOSING SUBDIVISION LEVELS

ONE OF ZBRUSH'S MAIN WORKFLOW ADVANTAGES is having the ability to step down to lower levels of subdivision to make quick global changes. In this section, I'll showcase a technique that lets you add details to a single-sided mesh at a high subdivision level, give the mesh a thickness, and then reconstruct your lower subdivision levels.

This technique was used to add thickness to the cape and clothing items as well as the numerous bits of floating flesh on this Bogman character from *Adaboy, The Sculpted Novel* (see Figure 2.79).

Figure 2.79 Final cape on Bogman

CREATING MESH THICKNESS WITHOUT LOSING SUBDIVISION LEVELS

Let's look at the creation of his torn cape:

1. Create a low-poly base mesh in ZBrush or any external modeling package. In ZBrush, you can start with a flat plane by using Plane3D in the Tool palette. Click the Make PolyMesh3D button in the Tool palette to convert the geometry into a polymesh, and then choose the Tool → Geometry → Reconstruct Subdiv button to achieve your desired mesh density.

2. Click the Tool → Geometry → Crease Edges button before you begin sculpting to help prevent the cape from shrinking when you create higher subdivision levels (see Figure 2.80).

Figure 2.80 Add creasing to the cape to prevent shrinking.

3. Begin to refine your form. At this stage, avoid all high-level detail and focus on the global low-subdivision-level masses.

4. Evaluate the overall shape, form, and gesture of the cape. Use the Move brush, Standard brush, and Transpose Mode to achieve the desired results.

In Figure 2.81, I blocked in the overall scale and gesture of the cape. Throughout this process, I turned on the visibility of the character and other costume subtools to evaluate their overall relationships.

5. Create higher levels of subdivision by using Tool → Geometry → Divide and then continue to refine the form.

6. Use the Move brush and Inflate brush on the main sections of the cape, and the Transpose mask to quickly rotate, scale, and reposition the long strands of tattered cloth.

Figure 2.81 Using the Move brush to block out the overall shape of the cape

CREATING MESH THICKNESS WITHOUT LOSING SUBDIVISION LEVELS

7. Continue to refine the mesh. Remember to step down to lower levels to make global changes. As a general rule, you will want to step down to the lowest level possible to achieve the desired changes.

8. Refine the sculpt to a level that shows your design intention, but don't add any finite surface detailing (see Figure 2.82). We'll save that for our final step.

Figure 2.82 Refine the cape with more subdivision levels.

9. Now let's add thickness. Press Shift+S or click the little camera icon in the Transform palette to take a screen capture of your mesh. This will allow you to see the amount of thickness we are about to create for our cape.

10. Without moving your mesh, store a morph target by choosing Tool → Morph Target → StoreMT.

11. After you save a morph target in the Tool → Deformation subpalette, use Inflate to offset your mesh. The amount of offset in the base-cape screen capture and the inflated cape will determine our new thickness.

    Figure 2.83 showcases the cape thickness we are about to create. It's important to note that we still have only a single-sided mesh. The screen capture we did in step 9 is only a visual cue.

12. To create a mesh with thickness, choose Tool → Morph Target → CreateDiff Mesh. Remember, if you have not stored a morph target, you will not be able to create a difference mesh.

13. The mesh is created as a new tool in your Tool palette. Select the new tool to view your cape with thickness! If you turn on the wireframe, you'll notice that ZBrush automatically created three polygroups: one for the outside surface, one for the inside surface, and one for the edge thickness. If you do not see all three sides of the mesh, just click Double in Tool → Display Properties (see Figure 2.84).

14. Using Tool → SubTool → Append, select the new cape mesh and append it as a new subtool. This will add it to our list of subtools for our character.

    With a clean, well-defined form, our sculpt could be complete, but let's take things one step further. Next we will use a trick that lets us reconstruct subdivision levels. In order to reconstruct subdivisions on the new mesh, we'll need to add a few edge loops to the edge thickness polygroup.

CREATING MESH THICKNESS WITHOUT LOSING SUBDIVISION LEVELS

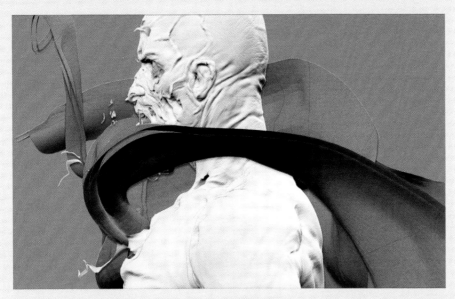

Figure 2.83 With a screen capture, adjust the cape to the desired thickness.

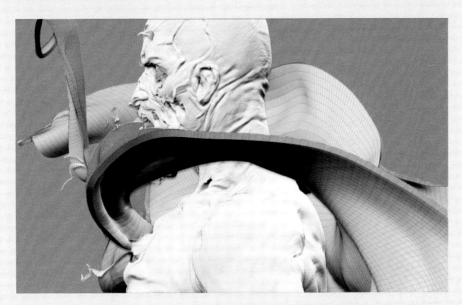

Figure 2.84 Turn Double on in Tool → Display Properties to see all three sides.

15. Shift+Ctrl-click on the edge thickness polygroup to isolate this section of the cape. You should now see only the polygroup representing the edge thickness.

16. Next we will insert edge loops. With the correct number of edge loops inserted in this poly-group, ZBrush will let us reconstruct lower levels of subdivision on the entire mesh. First let's figure out how many edge loops we need to add. Go back to your original cape mesh, step down to the lowest level, and hide everything except one polyface. Step back up to your high-est level. Count the number of spans added, and you'll know exactly how many spans we need

CREATING MESH THICKNESS WITHOUT LOSING SUBDIVISION LEVELS

to add to our new edge thickness polygroup. Figure 2.85 shows how many spans I have at the highest subdivision level of the original single-face cape. We need to add 15 edge loops.

Figure 2.85 Count the spans to figure out the number of edge loops needed.

17. Go back to the new cape subtool and isolate a selection on the edge thickness polygroup by holding Shift+Ctrl while clicking on a polygroup that represents the thickness. With the edge thickness polygroup visibility isolated, use Tool → Geometry → Edge Loop to insert 15 new edge loops.

Figure 2.86 shows the edge loops we are adding to the new polygroup on the new cape. So far, we've added four.

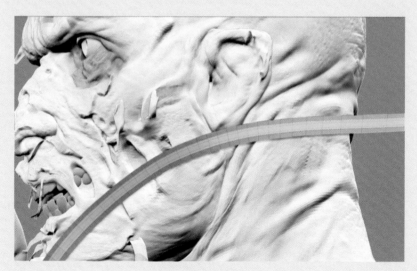

Figure 2.86 Four edges loops have been added.

18. After adding 15 new edge loops, use Tool → Geometry → Reconstruct Subdiv to re-create the lower levels of the subdivisions in the mesh.

CREATING MESH THICKNESS WITHOUT LOSING SUBDIVISION LEVELS

Figure 2.87 shows the final result of my cape on the lowest subdivision level and the highest subdivision level.

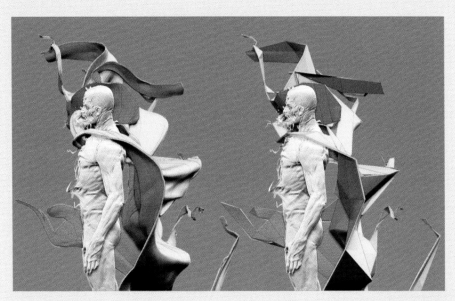

Figure 2.87 *Final result on the highest and lowest subdivision levels*

You should now be able to step up and down through all the levels of division on our new mesh with thickness. This is a great technique to use on everything from belts, boots, and pants, to bits of floating flesh. Good luck!

WITH A COMMITMENT *to driving the digital entertainment industry forward, Zack Petroc continues to develop new techniques that redefine how digital tools impact the art and design of storytelling. In 2005, he opened Zack Petroc Studios to focus on the development of unique new content and provide like-minded artists an avenue for creating an independent property (IP). The Studio's first IP, TheAdaboy.com, gives viewers direct access to behind-the-scenes story development techniques, allowing them to follow along as it evolves from concept to completed project. Additionally, his studio has worked on the development of several feature films and video games, with a recent client list that includes Disney Interactive Studios, Scott Free Productions, SCEA, Walt Disney Imagineering, Snoot Entertainment, Hasbro, and Paramount Pictures.*

Zack also has a passion for teaching and training digital artists. In addition to lecturing at universities across the US and abroad, Zack has headed several workshops and training seminars at leading industry companies. Recently he created one of a kind training tools and advanced Master Classes available via **www.zackpetroc.com***.*

Check the included DVD for details on a special Zack Petroc Studios Premium Member discount. Currently he enjoys spending his days as Model Supervisor and Studio Department Lead at Disney Feature Animation, interacting with some of the most talented artists in the industry.

www.zackpetroc.com

www.theAdaboy.com

three

Sculpting—
Developing Your Next Piece

The number one reason I *picked up ZBrush*
was for its sculpting brushes. ZBrush has changed how I create digital images. ZBrush gave me the freedom that I have never experienced before with any 3D application. It really made me have that real world feel of sculpting with clay. The many ways that ZBrush enables you to create should inspire you to develop your own workflow.

In this chapter, you will look further into ShadowBox, create your own brushes, use hard-surface tools, use Spotlight for sculpting, use ZSketch, and much more. So strap in with your Wacom pen in hand and get ready for the craziest, funniest ride of your digital sculpting life.

- Using hard-edge brush techniques
- Adjusting and creating brushes
- Understanding the power of ShadowBox
- Making difficult items with ZSpheres
- Using Morph Difference to create thickness

Using Hard-Edge Brush Techniques

When it comes to sculpting in ZBrush, everything starts and ends with the 3D brushes. There are more than 200 brushes that ship with ZBrush, and in the next few pages I will reveal how you edit brushes and create a brush from scratch.

With all the features in the Brush palette, you'd like to know how each button and slider affects your brush. Remember, you can access all brushes in ZBrush by tapping the letter B, and you will find the rest of the brushes in LightBox under the Brush tab.

ClipCurve Brush with BRadius

Let's take a look at some of my favorite brushes to play with in ZBrush, starting with the Clip brushes. Figure 3.1 shows the beginning of a mechanical soldier created entirely in ZBrush with the Clip brushes.

Figure 3.1 Mech soldier built with Clip brushes

Let's create two parts of this mech soldier, starting with the shoulder piece you see in Figure 3.2:

1. Make a polysphere in Edit mode in ZBrush. Make sure Symmetry mode is on in X-symmetry.

2. Make the first cut with the ClipCurve brush. You can see the cut I made in Figure 3.3.

Figure 3.2 Shoulder piece of mech soldier

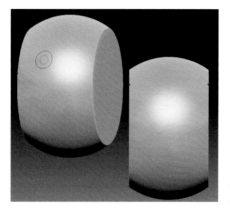

Figure 3.3 First cut with the ClipCurve brush

3. To get the offset look, activate BRadius by holding down Ctrl+spacebar or clicking the BRadius button in the Brush → Clip Brush Modifiers subpalette (see Figure 3.4).

Creating an offset on meshes is easy (see Figure 3.5), so experiment often with this feature.

4. To create the middle section, use the MaskRect brush to create a masked box and then use Move mode at the top of the interface to activate the Transpose line. Note that I did not use the Move brush to move the squared mask back into the shoulder piece. You can see the result in Figure 3.6.

Figure 3.4
BRadius
setting for
Clip brushes

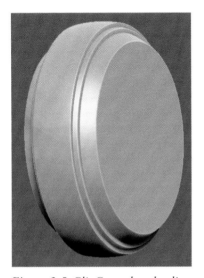

Figure 3.5 *ClipCurve brush edits with BRadius on*

Figure 3.6 *Shoulder piece with middle section*

I often use the spacebar with masking and clipping brushes to ensure an accurate position before applying the mask or clip. When you hold the spacebar while using a Mask brush or Clip brush, you can move the region around the document freely before you apply the mask or clip.

5. To make the grid pattern in the section that was just masked off in Figure 3.7, simply select the Standard brush with DragRect and the square alpha 28, as shown in Figure 3.8. Also, turn on V Tiles to 10 in the Alpha → Modify subpalette. This feature tiles the selected alpha along the vertical path. H Tiles would tile the alpha along the horizontal path.

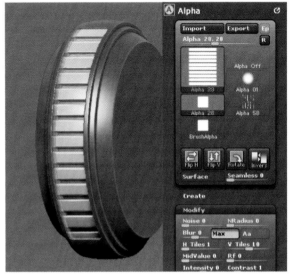

Figure 3.7 *A grid pattern is applied in the middle of the sphere.*

Figure 3.8
Standard brush with V Tiles applied to a square alpha

6. To build the center part of the shoulder piece, use MaskCircle with Square and Center on. These two buttons are in the Stroke → Shape subpalette (see Figure 3.9). Alternatively, click the Stroke icon on the left of the ZBrush interface (if you are using the default settings). The Square button keeps the stroke as a perfect circle, and the Center button sets the brush icon as the center of the stroke when drawn out.

Figure 3.10 shows the result of using the Center and Square features when you invert the mask.

7. To make the piece a bit wider, use Tool → Size Deformation along the X axis.

8. To finish the middle section, switch to the TrimHole brush. Start with a large brush stroke to push the surface in to create a hole. Then hold the Alt key so the brush pulls out the surface to create a circular center raised off the surface, as in Figure 3.11.

Figure 3.9 *Square and Center buttons of the Stroke palette*

Figure 3.10 *Center pushed in from masking with Center and Square on*

Figure 3.11 *Finished shoulder piece without color*

ZSketch Brushes for BaseMesh

To create the large pieces over the shoulders, the large piece in the front, or the pieces around the soldier's waist, use the Sketch 3 brush found in Sketch mode. With this quick technique, you can use any other mesh as a base to draw ZSpheres directly on the surface.

First you create the base of the whole character. This will help make your proportions correct. For this exercise, load SuperAverageMan_low.ZTL from the LightBox Tool menu. Of course, you could just use the base of your own character instead. Here are the steps:

1. Append a ZSphere as a subtool, as shown in Figure 3.12.

2. After you append a ZSphere, you may have to adjust its size to avoid drawing on the mesh instead of the ZSphere itself. Switch to Scale mode at the top of the interface and scale down the ZSphere, as shown in Figure 3.13.

3. With the ZSphere as the selected subtool, turn on ZSketch mode by pressing Shift+A or clicking EditSketch in the Tool → ZSketch subpalette (see Figure 3.14). As soon as you do this, the ZSphere will take on the characteristics of the selected material. In Figure 3.15, my ZSphere is in EditSketch mode.

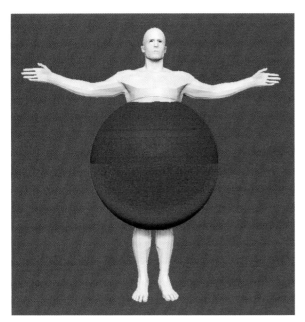

Figure 3.12 *ZSphere as a subtool to SuperAverageMan*

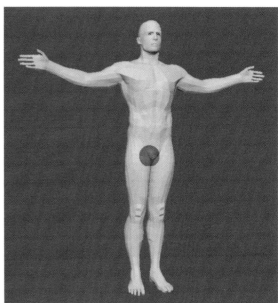

Figure 3.13 *ZSphere scaled to fit inside the SuperAverageMan mesh*

Figure 3.14
*EditSketch
on ZSketch
subpalette*

Now when I press the B key, the Brush palette will pop up only ZSketch brushes (see Figure 3.16).

4. In LightBox, click on the Brush menu. Open the ZSketch folder and select the Sketch 3 brush. Now draw directly onto the surface with ZSketch. Figure 3.17 demonstrates a quick way to create a piece of armor that may go around the waist.

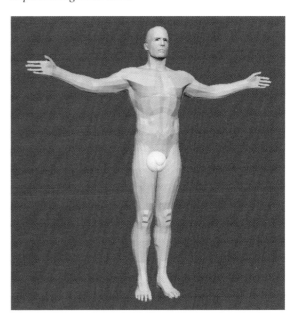

Figure 3.15 *ZSphere in EditSketch mode*

Figure 3.16
*ZSketch brushes when
in EditSketch mode*

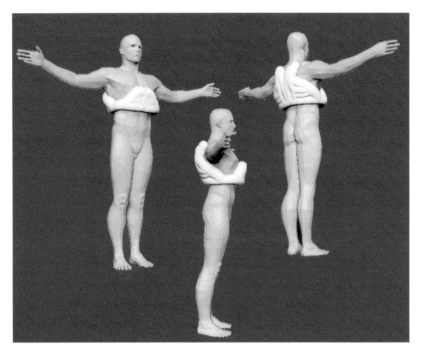

Figure 3.17 Armor base built from ZSketch

In ZSketch, draw out a stroke and then hold the Shift key to smooth the stroke. Repeat this process of drawing and smoothing over and over again. This technique creates a cleaner surface.

Now you need to turn the sketched ZSpheres into a mesh to further refine with the sculpting brushes.

5. Click the Preview button in the Unified Skin subpalette (see Figure 3.18).

6. Set the Polish Surface slider to **43**. This setting smooths out the mesh for a less lumpy look in Preview mode. Also, turn down the Border slider and turn off the Allow Tri button to avoid applying perfect border edges around each polygroup and to avoid allowing triangles in the mesh.

7. The Resolution slider controls the density of the unified skin (the number of polygons in the first subdivision level). Keep the resolution as low as possible while maintaining the silhouette. Remember that you are just previewing the mesh. To create a piece of geometry similar to Figure 3.19, you must click the Make Unified Skin button in the Tool → Unified Skin subpalette. A new tool is created at the top of the Tool palette. You must click this new tool in order to edit the mesh.

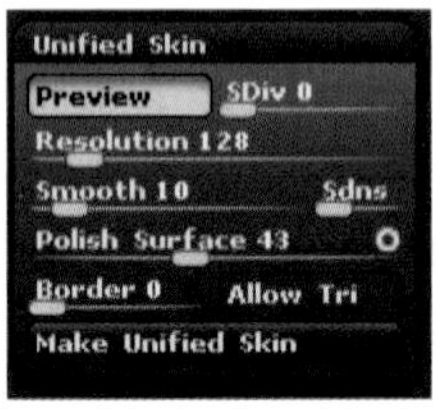

Figure 3.18 The Preview button will create a mesh for any ZSketch.

After playing around with the Clip brushes and using a lot of masking techniques, I came up with what you see in Figure 3.20.

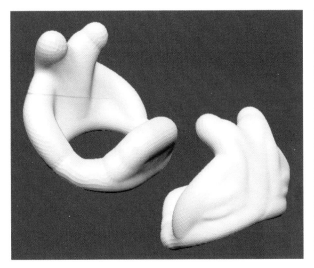

Figure 3.19 ZSketch unified skin mesh

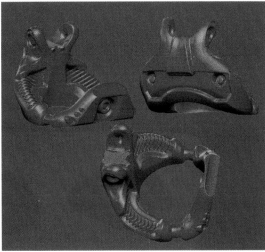

Figure 3.20 Finished model from the ZSketch process

Adjusting and Creating Brushes

The Brush palette can be overwhelming, so let's focus on some features that have always given me hours of discovery in ZBrush. By understanding the various features in the Brush palette, you will sculpt with a new outlook. This section presents some of my favorite features for creating a custom brush or editing brushes in ZBrush.

Using a Custom Brush with Tilt

When I first played with the Tilt feature, I created brush after brush, just as a challenge. In this exercise, you will create brushes much like the ScalesLizard, ScalesSnake1, and Scales C brushes in the LightBox → Brush menu.

First you will create a brush like the ScalesLizard brush. You can see in Figure 3.21 how the scales overlap in a direction that follows the brush stroke direction.

Figure 3.21 The ScalesLizard brush applies a realistic overlapping.

Start by creating the alpha. You will use the same effect as you did in Chapter 1, "Understanding the Basics," with the brick wall:

1. Make a scale out of the ZBrush polysphere to use for the alpha. You can see the finished scale and alpha in Figure 3.22. You can find the Scale tool and alpha in the Chapter 3 Assets folder. The tool is called ScaleAlpha.ZTL, and the alpha is called ScaleAlpha.PSD. In order to create this tillable alpha, I used the same technique in Chapter 1 in the Create a Tillable Alpha with 2.5D section.

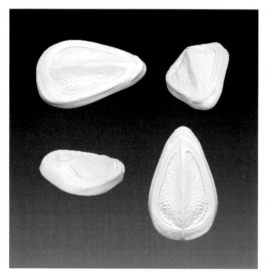 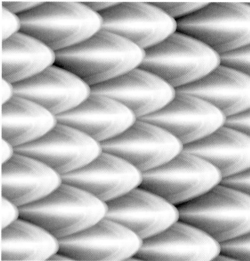

Figure 3.22 The scale (left) and the finished alpha (right)

2. Now let's assign the completed alpha to a brush. There are several base types in ZBrush. You can see any brush base type by hovering your cursor over any brush. In Figure 3.23, you can see that the Elastic brush is actually a base type.

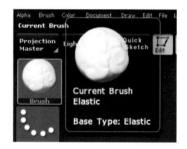

Figure 3.23 The Elastic brush is a base type.

Figuring out which base type to use when you create a custom brush is key. ZBrush has several base types that will react in many ways. Scroll over your favorite brush to see what base type it is; you will see the base type at the bottom of the icon.

For this project, the Elastic brush works the best.

3. Select the Elastic brush with a Dots stroke and ScalesAlpha.PSD selected as an alpha. Now when you apply the stroke to any surface, you will see the scales; however, there will be a major overlap of the alpha. To get rid of this, turn on the Roll feature in the Stroke palette. Also turn on the LazyMouse feature with the default settings. Figure 3.24 shows the difference with the brush stroke by just turning on these two features.

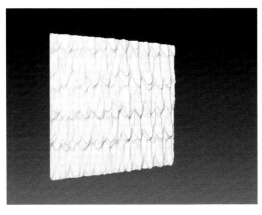

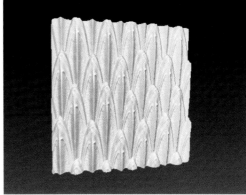

Figure 3.24 Roll and LazyMouse off (left), and Roll and LazyMouse on (right)

4. When you apply the stroke, the alpha does not follow the stroke direction. To fix this, rotate the alpha three times by clicking the Rotate button in the Alpha palette. Figure 3.25 shows the alpha facing toward the top after the rotation.

5. Repeat the alpha more than once along the vertical access. To do this, adjust V Tiles to **2** in the Alpha → Modify subpalette(see Figure 3.26).

6. Okay, now it's time to apply the Tilt to the alpha. The Tilt feature is in the Brush → Modifiers subpalette. Adjust the Tilt slider to 20 and keep Constant Tilt on (see Figure 3.27). Constant Tilt will maintain a tilt of 20, no matter what your pen pressure is.

7. To limit the alpha overlapping, go to the Brush → Auto Masking → Directional subpalette. Turn Directional on and make the following adjustments to the curve's Focal Shift and ByPressure settings (see Figure 3.28):

- Focal Shift = 90
- ByPressure = 0

8. Add another dot in the curve and push it to the lower-right corner. Also, change the Focal Shift at the top of the interface for the brush to -66.

Figure 3.29 shows the result after finishing with all the adjustments.

Figure 3.25 Clicking the Rotate button changes the alpha access to be facing upward.

Figure 3.26 Turning V Tiles to 2

Figure 3.27 Set the Tilt slider to 20 with Constant Tilt on.

Figure 3.28 Add another dot to the default curve and move it to the bottom-right corner.

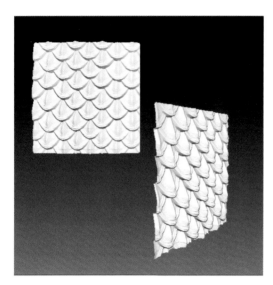

Figure 3.29 New Scale
brush applied to surface

You can find this brush, Scale.ZBP, in the Chapter 3 assets folder. Continue to play with the Tilt feature to discover its limits. To load the brush into your ZBrush program, click the Load Brush button in the Brush palette.

Creating a Stone Column

ZBrush is also a great tool for environment pieces. In this section, you will use the StoneWall brush to create a column. You will then apply some damage to the column by using the Surface feature along with a few more brush techniques, including creating a brush with Surface Noise applied. Follow these steps:

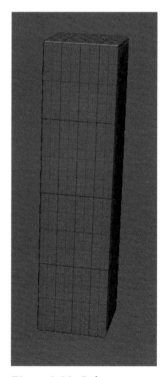

1. First you need to create the column. From LightBox load the DefaultCube.ZPR from the Project menu. This will give you a cube with five subdivision levels.

2. Now let's stretch out the cube, giving it a column form. With only Y selected, the cube size adjusts only along the Y axis. Move the Size slider to **100** twice in the Tool → Deformations subpalette. Our original cube becomes more column-shaped (see Figure 3.30).

3. Let's get some subdivision levels on the column now. Press Divide in the Tool → Geometry subpalette or use the shortcut Ctrl+D three times to get the column to level 8, which will equal 1.572 million polygons.

4. Select the StoneWall brush in LightBox → Brush Menu → Patterns folder.

5. If not already on, turn the X-symmetry mode on.

6. Adjust the brush Focal Shift to **-100**.

Figure 3.30 Column
form with Size along Y
applied twice

7. Under the Stroke palette, turn on Backtrack, and then turn on SnapToTrack and select the Line button.

8. Adjust your Draw Size so it is larger than your column.

9. Draw out the StoneWall brush, starting at the top of the column so that you have X-symmetry set to draw the front and back of the column simultaneously, as you can see in Figure 3.31.

10. Switch your symmetry to Z and apply another stroke, just as in step 10. You should have a finished-off column like Figure 3.32.

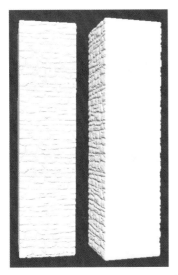

Figure 3.31 First stroke applied to the column, creating stone on the front and back

Figure 3.32 Finished column using the adjusted StoneWall brush

Applying Damage to the Column

You can now damage the column to make it look like part of a building that has been destroyed. The quickest way to apply surface detail to a mesh is to use the Surface features in ZBrush. Techniques such as the following can increase realism:

1. Use the ClayBuildup brush to create extreme damage, as shown in Figure 3.33.

2. Turn on Surface Noise in the Tool → Surface subpalette.

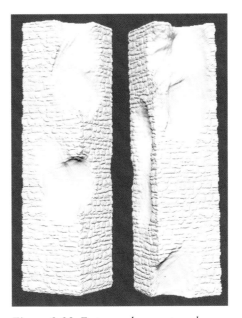

Figure 3.33 Extreme damage to column

3. Adjust the curve to look something like Figure 3.34, but have some fun and create your own curve.

4. Adjust the Noise Scale slider to something like **357**.

5. Keep the Strength slider low, such as **-0.073**. The Surface feature is just in Preview mode until you apply it to the surface. The higher the Strength, the more the surface inflates out.

6. Turn the Rel button off. This will adjust the Strength relative to Scale when pressed.

7. Mask off the parts of the mesh where you do not want the surface to be applied (see Figure 3.35). If you wish to have Surface applied to the entire mesh, don't do any masking on the surface.

8. Adjust the SNormal slider to **100**. This will limit the inflation when you apply this detail to the surface.

9. Click Apply To Mesh. This applies the Surface noise as a sculptural change. Check out the result in Figure 3.36.

Figure 3.34 Surface curve applied to surface

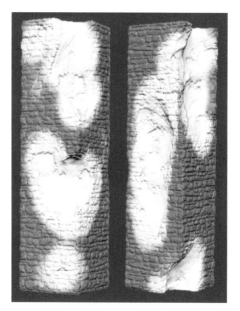

Figure 3.35 Mask out the parts where Surface will not be applied.

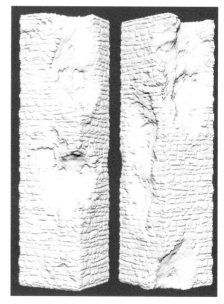

Figure 3.36 Surface Noise applied to the column

If you create a new 3D layer before clicking Apply To Mesh, you can make adjustments with the Layer Intensity and then bake in the layer to the model when you are happy with the results. You could also create a morph target before clicking Apply To Mesh so that you could use the Morph Target slider to decrease the result.

Creating a Surface Noise Brush

Surface noise can add all types of detail, even skin texture. Let's create a brush that lets us define where to apply surface noise. In your Brush palette, you will see a subpalette called Surface; let's take a quick look at this amazing feature:

1. Go to LightBox in the Brush menu and load the Surface Noise brush called Noise06. Apply this brush to the column. You can see the changes in Figure 3.37.

2. Adjust the curve in the Noise06 brush to look more like Figure 3.38.

3. Turn the Noise Scale to 512. You can see the subtleness that the brush gives to the surface in Figure 3.39.

4. One more brush is great for a model like this. Load the SoftConcrete brush and play around with it until you have something that looks like Figure 3.40.

   There you have it. You just created a pretty cool-looking column from start to finish in ZBrush.

Figure 3.37 Column with brush noise applied

Figure 3.38 Noise curve for the brush

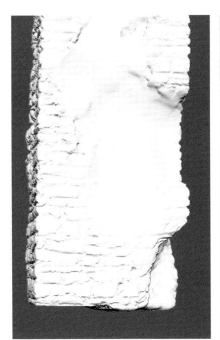

Figure 3.39 Column with brush noise applied

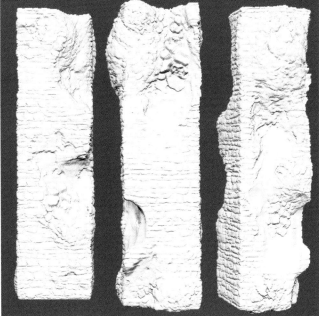

Figure 3.40 The SoftConcrete brush gives a great look to a model like this one.

Understanding the Power of ShadowBox

ShadowBox lets you create extremely complex shapes in just a few quick strokes of any of the masking brushes. ShadowBox is covered extensively throughout the book, but I want to cover a few cool ways to use ShadowBox in this chapter.

Getting Started with ShadowBox

First we need to touch base on the basics of ShadowBox before diving into more complex techniques. Having Symmetry mode in ZBrush can be convenient, but with ShadowBox it can be outright fun to use:

1. Load ShadowBox128.ZTL from the LightBox Tool menu.

   The 128 stands for the resolution of the ShadowBox when it is created. Adjust the resolution of any ShadowBox by turning off the ShadowBox button in the Tool → Geometry subpalette. The lower you go, the less detail you can achieve when masking. Turn off the ShadowBox button and change the Res slider to 256 (See Figure 3.41).

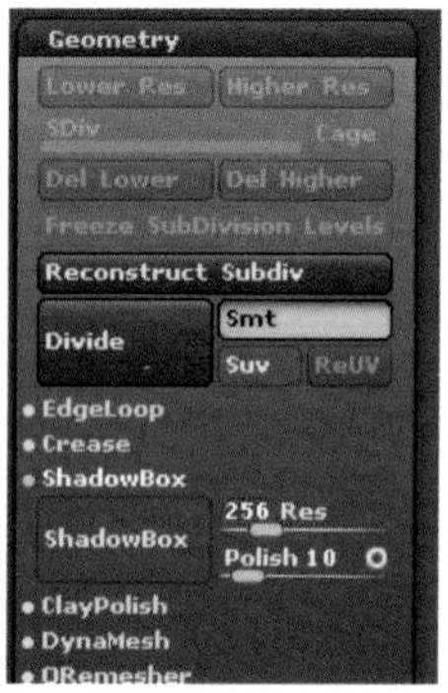

2. Turn the ShadowBox button back on.

3. ZBrush will create a cube in the middle of the ShadowBox. (see Figure 3.42).

4. Hold the Ctrl key and click-drag anywhere in the open document to clear the mask of ShadowBox. This will clear the cube from ShadowBox. Okay, enough technical stuff, let's have some fun.

5. Turn on Symmetry mode in the palette's Z axis and turn on Radial Symmetry with a RadialCount of **16**.

6. Turn on Transparency mode and Ghost on the right side of the interface (see Figure 3.43). This is key to using ShadowBox: with these buttons activated, you can mask through the geometry.

Figure 3.41 ShadowBox settings in the Tool Geometry subpalette

Figure 3.42 When adjusting the Res, ZBrush will automatically create a cube when the ShadowBox button is turned back on.

Figure 3.43 Transparency mode with Ghost on

7. If it's on, turn off Perspective mode when using ShadowBox.

8. Now while ShadowBox is oriented so you are looking at the panel labeled Back, select the MaskPen brush as your masking brush, hold the Ctrl key, and draw out something similar to Figure 3.44.

9. To convert this masking into a tool, just click the ShadowBox button in the Tool → Geometry subpalette off. With a little fun with the ClipCurve brush—that's right, it too can be in Radial Symmetry mode—you can make something like Figure 3.45.

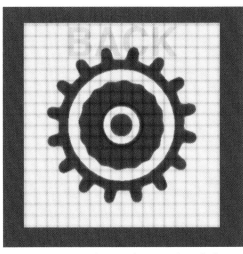

Figure 3.44 *Mask gear shape with radial symmetry on.*

Figure 3.45 *Finished tool using ShadowBox and ClipCurve*

Silhouette Drawing with ShadowBox

Now that you understand the ShadowBox basics, you're ready to try a few more techniques. Because ZBrush can also apply paint detail, you can use this to your advantage in the next exercise.

How often do we make digital creations that we would love to sculpt from a blueprint? You will use a blueprint to create a silhouette of the item we want—in this case, a plane. The plane.PSD file used throughout this technique is in the Chapter 3 assets folder. So let's get started:

1. Load ShadowBox128.ZTL from the LightBox project menu if you do not have a fresh one in Edit mode.

   Notice the grid and the Back, Right, and bottom indicators; these are actually a texture file that is applied to the ShadowBox tool. You can access this texture by going to the Tool → Texture Map subpalette (see Figure 3.46).

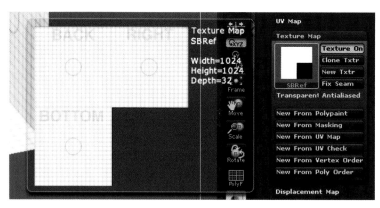

Figure 3.46 Texture map applied to ShadowBox tool

2. Export this texture from ZBrush to use in Photoshop to line up textures: click the Clone Txtr button in the Texture Map subpalette. This button sends the file to the Texture palette, where you can export the file.

3. After you align your file in Photoshop to work with the ShadowBox file, save it as a PSD file and import the file through the Texture palette, in this case the plane.PSD file (see Figure 3.47). The Import button is at the top of the Texture palette.

4. After you import the file, click the small icon in the Tool → Texture Map subpalette and select the newest imported file (see Figure 3.48).

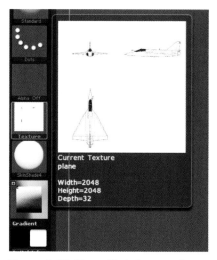

Figure 3.47 Plane file is imported through the Texture palette.

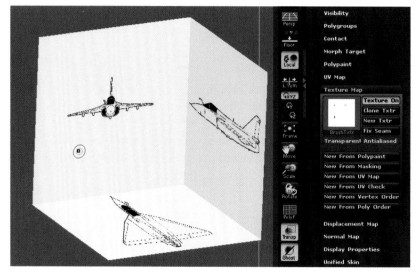

Figure 3.48 Plane.PSD assigned to the ShadowBox by selecting the image in the Texture Map subpalette

5. The texture is applied to the ShadowBox. Now assign this texture as paint information. Make sure to turn RGB on at the top of the interface, as shown in Figure 3.49.

6. Under the Tool → Polypaint subpalette, click Polypaint From Texture. This will use the texture as paint to be applied to the ShadowBox. Even if you turn off the texture in the Texture Map subpalette, the plane will still be seen on the ShadowBox.

Figure 3.49 RGB button at the top of the interface

7. Select the Standard brush with just the Dots stroke on and only RGB on. You imported the plane texture earlier, so it may still be on in the Texture palette; make sure to turn it off.

8. Press V to switch the main color from white to black (see Figure 3.50).

9. Now paint out the plane's silhouette as in Figure 3.51. Of course, you can do this with any silhouette. Remember, you can press V to switch back and forth between black and white colors.

Figure 3.50 Main and secondary colors should be set as the same in the image.

10. In the Tool → Masking subpalette, click the Mask By Intensity button. This will use the black color as 100 percent mask, but you will not see it applied to the ShadowBox.

11. Now if you hold the Ctrl key and mask wherever black color is applied to the ShadowBox tool, you will see the magic happen. Don't forget to pick up your jaw when you see the results. As you can see in Figure 3.52, a full plane is created instantly.

12. To make the plane an actual mesh, turn off the ShadowBox button (see Figure 3.53).

Figure 3.51 Silhouette of plane on ShadowBox tool

I hope you can imagine the power of this technique. You can easily turn any images that create a silhouette into geometry in ZBrush in a matter of minutes.

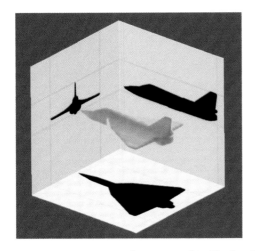

Figure 3.52 Instant plane created in ShadowBox

Figure 3.53 Finished plane from silhouette

Using ShadowBox to Create Accessories

You have looked at two ways to use ShadowBox. Now you will use ShadowBox to create some glasses for the DemoHead.ZTL file that ships with ZBrush in the LightBox → Tool menu.

With the DemoHead in Edit mode, you can begin creating glasses for him. First you need to load ShadowBox128.ZTL again, unless you already have it in the Tool palette. ZBrush will automatically switch to the Shadowbox128 tool when loaded, so just select the DemoHead again.

1. Append and select the Shadowbox128 tool to the DemoHead (see Figure 3.54). The Append button is in the Subtool palette. Also make sure to have the Ghost Transparency on at this time.

2. Draw on all three sides of ShadowBox to get what you see in Figure 3.55. This will take some experimenting, but trust me, you will get it. ShadowBox is also meant to give you a simple starter base mesh. Don't try to get it perfect in ShadowBox. You have the ZBrush 3D brushes to help you with that.

Figure 3.54 ShadowBox tool appended to the DemoHead

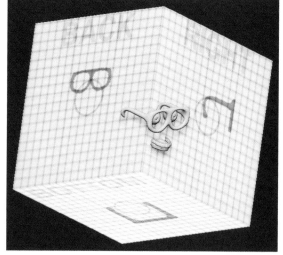

Figure 3.55 ShadowBox masking creating the glasses

3. Unclick the ShadowBox button for your results (see Figure 3.56).

4. With a little touch-up with the ClipCurve brush, you can easily give the DemoHead some glasses (see Figure 3.57).

These are very simple glasses, but you have to admit, the DemoHead looks great with glasses. Continue to push yourself to discover how you can make accessories and more with ShadowBox.

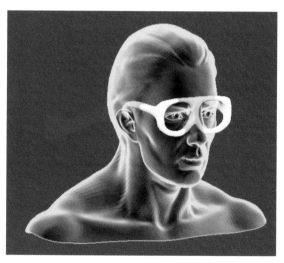

Figure 3.56 ShadowBox turned off creates the mesh that is glasses.

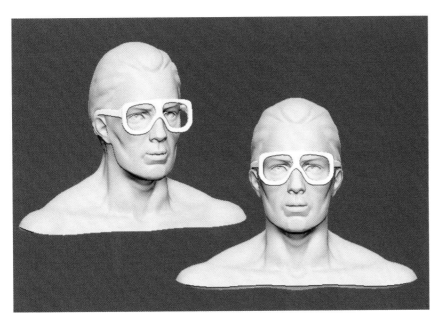

Figure 3.57 *Finished glasses for the DemoHead*

Making Difficult Items with ZSpheres

A ZSphere is one of the greatest assets of ZBrush. You have already used ZSketch to create base meshes; now you'll use the ZSpheres themselves to create chain mail and a string of bullets on the DemoSoldier that ships with ZBrush. This technique will also show how the mannequin's tools were created in ZBrush.

Putting together complex objects such as chain mail or a string of bullets can be a bit grueling. But with this technique, you will gain a quickness and accuracy that you never thought possible.

Creating Chain Mail

Chain mail takes some time to put together, especially if you are creating a knight from medieval times. If you follow these steps for creating a repetitive complex object, you have endless possibilities with this technique:

1. Make an individual link for the chain mail by selecting the Ring3D tool in ZBrush.

2. In Edit mode, draw out the Ring3D on the ZBrush document.

3. Now click Make Polymesh3D; your ring will look the same but now it is a sculptable mesh. The name should change to something like PM3D_Ring3D.

4. Switch to Move mode, draw out an action line, and hold the Ctrl key while clicking on the middle circle when moving. This will create a duplicate of the ring. You can also hold Shift in this process to keep the ring aligned along the action line. As long as you have something like Figure 3.58, you will be fine.

5. Rotate the ring you just moved. Using the Tool → Deformation → Rotate slider, rotate by **90** with only the Y highlighted (see Figure 3.59).

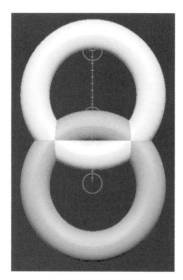

Figure 3.58 Offsetting the two rings

Figure 3.59 The upper ring with a 90-degree rotation

Figure 3.60 Rename the rings Link.

7. Rename the rings Link in the Tool → SubTool subpalette. You should have what I do in Figure 3.60.

8. Select a ZSphere. You should see your tool switch from Link to a ZSphere.

9. Now make sure you are in Draw mode. Begin to draw out a second ZSphere; hold the Shift key while drawing out the ZSphere. This will snap the second ZSphere to be the exact size of the original (see Figure 3.61).

10. Open the Tool → Adaptive Skin subpalette and find a button called Use Classic Skinning.

11. Turn on Use Classic Skinning (see Figure 3.62).

12. Click Insert Local Mesh. A menu pops up (see Figure 3.63). Find the Link tool and click it to replace the second ZSphere with the Link tool.

Figure 3.61 Second ZSphere drawn out to match the size of the original by holding the Shift key when drawing

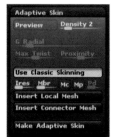

Figure 3.62 Adaptive Skin subpalette with Use Classic Skinning on

Figure 3.63 Selecting the Link tool to replace the ZSphere chains

Make sure the second ZSphere is selected when using this technique. The selected ZSphere will be red. To select a ZSphere, just switch to the Move mode at the top of the interface, click the second ZSphere, and then click Draw mode.

Depending on the distance between your two ZSpheres, you will get something like Figure 3.64.

You can clearly see a problem. The link is not going in the right direction. This is easy to fix in ZBrush.

13. Select Link in the Tool palette again. Open the Tool → Preview subpalette and click in any open space in the Preview window (see the left image of Figure 3.65). Click and drag to start rotating the link, and then hold the Shift key (see the right image of Figure 3.65).

14. Click the Store button below the Preview window. You should see your link change orientation in the ZBrush document.

Figure 3.64 Second ZSphere is replaced by the Link tool.

Figure 3.65 The link orientation at the start (left), and the link orientation after rotating it in the Preview window (right)

15. Switch back to the ZSphere with the link going in the wrong direction. Undo by pressing Ctrl+Z so all you have are the two ZSpheres again. Make sure the second ZSphere is selected again.

16. Click the Use Classic Skinning option again in the Adaptive Skin subpalette. Click the Insert Local Mesh option again and select the link (see Figure 3.66).

17. Continue to draw out ZSpheres to create a long chain. Remember to hold the Shift key when drawing out the ZSpheres so the chain link will always be the same size. After you draw all you want, the chain mail will look similar to Figure 3.67.

Figure 3.66 ZSphere is replaced by the Link tool with the correct orientation.

You aren't quite done yet. You need to make this chain mail an actual mesh.

Figure 3.67 *Finished-off chain mail*

Figure 3.68 *Finished chain mail after clicking Make Adaptive Skin*

18. Click the Preview button in the Adaptive Skin subpalette or press A to convert everything into a mesh.

19. In Preview mode, click the Make Adaptive Skin button to create a chain mail tool that will be placed automatically in the Tool palette. As you can see in Figure 3.68, you have the finished chain mail.

   Just a few more steps. The half-circle at the beginning of your chain is from the root ZSphere that was drawn out. Deleting this piece is easy.

20. Turn on Polyframe mode (see the left image of Figure 3.69), hold down Ctrl+Shift, and select the half-circle. You now only have a half-circle visible (see the middle image of Figure 3.69).

21. Continue to hold Ctrl+Shift. Click and drag anywhere in the canvas without letting go of Ctrl+Shift. This switches the viewable mesh to the chain shown in the right image of Figure 3.70.

22. Go to the Tool → Geometry subpalette and click the DelHidden button. If you get a warning when you click DelHidden, it's most likely because you are on subdivision level 2. Switch to level 1, and you can delete the hidden half-circle.

There you have it, a simple way to use ZBrush to create chain mail. Now just think about all the cool stuff you can make by swapping out ZSpheres with actual geometry.

Figure 3.69 *The three steps to deleting hidden geometry in ZBrush*

Creating a String of Bullets

Let's really put this technique to work by creating a string of bullets along the chest of the DemoSoldier tool that ships with ZBrush. Unlike the preceding exercise, this task is not presented step-by-step. I will just walk you through the major points to make our DemoSoldier become Rambo.

I have included the Bullet.ZTL file used in this example in the Chapter 3 assets folder. The file has several polygroups, and the outer piece of geometry is meant to be the leather that holds the bullet. If you wish to follow along, load Bullet.ZTL into ZBrush in Edit mode.

---

1. Make a very simple strap that is wrapped around the DemoSoldier (see Figure 3.70). I didn't create anything really detailed here; I just want to give you the idea of what you can do with this technique.

2. Next you need to Append or Insert a ZSphere to the DemoSoldier tool. The Append button will add the ZSphere to the bottom of the Tool → Subtool palette, whereas the Insert button will place the ZSphere directly below the currently selected subtool.

3. Adjust the size and location of the ZSphere by using the Move and Scale modes at the top of the interface. Position the ZSphere where you want the bullets to begin. Remember, these ZSpheres will become your bullets. Figure 3.71 shows where I placed the first ZSphere, often known as the root ZSphere.

   Now you can actually use the geometry of the strap, or any other geometry for that matter, to draw your ZSpheres onto.

4. As long as Draw mode is on, you can click anywhere on the strap, and the next ZSphere will begin to draw there. Remember to hold the Shift key so every ZSphere drawn will be an identical size (see Figure 3.72).

5. Click Insert Local Mesh for this ZSphere with an already loaded bullet tool; the bullet does not have the correct axis to the strap, as you can see in Figure 3.73.

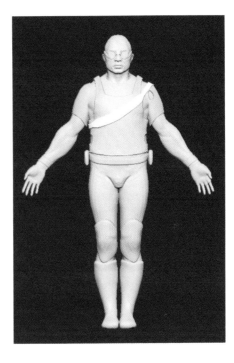

Figure 3.70
DemoSoldier tool with a strap wrapped around his body

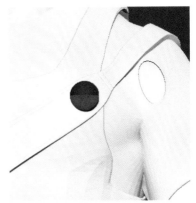

Figure 3.71
Root ZSphere in position for the first bullet

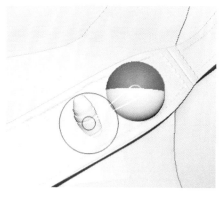

Figure 3.72 The second ZSphere drawn on the strap

Figure 3.73 Bullet with the incorrect axis after clicking Insert Local Mesh

6. This is a very easy fix. Undo your last operation so you are back to just two ZSpheres.

   The ZSpheres themselves have two shades of red; this indicates the centerline of the ZSphere. In the left image of Figure 3.74, the centerline is not parallel with the strap. This is why the bullet is on the incorrect axis when inserting.

7. To fix the axis, switch to Rotate mode at the top of the interface and rotate your ZSphere until the centerline is parallel with the strap (see the right image of Figure 3.74).

   Figure 3.75 shows a bullet that lines up with the strap.

8. Draw out as many bullets as you want. You can see my finished line of bullets in Figure 3.76.

Figure 3.74 ZSphere centerline not parallel with the strap (left), and the centerline made parallel with the strap in Rotate mode (right)

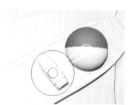

Figure 3.75 The bullet will now line up with the strap.

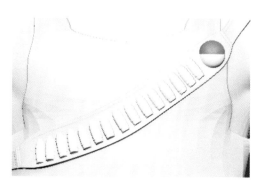

Figure 3.76 Finished line of bullets

9. After clicking Make Adaptive Skin with the bullets, I decided to duplicate the bullets and strap and mirror them onto the other side by using the Mirror feature in Subtool Master. If not already installed in the Zplugs Palette it can be downloaded from Pixologic's website at `www.pixologic.com/zbrush/downloadcenter/zplugins/`.

Take a look at the finished Rambo version of the DemoSoldier in Figure 3.77.

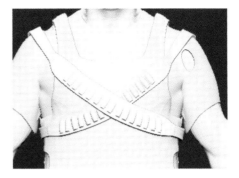

Figure 3.77 Rambo version of the DemoSoldier

Using Morph Difference to Create Thickness

Morph targets can be a very powerful tool when you sculpt with ZBrush. If you are unfamiliar with morph targets, visit the Pixologic wiki on morph targets at `www.pixologic .com/docs/index.php/Tool:Morph_Target_Subpalette`.

A morph target is essentially a stored state of your mesh at any level of subdivision. Artists often use a morph target with the Morph brush, which is a very powerful workflow, but few artists use the CreateDiff Mesh button in the Morph Target subpalette.

Many industries use ZBrush because of its unique tool set, but one that can really play with the CreateDiff Mesh button is the jewelry industry. Let's use this unique feature in ZBrush to create a bracelet:

1. Load a cylinder with the measurements for a woman's wrist. If you do not have a cylinder with accurate measurements for a woman, convert Cylinder3D into a polymesh by selecting Cylinder3D and clicking Make PolyMesh3D to follow along and see how this works.

2. Import an alpha of a flower pattern (see Figure 3.78). You can find this alpha in the assets for Chapter 3. The file is called `Flower.PSD`.

3. You will use the flower alpha as a mask for the entire bracelet. Hold Ctrl, turn on Z-symmetry, and set Radial Count to **10** in the Transform palette (see Figure 3.79).

Figure 3.78 Flower pattern for the bracelet

Figure 3.79 Z-symmetry on with RadialCount set to 10

4. Continuing to hold Ctrl, select the MaskPen brush with a DragRect stroke and the flower alpha in the Alpha palette (see Figure 3.80).

5. Still holding Ctrl, adjust the Focal Shift to **-100** and draw out the flower pattern onto the cylinder (see Figure 3.81).

6. Head to the Tool → Visibility subpalette and click HidePt to hide everything that is not masked (see Figure 3.82).

7. Delete the hidden geometry: open the Tool → Geometry subpalette and delete all lower subdivision levels.

   You must be on the lowest subdivision level to delete hidden geometry in ZBrush. However, if you walked down to the lowest level in this example, you would lose the preciseness of the masking. This is why I have deleted the lower levels of my model.

8. Click the DelHidden button.

9. Turn on Double in Tool → Display Properties so you can see the other side of the bracelet.

10. Head to the Tool → Deformation subpalette to apply a Polish of 1 to the whole surface.

Figure 3.80
MaskPen brush selected with DragRect and the flower alpha

Figure 3.81 Drawn-out flower alpha wrapped around the cylinder

Figure 3.82 HidePt hides everything not masked.

11. Store a morph target of the bracelet by clicking StoreMT in the Tool → Morph Target subpalette.

12. Take a snapshot by clicking the little camera icon in the Transform palette or use the Shift+S shortcut.

A snapshot creates a copy of the tool that is dropped to the canvas. You can use the snapshot as a reference while you determine the thickness of the bracelet. You could also duplicate the subtool before using the Deformer so you can rotate the tool in Edit mode while adjusting the thickness.

---

13. When you have the snapshot, you can play with the thickness of the bracelet by moving the Size slider in the Tool → Deformation subpalette to any positive value. You can clearly see how thick this bracelet will be in Figure 3.83.

14. Click the CreateDiff Mesh button in the Tool → Morph Target subpalette. Voila! A new tool is created that will become your bracelet (see Figure 3.84).

You have a finished bracelet to give to your loved one or to start your own jewelry company. Who would think this was so easy, right? I will share many techniques for creating jewelry throughout this book; this one gave us a great start.

Figure 3.83 A snapshot will drop an instance to the ZBrush document so you see the change in thickness.

Figure 3.84 Finished bracelet with a thickness from the CreateDiff Mesh

ARTIST SPOTLIGHT: TOMAS WITTELSBACH
JEWELRY CREATION PROCESS WITH MODO AND ZBRUSH

I USUALLY START WITH rough design sketches to plan out my ideas. Here is a quick overview of how to take a piece of jewelry from design to fabrication:

1. I draw out three views of the ring: the front, side, and top. I can't tell you how much this first step will help you along this journey (see Figure 3.85).

2. Because of the measuring capabilities in modo, I create cylinders ahead of time that are calibrated to common ring and stone sizes, as shown in Figure 3.86. This makes it easy for me to bring over a simple object into ZBrush that already has a true size.

3. I also do the same thing with stone sizes (see Figure 3.87).

4. In modo, I create a smooth block-out of the stone I'm creating the piece around. You can see the simplicity of this block-out in Figure 3.88.

Figure 3.85 Three views of the ring

JEWELRY CREATION PROCESS WITH MODO AND ZBRUSH

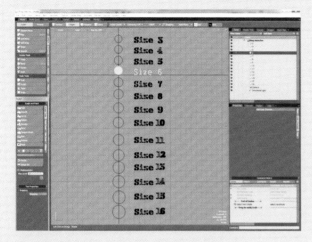

Figure 3.86 *Common ring and stone sizes*

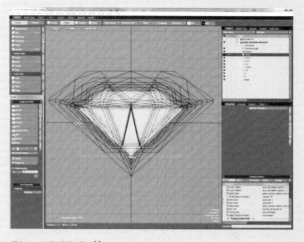

Figure 3.87 *Different stone sizes*

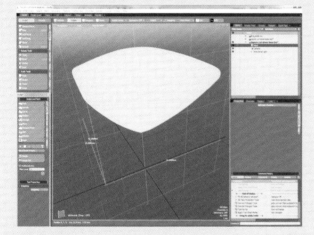

Figure 3.88 *Block-out of a stone*

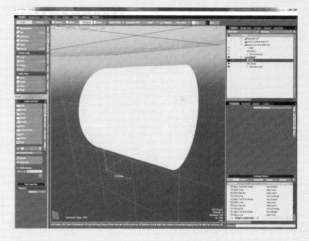

Figure 3.89 *Example of a ring base*

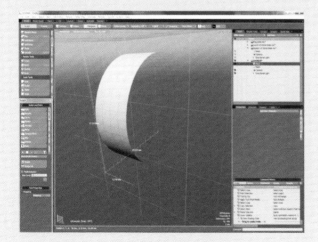

Figure 3.90 *Creating a new mesh*

5. Now I use my cylinders to select the amount of geometry for the ring base (see Figure 3.89).

6. I create the previous selection into a new mesh (see Figure 3.90).

7. After determining the band measurements, I extrude it to the desired thickness. In Figure 3.91, I have decided to make the thickness 2.3 mm.

8. With a base ring started, I block out the look of the ring. Keep in mind that you never move any of the vertices in the inner part of the ring. This would change the ring size and cause some major issues down the road. You can see the direction this ring is going in Figure 3.92.

JEWELRY CREATION PROCESS WITH MODO AND ZBRUSH

Figure 3.91
Determining
thickness

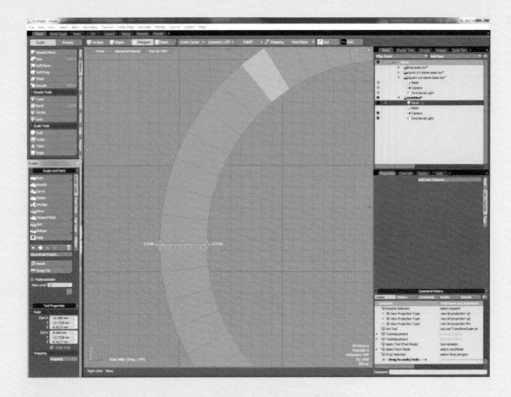

Figure 3.92
Ring progression

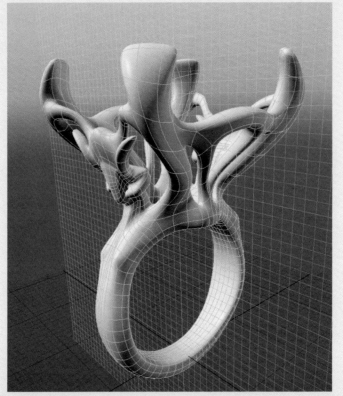

JEWELRY CREATION PROCESS WITH MODO AND ZBRUSH

9. A great advantage to using modo is GoZ. With one click of the button, I can send my base block-out over to ZBrush, as shown in Figure 3.93. All the measurements done in modo will translate just fine into ZBrush. No accuracy is lost.

To familiarize yourself with GoZ, visit `www.pixologic.com/zbrush/features/GoZBrush/`. If you do not have GoZ installed on your system, you can download it from `www.pixologic.com/zbrush/downloadcenter/zplugins/`.

10. I want extra geometry in the area where I want to add details such as scales, so before I divide, I will mask the area. I would like to locally subdivide the mesh. Chapter 1 covers local subdivision in detail. I invert the mask so everything else but that selection is now masked. You can invert a mask by Ctrl-clicking or by tapping the pen in an open area in ZBrush. Figure 3.94 shows the result.

Figure 3.93 Using modo

Figure 3.94 Inverting a mask

JEWELRY CREATION PROCESS WITH MODO AND ZBRUSH

Figure 3.95 *Only the unmasked area divides.*

11. I divide the tool, and ZBrush will divide only the unmasked area, as shown in Figure 3.95. (Again, this is a local subdivision that is explained in Chapter 1). I can now proceed with sculpting the details of the ring in this area.

12. I create a single scale. As shown in Figure 3.96, I made a surface and sculpted it into a unique pattern.

13. To tile the scale into a repeating pattern, I use the 2.5D technique (explained in detail earlier in this chapter, in the "Adjusting and Creating Brushes" section). You can see the detail possible with creating just one piece of mesh in ZBrush (see Figure 3.97).

14. In the Alpha palette, I click the GrabDoc button, which creates a custom alpha that tiles perfectly (see Figure 3.98).

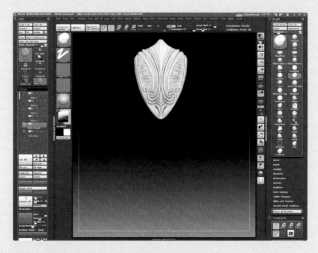

Figure 3.96 *A single scale*

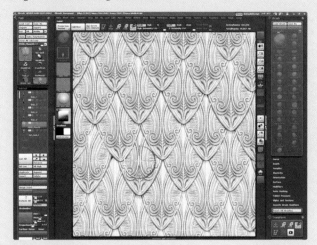

Figure 3.97 *A repeating pattern*

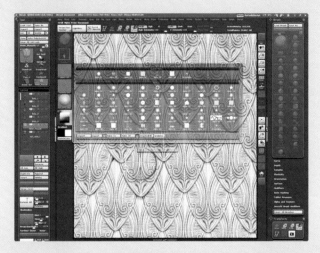

Figure 3.98 *Custom alpha*

JEWELRY CREATION PROCESS WITH MODO AND ZBRUSH

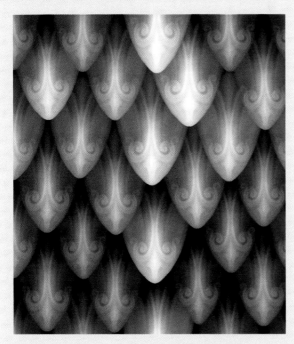

Figure 3.99 Effect of the GrabDoc button

Alpha library, I select the Scale alpha. With this combination of options, I can place the scales design in the right spot.

Sometimes I need to switch to Move mode to place the alpha that was just drawn out in the right location. When I am all set, I click the Projection Master button again and select Pick Up (see Figure 3.101).

Figure 3.100 Projection Master dialog box

The highly detailed alpha that was created using the GrabDoc button appears in Figure 3.99.

15. I select the ring I have been sculpting and mask everything out from the spot where I want to apply the scales.

    When you have a mask, enter Projection Master to use the alpha previously created as a way to add detail quickly and with accuracy. Either click the Projection Master button at the top of the interface or click Ctrl+G to launch the dialog box you see in Figure 3.100. In the Options box that appears, turn Colors off, and turn on Double Sided, Fade, Deformation, and Normalized. Then click the Drop Now button to enter Projection Master.

16. Now I choose the SingleLayer brush from the Tool palette. In the Stroke Type library, I select the DragRect stroke style, and in the

Figure 3.101 Selecting Pick Up option

JEWELRY CREATION PROCESS WITH MODO AND ZBRUSH

17. After leaving Projection Master mode by clicking G or the Projection Master button, ZBrush will pick the ring back up.

    After you pick up any model from Projection Master mode, you'll reenter 3D mode. In Figure 3.102, the scales are applied only where the mesh was not masked. Now it's time to decimate the ring for printing.

    The ring needs to be decimated because ZBrush can handle millions of polygons, but the software used with the 3D printing machine cannot handle a high poly count. The Decimation Master will reduce the overall polygon count but keep the high detail that you get in ZBrush.

    I go to ZPlugin and select Decimation Master. I set the sliders to the desired setting and click Preprocess Current. If you do not already have Decimation Master installed, you can download this plug-in from the Pixologic website at **www.pixologic.com/zbrush/ downloadcenter/zplugins/**.

18. After the preprocess is complete, I need to use the Decimate Current tool. Preprocess will actually evaluate the entire mesh and prepare it for decimation when you select Decimate Current or Decimate All. I usually wind up in the 2–5 percent range for the number of polygons to decimate the ring to for an appropriate print size. We are looking for a finished range under 300,000 polys. Most growing machines or 3D printers don't like huge files. In Figure 3.103, I ended up decimating this ring in the 219,000 polygon range at a 3 percent decimation.

19. By clicking the GoZ button, I send the model back to modo and I can check the scale and thicknesses. It's easy to sculpt away the tolerances of an accurate ring size. As shown in Figure 3.104, I write down my overall measurements.

20. Now I press the GoZ button in modo to send the model back to ZBrush. In the ZPlugin drop-down menu, open the 3D Print Exporter plug-in. If 3D Print Exporter is not installed, you can download this plug-in from the Pixologic website.

Figure 3.102 *Scales where mesh was not masked*

Figure 3.103 *Three percent decimation*

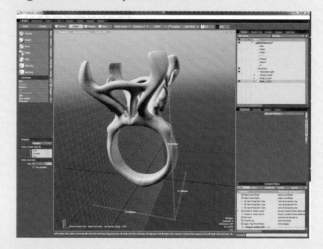

Figure 3.104 *Overall measurements*

JEWELRY CREATION PROCESS WITH MODO AND ZBRUSH

As shown in Figure 3.105, I need to put in only one measurement and then click the Update Size Ratio button to have an accurate ratio. I put in a measurement of 23 mm and then update my ratio. By typing in one of the measurements I got from modo, I can export an accurate ring from ZBrush. I export this ring as a Binary STL because this is the file type that 3D printers need in order to print out our masterpiece.

This ring was grown on an EnvisionTec Perfactory at 15 microns. In Figure 3.106, you can see the result that you get straight from the printer.

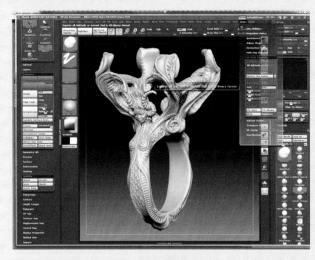

Figure 3.105 *Update Size Ratio button*

Figure 3.106 *The end result*

TOMAS WITTELSBACH *is a former sculptor in the film industry who transitioned into jewelry creation. He uses ZBrush to create sculptural jewelry produced with modern fabrication to emulate an old-world craft that would be time- and cost-prohibitive if created with traditional techniques. By joining his company, House of Wittelsbach ,with Green Lake Jewelry Works, he now has the benefit of a world-class fabrication jewelry workshop, helping to create some unique pieces of art jewelry.*

Tomas is a jewelry designer at Green Lake Jewelry Works in Seattle as well as running House of Wittelsbach through Green Lake.

www.greenlakejewelry.com

www.tswittelsbach.com

ARTIST SPOTLIGHT: VITALY BULGAROV

USING DYNAMESH WITH DECIMATION MASTER FOR HARD-SURFACE MESHES

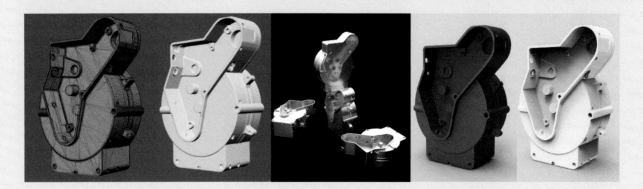

THIS IS A QUICK TIP on how to use DynaMesh with Polish mode and Decimation Master to create complex hard-surface models from low-polygon, non-subdivision-based meshes created in other software.

The advantage of this technique is that for those who may prefer poly modeling for base mesh creation, DynaMesh will help to establish smoothed edges without the long process of creating supporting edge-loops and clean topology.

1. Start with different meshes merged together without welding any vertex points or any cleanup. Triangulate the mesh before importing into ZBrush, as shown in Figure 3.107.

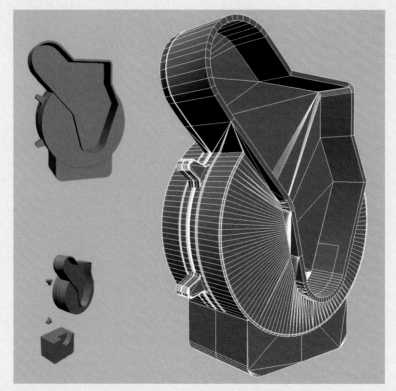

Figure 3.107 Start with a base mesh from other applications or within ZBrush.

USING DYNAMESH WITH DECIMATION MASTER FOR HARD-SURFACE MESHES

2. Import the mesh into ZBrush and then activate the DynaMesh button in the Tool →
   Geometry subpalette. Adjust the Resolution slider to higher settings to maintain the
   overall hard edge. I find that resolutions between 250 and 350 work best. DynaMesh
   will create a new mesh with evenly distributed topology so you can start adding additional
   details to the surface. In Figure 3.108, you can see the evenly distributed topology on my
   imported mesh.

3. Now that you have a DynaMesh, you can use the InsertCylinder brush to create holes by holding the Alt key, and also add cylindrical shapes to the mesh. Use the ClipCircle brush while
   holding the Alt key to create cylindrical shapes (see Figure 3.109).

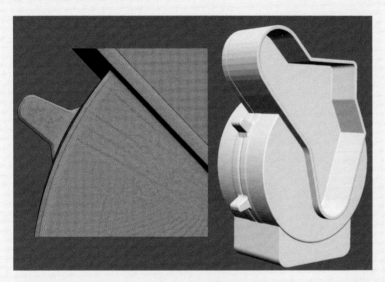

Figure 3.108 *Convert to DynaMesh for evenly distributed polygons.*

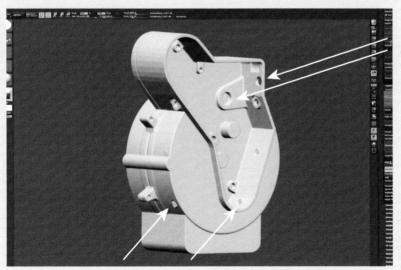

Using Insert Cylinder brush
with ZAdd and ZSub mode
to add details

Using ClipCircle brush to cut in cylindrical shapes

Figure 3.109 *Use the InsertCylinder to create holes and use the ClipCirlce brush to
create cylindrical shapes.*

USING DYNAMESH WITH DECIMATION MASTER FOR HARD-SURFACE MESHES

4. After adding the details, use the Decimation Master to reduce the poly count and convert all quads into triangles (see Figure 3.110).

5. When you're finished with ZBrush, export the mesh into another application to do some render tests with a raytracing render engine such as mental ray or RenderMan.

   You can see the final renders I completed in Figure 3.111.

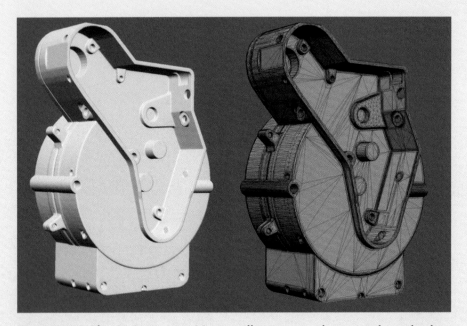

Figure 3.110 *Plug-In Decimation Master will convert quads to triangles and reduce the polygon count.*

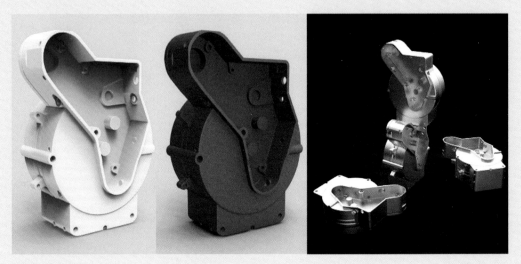

Figure 3.111 *Finished render in external render*

USING DYNAMESH WITH DECIMATION MASTER FOR HARD-SURFACE MESHES

VITALY BULGAROV *is an award-winning 3D artist who is currently working at Blizzard Entertainment as a cinematic artist. He started his career in Moldova as a freelance artist about six years ago. After moving to Moscow, he worked in major Russian game development studios as a full-time artist, while at the same time continuing to freelance for American and European studios. Vitaly regularly contributes to online CG artist forums and has won many awards, including a CGChoice Award as well as the 3DTotal Excellence Award.*

`www.bulgarov.com`

SPECIAL PROJECT | SCULPTING HARD SURFACE DETAILS

CREATING A HOSE CON

CREATING THE FRONT

USING NOISEMAKER FOR

Sculpting Hard-Surface Details

During my travels, I am *often asked how to use ZBrush to create hard-edged shapes. This chapter shows you how to create something inspired by the work of Andrew Ley. You can find the original piece at* andrewley.cgsociety.org/gallery/437338/. *The piece has always captured my attention, so why not use it as a source to create something like a mechanical helmet in ZBrush? I also took some inspiration from the Gundam series for this piece.*

The most important part of creating a hard-edged piece in ZBrush is to develop a workflow that maintains the quality you seek. In this chapter, you will find a few ideas for workflows for creating some cool hard-edged pieces.

- Creating a hose component
- Creating the front eye piece
- Using NoiseMaker for patterns

Creating a Hose Component

In this section, you will re-create the piece you see in Figure 4.1. This piece holds up a hose that travels around a helmet.

After you break down how it is created, the piece is fairly simple: all components were created in ZBrush from scratch. So let's move on, without further ado, to creating a hose component:

1. Select Cylinder3D in the Tool palette, as shown in Figure 4.2.

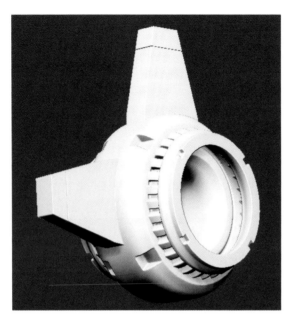

Figure 4.1 *Finished hose component from the helmet*

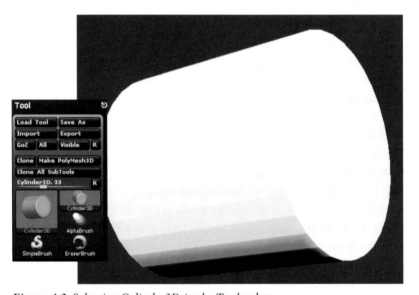

Figure 4.2 *Selecting Cylinder3D in the Tool palette*

2. We cannot sculpt on any tool in ZBrush with *3D* at the end of the name, because it is not a mesh. It is a primitive shape with dimensions that we can reshape by using a special set of controls. Access these controls by opening the Tool → Initialize subpalette. Now you can make quick adjustments to the cylinder.

3. Turn on the Polyframe button at the right side of the interface. You can see the wireframe of the default Cylinder3D primitive.

4. To adjust the divisions of the cylinder, use the Initialize states. I adjusted two sliders to get a smoother cylinder. As shown in Figure 4.3, increase HDivide spans to **256** and adjust the Inner Radius to **70** to create an opening through the cylinder.

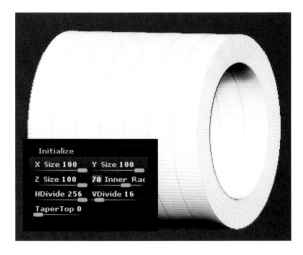

Figure 4.3 Adjusting the HDivide and Inner Radius in the Initialize subpalette to create a totally different cylinder

5. Now that I have created the basic shape by using the Initialize sliders, I can turn the primitive into a sculptable mesh by clicking the Make PolyMesh3D button at the top of the Tool palette.

6. If Perspective is on, turn it off by pressing the P hot key.

7. Turn on Symmetry mode in the Transform palette. Because this model is facing the Z axis, change the axis in the Transform palette to Z, as shown in Figure 4.4.

Figure 4.4 Changing symmetry to the Z axis in the Transform palette

8. Hold Ctrl+Shift to select the SelectRect brush and then draw out a selection rectangle like that in Figure 4.5 to create the selection you see in Figure 4.6.

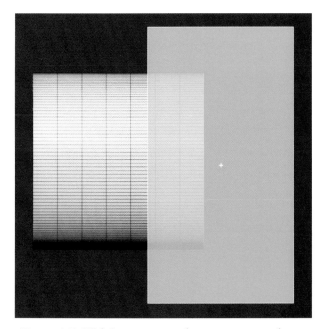

Figure 4.5 With Symmetry mode on, you can make identical selections on either side of the cylinder.

Figure 4.6 The result of the selection on the cylinder when using Symmetry mode

9. Make a similar selection by holding Ctrl+Shift, begin to draw out a square, and then let go of Ctrl+Shift so you can hold down the Alt key to convert the green square into a red square (the red square indicates that whatever is in the red will be hidden). Drag the rectangle up to the first row of polygons, as shown in Figure 4.7. Only the middle row will now be visible (see Figure 4.8).

Figure 4.7 *Holding Alt after you start drawing the selection rectangle tells ZBrush to hide what is in the rectangle.*

Figure 4.8 *Selecting out the outer ring of the cylinder to get only the inner row of polygons*

10. Click the Edge Loop button in the Tool → Geometry → EdgeLoop subpalette to add a row of new polygons through this ring (see the left image of Figure 4.9).

11. Now shrink the selection by clicking Ctrl+Shift+S once or click the Shrink button in the Tool → Visibility subpalette to get something similar to the right image of Figure 4.9.

Figure 4.9 *The Edge Loop button adds a ring of polygons on visible polygons (left). Use Ctrl+Shift+S to shrink the selection to only one row of polygons (right).*

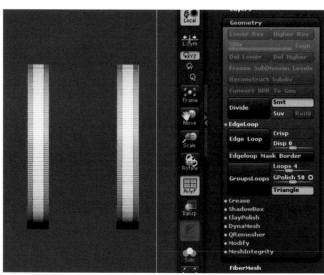

12. Send the Inflate slider to **-100** once in the Tool → Deformation subpalette. After you inflate this row of polygons, unhide everything again by holding Ctrl+Shift and clicking anywhere in the open document. You should have results similar to Figure 4.10 from the negative inflation.

13. Select the inner ring of the mesh, as shown in Figure 4.11. With this ring selected, move the Inflate slider to **100** in the Deformation subpalette again. Then you should have results similar to Figure 4.12.

Figure 4.10 The Inflate slider creates a nice cut into the surface of the cylinder.

Figure 4.12 Using the Inflate slider in the Deformation subpalette to increase the center of the cylinder radius

Figure 4.11 Selecting the inner section of the ring to isolate it and inflate the center

14. When using the SelectLasso brush, you can select geometry rings by Ctrl+Shift-clicking on the edges of the geometry. Use SelectLasso to click the edge that is horizontal on the cylinder to create a selection similar to the left image in Figure 4.13. Then invert the selection by holding Ctrl+Shift while you click-drag in any open part of the document, to create a selection like that shown in the right image of Figure 4.13.

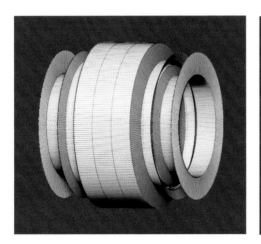

Figure 4.13 Using the SelectLasso tool to isolate the outer ring (left), and the inverse of the selection (right)

If you selected horizontal edges, ZBrush will continue to select the ring of geometry that is parallel to the edge that is selected. In this case, ZBrush selects the geometry that wraps around the cylinder. If you had selected a vertical edge, ZBrush would select geometry that wraps in the other direction (see Figure 4.14).

15. Add an edge loop by clicking Edge Loop in the Tool → Geometry subpalette (see Figure 4.15).

16. Now with only the ring of polygons showing (see Figure 4.16), move the Size slider in the Deformation subpalette to -20 to get results similar to Figure 4.17.

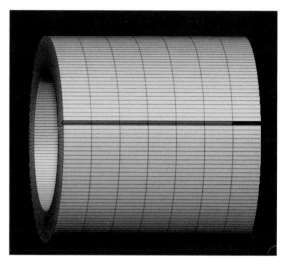

Figure 4.14 By selecting the vertical edge, you get a selection that follows the geometry horizontally around.

Figure 4.15 Adding an edge loop to create a nice new loop of geometry

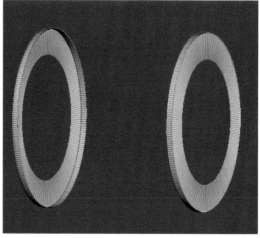

Figure 4.16 Isolating the outer section of the ring and using the Size slider in Deformation to change the outer ring size

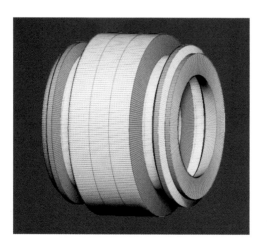

Figure 4.17 Moving the Size slider to -20 to make the visible rings of geometry smaller than the whole cylinder

17. To add volume in the middle of the cylinder, make a selection as shown on the left in Figure 4.18. Then shrink the selection again by pressing Ctrl+Shift+S to get results like the middle image in Figure 4.18.

18. Hold Ctrl and click anywhere in the open document to completely mask off the middle ring, as shown in the right image of Figure 4.18.

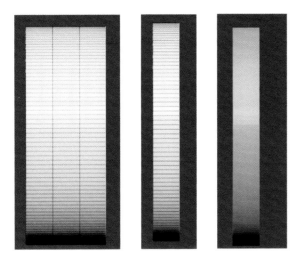

Figure 4.18 Selecting the middle of the cylinder (left), using the Visibility Shrink button again (middle), and masking off all visible geometry (right)

19. Ctrl+Shift-click anywhere in an open spot in the document to bring the whole cylinder back, as shown in Figure 4.19.

20. You need to invert the masking. To do this, hold the Ctrl key and click anywhere in the open document. Figure 4.20 shows the inverted masking.

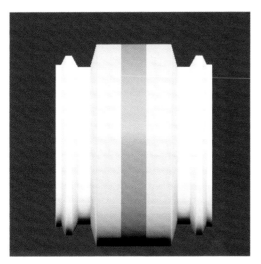

Figure 4.19 By clicking anywhere in the open document when holding Ctrl+Shift, the whole mesh displays again.

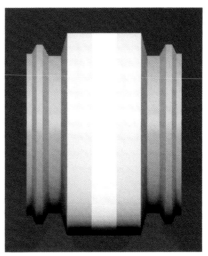

Figure 4.20 Inverting a mask by Ctrl-clicking anywhere on the document

21. Now move the Inflate slider in the Deformation subpalette up to **100** again. Your results should be similar to Figure 4.21.

22. Now for the fun stuff. In the Tool → Geometry subpalette, move the Res slider (next to DynaMesh) to 248 and then click the DynaMesh button to turn this mesh into a DynaMesh (see Figure 4.22). Figure 4.23 shows how the cylinder was converted into an equally distributed mesh.

    Converting the geometry into a DynaMesh creates a surface with equally distributed polygons that you can reorder at any point. The DynaMesh also lets you add to this mesh by using insert brushes.

23. Select the InsertCube brush by pressing B; then press the I key to isolate brushes that start with the letter *I* so you can select the InsertCube brush (see Figure 4.24).

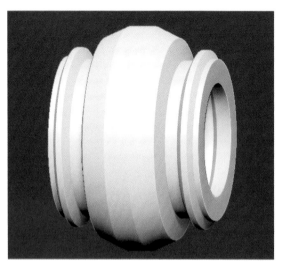

Figure 4.21 *Using the masking to inflate the inner section of the cylinder*

Figure 4.22 *The Res slider in DynaMesh controls the number of polygons used to distribute through the mesh.*

Figure 4.23 *The cylinder turned into a DynaMesh with Res set at **248***

Figure 4.24 *Select the InsertCube brush by pressing B; then press I to isolate brushes that start with the letter I.*

24. In the Transform palette, make sure to turn on all three axes for Symmetry (see Figure 4.25).

25. In the Picker palette, change the Picker orientation arrow to face straight ahead (see Figure 4.26) so your cubes will face the correct direction in relation to the cylinder when drawn out. Hold the Alt key as you draw out these cubes to use them as a type of Boolean option—that is, to subtract the cube shape from the cylinder (see Figure 4.27).

Figure 4.25
Turning on X, Y, Z axis symmetry in the Transform palette

26. Now for the really cool part. Holding Ctrl, click and drag anywhere on the open part of the document. ZBrush uses the cubes to cut into the cylinder, but also makes sure the polygons are evenly distributed (see Figure 4.28).

Figure 4.26
Changing the picker orientation to be straight on

27. Repeat the preceding step again on the middle section (see Figure 4.29). Hold Ctrl as you click and drag in an open part of the document to redistribute the polygons with DynaMesh. There is no best time to re-DynaMesh, but for this piece, you may want to DynaMesh each time you insert a new piece so you see the results.

Figure 4.28
DynaMesh will readjust the polygons.

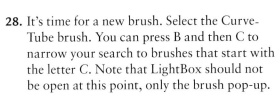

Figure 4.27 Draw out cubes while holding the Alt key for a subtractive result.

28. It's time for a new brush. Select the Curve-Tube brush. You can press B and then C to narrow your search to brushes that start with the letter C. Note that LightBox should not be open at this point, only the brush pop-up.

29. With the CurveTube brush selected, go to the Brush → Modifiers subpalette. Turn the Brush Modifier slider to **4** (see Figure 4.30). This slider controls how many faces the CurveTube will have when used; in this case we just changed it to be cubes when drawn out.

Figure 4.29
Using InsertCube to keep cutting into the mesh

Figure 4.30
Move the Brush Modifier slider to 4 in the Brush → Modifiers.

30. In the Stroke palette, CurveMode shows Bend and Intensity on by default (see Figure 4.31). Turn off both of these buttons so that in the next few steps you can create symmetrical grooves around the inner edge of the surface. (With Intensity on, the mesh will have intensity change from the point of clicking on the surface and then out. We want a consistent intensity along the whole brush. With Bend off, you avoid changing the curve points each time you press on the curve you are about to draw out. We want the curve not to be edited at all after it has been drawn out.)

Turn on the AsLine button so that when you draw out your curve, it will always be a straight line.

31. In the Transform subpalette, only Z-symmetry should be activated with Radial Symmetry set to **32**.

32. With the floor grid on, draw on the side with the blue line of the floor grid: this is the side that will be the positive Z direction of the cylinder. You can see the brush on the correct side of the cylinder.

33. When drawing out your curve, you will get **32** instances of your brush along the cylinder that will be **32** cubes (see Figure 4.32).

34. We have results on only one side (see Figure 4.33). Create this geometry on the other side by using the Tool → Geometry → Modify Mirror And Weld button on the Z axis (see Figure 4.34). This button, near the bottom of the Geometry subpalette, creates the same geometry on both sides of the object (see Figure 4.35).

Figure 4.31 *Turning off Bend and Intensity in the Stroke palette*

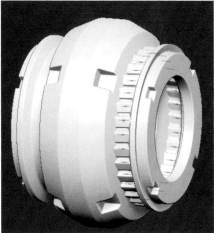

Figure 4.33 *The new geometry appears on only one side of the cylinder.*

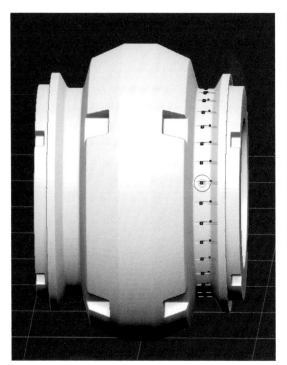

Figure 4.32 *Drawing out the curve produces 32 cubes.*

Figure 4.34 *Turning on the Z in the Mirror And Weld button*

Figure 4.35 *After clicking Mirror And Weld, ZBrush duplicates the geometry to the other side.*

Now you need to build the fins at the top and side of the component.

35. Select Cube3D and turn it into a polymesh by clicking the MakePolyMesh3D button. Then create a DynaMesh with the default settings by clicking the DynaMesh button in the Tool → Geometry → DynaMesh subpalette.

36. Make sure Symmetry is on and use the ClipCurve brush while holding the Ctrl+Shift keys to cut the cube into more of a rectangle (see Figure 4.36).

37. With the rectangle turned to the side, use the ClipCurve brush to cut an angle into the rectangle. Be free with this; don't worry about getting exactly what I have. Figure 4.37 shows the angle I chose and my results.

Figure 4.36 *Using the ClipCurve brush to change the shape of the cube into a rectangle*

Figure 4.37 *The angle used with the ClipCurve brush (left), and the results of using ClipCurve (right)*

38. Switch to the other side of the rectangle. Change your Symmetry to the Z axis from the X axis in the Transform palette and make another cut with the ClipCurve brush (see Figure 4.38). Remember, feel free to cut this any way. When you are finished with the cuts, hold Ctrl while you click-drag anywhere on the ZBrush document to DynaMesh the mesh again.

39. Hold Ctrl+Shift while you open the Brush palette and select the SliceCurve brush (see Figure 4.39). Activate the Group button in DynaMesh, as shown in Figure 4.40. The Group button tells ZBrush to separate the DynaMesh based on polygroups.

40. Draw out a slice straight across the top of the shape and then re-DynaMesh; because the Group button is on, ZBrush will make two separate pieces (see Figure 4.41).

Figure 4.38 Using ClipCurve to change the shape

Figure 4.39 Holding Ctrl+Shift to select the SliceCurve brush

Figure 4.40 Turning on Group in the DynaMesh section

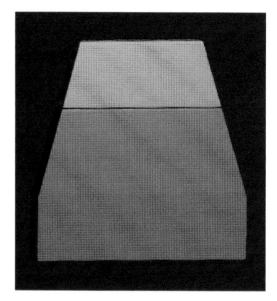

Figure 4.41 With Group on, ZBrush makes each polygroup into a separate section when DynaMeshing.

Creating a Hose Component

41. In the Tool palette, select the cylin-drical model you've been working on before this piece. In the SubTool palette, click the Append button and select the remeshed cube to add it to the cylindrical model as a subtool (see Figure 4.42).

42. Move using Move mode so that the rectangle sits straight over the cylindrical model. Also use Tool → Deformation → Rotate along the X axis only by 90 to position the rectangle into place (see Figure 4.43). Then dupli-cate the rectangle subtool and rotate the new copy so it is perpendicular to the first rectangle; your results should be similar to Figure 4.44.

Figure 4.42
Appending the rectangle shape to the cylinder

You just re-created the finished piece of the helmet.

You can also turn these three subtools into one mesh by clicking the MergeDown but-ton in the Tool → SubTool → Merge subpalette (see Figure 4.45).

Figure 4.43 By moving the rectangle shape into place with the Move and Rotate modes of ZBrush, you can place this subtool anywhere.

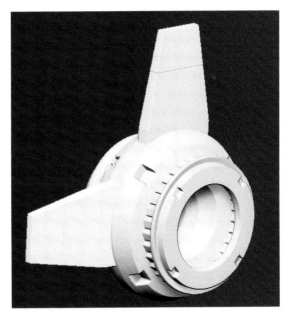

Figure 4.44 Duplicating the subtool with the Duplicate button and then rotating the copied piece into place

Figure 4.45 Using MergeDown in the SubTool subpalette to make the three subtools one

Creating the Front Eye Piece

When you create a mech-style mesh in ZBrush, you must think about tools that you can combine to get your desired results. The eye piece is a great example of how to combine several tools and techniques. You can see the whole eye in Figure 4.46, but I want to focus on creating the front of the eye, using ShadowBox, DynaMesh, SliceBrush, and primitives.

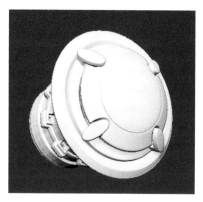

Figure 4.46 The entire eye front, constructed in ZBrush from scratch

Follow these steps to create the eye front:

1. You want to start with the very front of the eye, so you will again use a 3D primitive from ZBrush. Load SweepProfile3D, shown in Figure 4.47.

Figure 4.47 Loading SweepProfile3D from the Tool palette

2. You start with a shape similar to Figure 4.48. Notice in the Initialize subpalette in Figure 4.49 some significant differences in this subpalette compared to the one for Cylinder3D in the previous section. These options make the SweepProfile3D primitive a very powerful tool.

Figure 4.48 The default shape of the SweepProfile3D primitive

Figure 4.49 The Initialize state has many more controls for SweepProfile3D.

3. To get the basic shape, you want to change the S Profile to something similar to Figure 4.50 and adjust the Z Size to **31**, the HDivide to **128**, and the VDivide to **11**. Your results should look similar to the image on the right of Figure 4.50.

4. Convert the shape into a mesh by clicking the MakePolyMesh3D button in the Tool palette.

5. Now turn the shape into a DynaMesh: set the Res slider to **200** and turn on Group (see Figure 4.51).

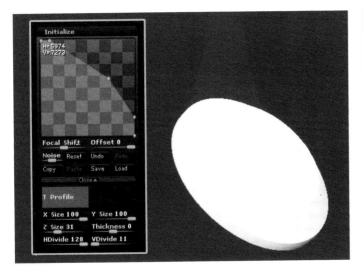

Figure 4.50 *Making adjustments to the S Profile to create unique shapes*

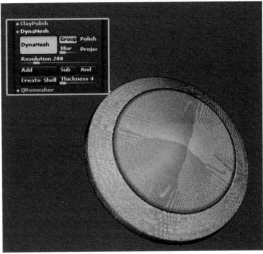

Figure 4.51 *Before turning on DynaMesh, changing the Res slider to 200, and turning on the Group button*

6. Hold Ctrl+Shift to select the SliceCurve brush.

7. Draw a line that cuts across the top of the shape, then re-DynaMesh by holding Ctrl and dragging anywhere on the open document. Your results should be similar to the image on the right of Figure 4.51. Remember, because you have Group on in DynaMesh, you will actually separate the mesh into two pieces.

8. You still have two polygroups, so let's use this to your advantage. Hold Ctrl+Shift and click one of the polygroups to hide the other polygroups. (Press Shift+F to activate Polyframe mode and turn on polygroups.)

9. Next, click the Split Hidden button in the SubTool subpalette to create two separate subtools.

10. Turn on Transp and Ghost on the right side of the interface (see Figure 4.52). You should get results similar to Figure 4.52, where the bottom part of the chopped eye is the selected subtool.

Figure 4.52 *Activating the Transp and Ghost buttons*

11. Open the Brush palette and select the InsertCylinder brush. Hold the Alt key as you draw out the cylinder and look straight at the top of the bottom section (see the left image in Figure 4.53). Also turn the model to make sure the cylinder goes all the way through the bottom, as shown in the image on the right in Figure 4.53.

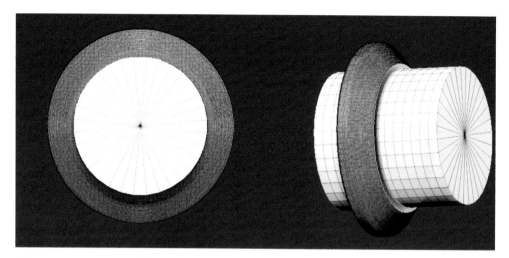

Figure 4.53 *Position of the model when drawing out the cylinder while holding the Alt key (left), and verifying that the cylinder went through the whole bottom section (right)*

12. Hold Ctrl and click-drag anywhere in the open document to use the cylinder as a cutting tool. You can make a perfect hole in the bottom part of the mechanical eye (see Figure 4.54).

Figure 4.54 *By Ctrl-click-dragging on an open part of the document, the cylinder is used to create a hole.*

13. Switch to the InsertSphere brush and make sure you are looking straight onto the bottom section. Turn on X- and Y-symmetry in the Transform palette. While holding the Alt key, draw out a sphere as shown in Figure 4.55 on the left.

14. Once again, re-DynaMesh by holding Ctrl and click-dragging anywhere on the open document. Use the spheres to cut out a section. Check out Figure 4.55 on the right.

15. Open LightBox. Under the Tool menu, find ShadowBox128.ZTL. Double-click to load this into the Tool palette.

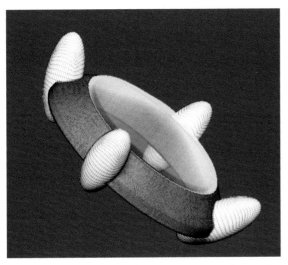

Figure 4.55 With X- and Y-symmetry on, four spheres are drawn out at once (left). The spheres cut a shape in the bottom section (right).

Now you'll create the piece that holds the eye piece in place.

16. ZBrush automatically switches to this tool because the Edit button is on. Switch back to your eye and append the ShadowBox you just loaded (see Figure 4.56).

17. Make sure ShadowBox is your selected subtool. Turn off the PolyF button. Notice that the ShadowBox is about the same size as the eye, so visit the Deformation subpalette and move the Size slider to **100** once (see Figure 4.57) to make room for masking.

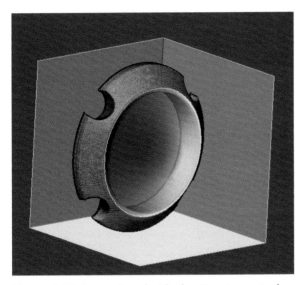
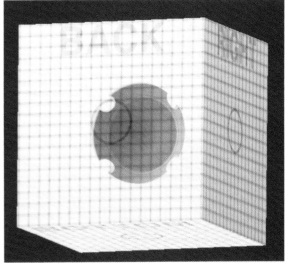

Figure 4.56 Appending the ShadowBox to create the pieces that hold up the eye

Figure 4.57 Moving the Size slider in the Deformation subpalette to resize the ShadowBox

18. ShadowBox creates a mesh based on the masks you draw on the wall of the box, so while holding the Ctrl key, select MaskCircle with X- and Y-symmetry turned on in the Transform palette. Then draw out a circle similar to Figure 4.58.

19. Turn to the side of ShadowBox; you need to make these posts longer. Holding Ctrl, switch to the MaskRect brush. Don't worry about the symmetry; what you have will work. Also don't worry about being perfect with this next masking job. Just draw out a box that is long enough and wide enough so you do not lose the round shape you already drew out before this mask (see Figure 4.59).

20. Turn off the ShadowBox button in the Tool → Geometry subpalette. You should see results similar to Figure 4.60. However, you may want to change the shape of the pegs by cutting them in half about three-quarters of the way up the posts.

21. Convert this mesh into a DynaMesh with Res set at **152**.

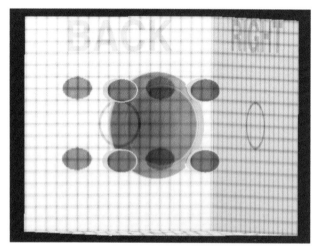

Figure 4.58 *With X- and Y-symmetry activated, using the MaskCircle brush to create four posts for the mechanical eye*

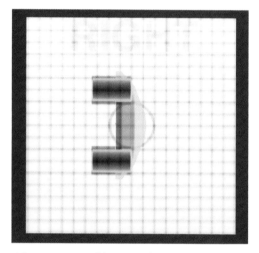

Figure 4.59 *Adding another mask on a different wall lets ShadowBox use both masks.*

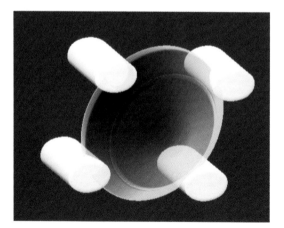

Figure 4.60 *With the ShadowBox button off, ZBrush gives a mesh from the masked parts on the ShadowBox walls.*

22. Select the InsertCube brush. While holding the Alt key, draw out a cube similar to the left image of Figure 4.61. Make sure the cube cuts all the way through the posts.

23. Ctrl-click and drag on an open area to re-DynaMesh the shapes. You should get results similar to the right image of Figure 4.61.

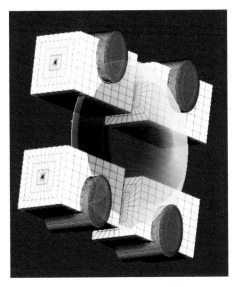

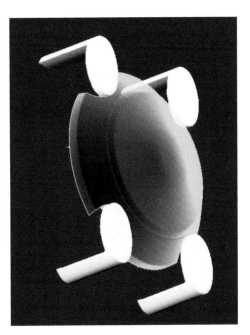

Figure 4.61 Drawing InsertCube as a subtraction (left), and creating a nice new post by Ctrl-click-dragging

All you have left to create is the base ring to attach the posts. This is easy. You will use Cylinder3D again.

24. Select Cylinder3D. Adjust your Initialize values to the following:

- X Size = 100
- Y Size = 100
- Z Size = 11
- Inner Radius = 80
- HDivide = 256
- VDivide = 8
- TaperTop = 0

Click the Make Polymesh button. Figure 4.62 shows the results.

Figure 4.62 Making a simple ring for the base of the posts by using Cylinder3D

25. Select the eye holder we finished in step 23, append the new ring, and resize it (see Figure 4.63). Also, turn off transparency to get a better idea of how the shape really looks.

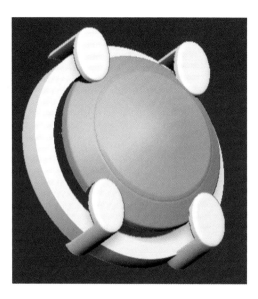

Figure 4.63 *Appending the ring to the eye to move and size the base to fit for the posts*

26. Now you need to move the posts into a better position. Make the posts the selected subtool, with X- and Y-symmetry on in the Transform palette. In Rotate mode, draw out a transpose line, as shown in Figure 4.64.

27. Rotate and move the posts to position them the way you like. Merge the ring and posts as one and then convert them into a DynaMesh with a Res setting at **128** (see Figure 4.65).

As you can see, combining a few simple tools in ZBrush can create a very complex model.

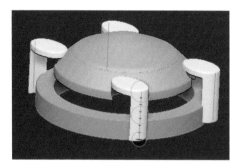

Figure 4.64 *By switching to Rotate mode at the top of the ZBrush interface, you can draw out a transpose line.*

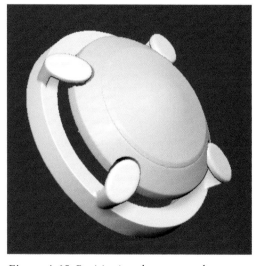

Figure 4.65 *Positioning the posts and then merging the ring and posts as one to make a DynaMesh*

Using NoiseMaker for Patterns

Creating patterns that are clean and look realistic on a mesh can be difficult. However, with the ZBrush NoiseMaker, all you need is a model with a well laid-out UV to achieve a very realistic pattern on any model. In this section, you will learn how easy it is to quickly apply a pattern to the tubes for the helmet:

1. Start by loading the Hose.OBJ asset from the Chapter 4. Assets folder. Import Hose. OBJ and draw it on the document. Then turn the Edit button on.

2. A key component to this hose is that I laid out UVs in Maya; the UVs are evenly distributed so that I get a perfect wrap with the pattern (see Figure 4.66).

3. Subdivide the hose up to level 8 so you have 1.836 million polygons.

4. In the Tool → Surface subpalette, turn on the Noise button so that the NoiseMaker dialog box pops up (see Figure 4.67).

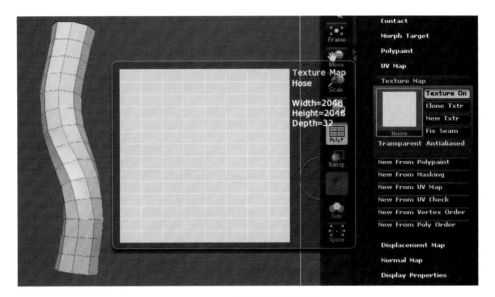

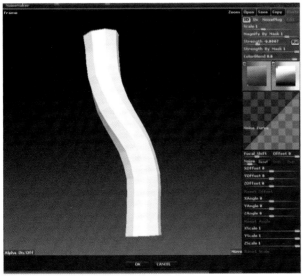

Figure 4.66 By laying out UVs that are evenly distributed, we get a perfect pattern wrapped around the hose.

Figure 4.67 The Noise button in the Tool → Surface subpalette activates the NoiseMaker pop-up.

5. Select UV at the top of NoiseMaker instead of the default 3D button.

6. Click the Alpha On/Off button in the lower-left corner of the NoiseMaker preview window so you can search for a file. When the dialog box opens, browse to the `Chapter 4 Assets` folder and load `Weave04.psd` (see Figure 4.68).

7. After you apply the weave file, you will see it wrapped around the hose in the preview window. Adjust the Scale slider close to **0.5** to repeat the pattern more and then adjust the Strength slider close to **-0.06** to make it stronger (see Figure 4.69).

8. Now make sure the hose is at the highest subdivision level and create a layer in the Tool → Layer subpalette, as shown in Figure 4.70. Make sure the layer is in REC mode. The pattern will be applied to a layer so you can turn it on and off or change its intensity.

9. Turn the SNormal slider all the way up to **100** (see Figure 4.71). This will limit the amount of inflation that occurs when the pattern is applied. Then click the Apply To Mesh button.

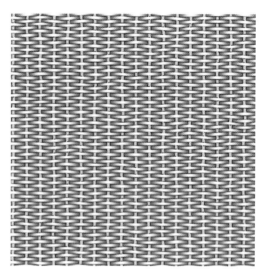

Figure 4.68 `Weave04.PSD` *in the* `Chapter 4 Assets` *folder*

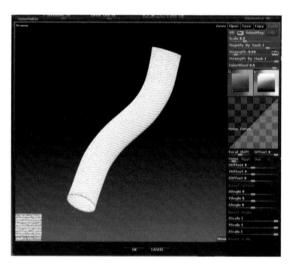

Figure 4.69 *Playing with your Scale and Strength sliders to get different results*

Figure 4.70 *When a layer is created on the highest subdivision level, it will automatically be placed in REC mode.*

Figure 4.71 *Turning the SNormal slider up to 100 to limit the inflation to the hose*

Notice that the detail is too intense. This is where having a layer comes in handy.

10. Change the Intensity of the layer to **0.5** to improve the quality of the pattern on the hose. Figure 4.72 shows the results.

Now you know a quick way to apply a pattern to a 3D mesh based on UV layout and using the NoiseMaker for the pattern. Try the same workflow with layers for a few different patterns to get the hang of it.

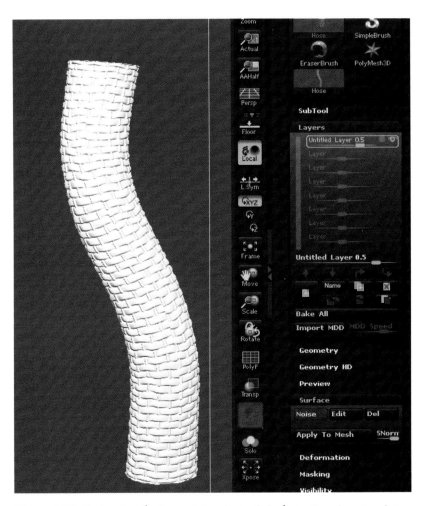

Figure 4.72 By turning the Layer intensity to 0.5, the pattern is not so intense.

ARTIST SPOTLIGHT: SEBASTIEN LEGRAIN
USING PROJECTION MASTER TO CREATE MECHANICAL PARTS

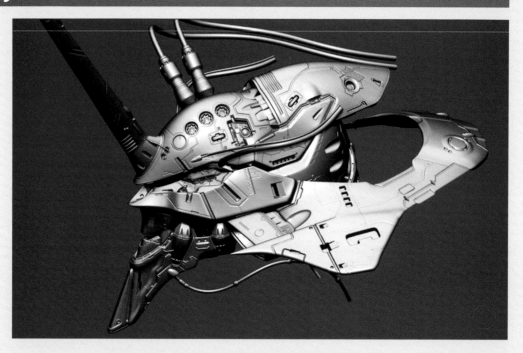

IN THIS TUTORIAL, I'll show you how to make a mechanical panel you can use for ships or robots, much like various panels on the image above. I'll mainly be using Projection Master for this technique.

1. We'll begin with the making of a custom alpha. Draw a shape in Photoshop on a layer using a mask. Then reduce this mask, removing some areas, and blending this layer at 50 percent to make a two-level pattern (see Figures 4.73 and 4.74). Having different levels of gray will create a difference of depth in the alpha that will eventually be applied in Projection Master.

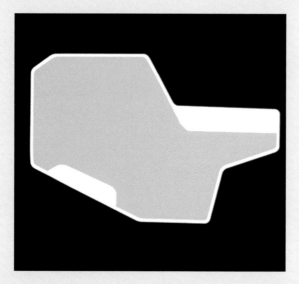

Figure 4.73 Masking off a section to create two levels of detail

USING PROJECTION MASTER TO CREATE MECHANICAL PARTS

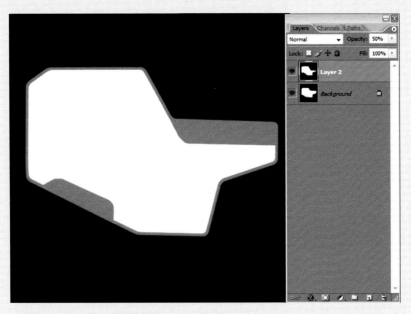

Figure 4.74 *Finished alpha read for ZBrush, with gray layer to add the two levels when applied as an alpha in ZBrush*

2. Make a plane by clicking the Plane3D button and then click the MakePolymesh button in the Tool palette. Make sure to have Smt off next to Divide in the Tool → Geometry subpalette and subdivide this plane to level 5 to get 263,169 polygons (see Figure 4.75).

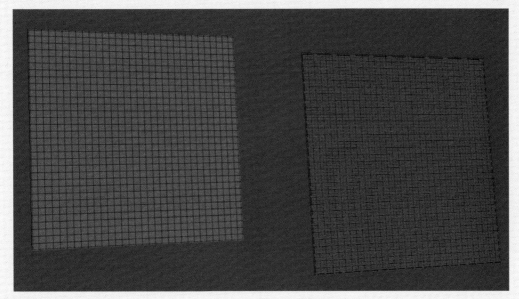

Figure 4.75 *Plane on the left is before subdividing and the plane on the right is after subdividing to level 5 with 263,169 polygons.*

USING PROJECTION MASTER TO CREATE MECHANICAL PARTS

3. Make sure to have the plane facing the camera, as shown in Figure 4.76. To open the Projection Master plug-in, click the Projection Master button at the top left of the interface. Within the options window for Projection Master, make sure that Deformation is on and Normalize is off. It is also important to deactivate the Persp button on the right shelf so that perspective distortion does not affect the model when you use the plug-in.

4. Use the SingleLayer brush with the DragRect stroke to drop the alpha that you made onto the plane, making sure the alpha covers most of the area and the SingleLayer brush has ZSub on (see Figure 4.77).

5. Press the W hot key to activate the Move gyro. You'll see it appear at the center of the depression in the surface. Drag on the handles of the gyro to reposition the brush stroke on the plane (see Figure 4.78).

Figure 4.76 Plane is facing the camera.

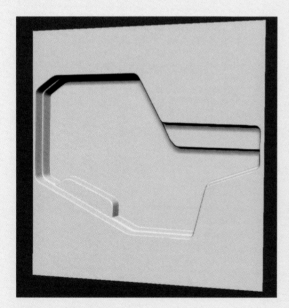

Figure 4.77 ZSub

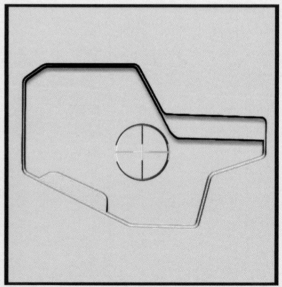

Figure 4.78 Repositioning the brush stroke

USING PROJECTION MASTER TO CREATE MECHANICAL PARTS

6. Now exit Projection Master by clicking the Projection Master button and choosing Pick Up Now. This sends the model back to 3D sculpting mode, as shown from the side in Figure 4.79. Mask the upper plane part. You add the mask by turning the plane on its side and dragging out a masking rectangle.

7. Now that the mask is created, send the object back to Projection Mask for more detailing. Use the Single Layer brush again, with the Line stroke selected to paint a network of assembly lines, adding a few details such as rivets and random squares and rectangles as shown in Figure 4.80.

8. Exit Projection Master again. The details you created in Projection Master are applied only to the unmasked section of the surface. Rotate the model to the side view and mask the upper plane, as shown in Figure 4.81. With the surface masked, enter Projection Master once more for even more detailing.

You can use 3D tools inside Projection Master. I take advantage of this to create even more complex details for my models.

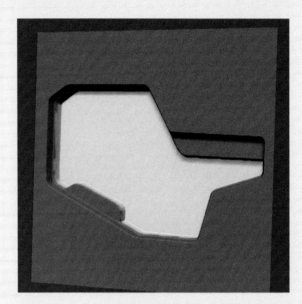

Figure 4.79 3D sculpting mode

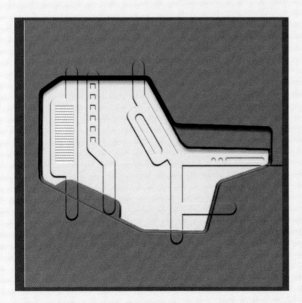

Figure 4.80 Line stroke option

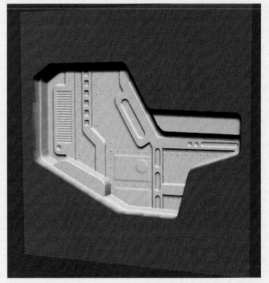

Figure 4.81 Rotate and mask the upper plane

USING PROJECTION MASTER TO CREATE MECHANICAL PARTS

9. While in Projection Master, select Cylinder3D from the Tool palette. In the Tool → Initialize subpalette, set HDivide to **256** to make sure the cylinder is smooth. Draw the cylinder parallel to the plane section that is flat to the camera. If you apply the cylinder on a normal face that is not facing the camera, the cylinder will be on an angle. Press the R key to enter Rotation mode. Hold the Shift key while rotating to snap the cylinder at a 90-degree angle. Press E to scale the cylinder. So, make a very small cylinder and stretch it vertically, as shown in Figure 4.82.

10. By using the Gyro tool in Move mode (hot key = W), you can position the cylinder on the canvas. Clicking in the gray circle of the locator as you move will maintain the cylinder's orientation. When you are working in Move mode within Projection Master, clicking outside in an open area when the gyro is activated changes the cylinder's Z-position forward or backward, which is extremely efficient and accurate. Moving in Z-position will allow you to move the cylinder back and forth in the depth of the plane.

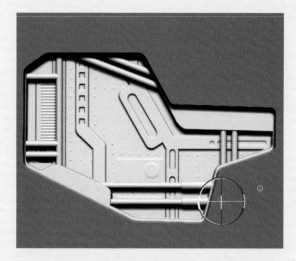

11. Create the additional details you see in Figure 4.83 by using a subdivided box and some polymesh wires created from ZSphere. By taking advantage of the fact that you can use any type of 3D mesh object as a brush stroke within Projection Master, you can easily create some very intricate and interesting details.

Figure 4.84 shows how the details look when you exit the Projection Master plug-in.

Figure 4.82 Creating a cylinder

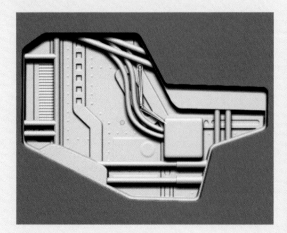

Figure 4.83 ZSphere creations

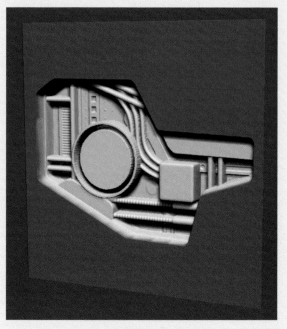

Figure 4.84 Projection Master plug in

USING PROJECTION MASTER TO CREATE MECHANICAL PARTS

12. Figure 4.85 shows another object you can create using these same techniques. Use Radial Symmetry to create a circular design. Using the Masking brush, hide the parts of the model that you do not want to be affected by the Projection Master plug-in.

13. Using the same Projection Master technique, merge the preceding model into your plane, as shown in Figure 4.86. With ZSub, you need to rotate your ZTool to make sure it's facing the direction that you wish to draw out this new piece to become a part of the metal.

14. Break the original shape of the highest point of the plane with a few cube strokes to add some detail elements as shown in Figure 4.87.

15. After you create your detailed panel, you can make a custom brush that will stamp the design on other surfaces. To do this, generate an alpha from the panel design and apply the alpha to a custom brush.

Figure 4.85 Radial Symmetry to create designs

Figure 4.86 Merging the model and plane

Figure 4.87 More details

USING PROJECTION MASTER TO CREATE MECHANICAL PARTS

Align the panel tool so that it is flat on the canvas. Drop the panel tool by exiting Edit mode (hot key = T). Then select MRGBZGrabber in the Tool palette. Make sure the Auto Crop option is disabled in the Modifiers subpalette of the Tool palette. Hold the Shift key while dragging on the canvas over the panel design to maintain a square selection. After you complete the selection, let go of the tool. The MRGBZ Grabber creates an alpha based on the depth of the design and places the new alpha in the Alpha library (see Figure 4.88).

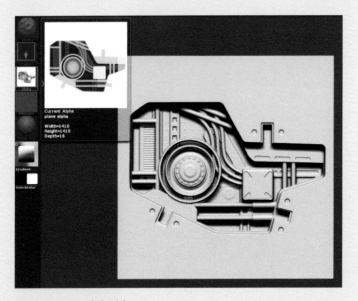

Figure 4.88 Alpha library

16. Now you can either project the tool onto another surface while in Projection Master, or apply the alpha to a brush and stamp all over another surface, as shown in Figure 4.89.

Figure 4.89 Applying the alpha to a brush

USING PROJECTION MASTER TO CREATE MECHANICAL PARTS

The advantage of having an alpha on a tool is that the alpha will respect the curvature of the surface. In Figure 4.90, I used the alpha we just created on my robot.

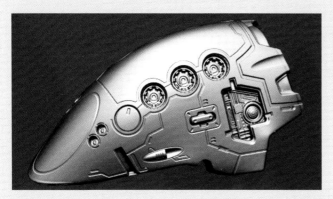

Figure 4.90 *Finished robot*

As you can see from the preceding workflow, Projection Master is a neglected tool in ZBrush that can still help you create some really dynamic pieces. Give Projection Master a try, and you may surprise yourself.

FRENCH NATIVE *Sebastien Legrain is the lead character modeler for Eidos-Montreal in Canada. He recently finished work on the video game* Deus Ex Human Revolution. *For more than eight years, he has worked in the video game industry, on AAA titles for companies including Microsoft, Ubisoft, and THQ. As a ZBrush user, he has been a feature presenter at SiGGRAPH for Pixologic. He has also contributed an artist tutorial for the Pixologic ZClassroom that can be viewed at* `www.pixologic.com/zclassroom/` `homeroom/tutorial.php?lesson=sebastien`.

Sebastien has been pushing pixels since ZBrush 2. Since ZBrush 3 introduced integrated 3D sculpting tools, many artists have stopped using the Projection Master plug-in, and the old 2.5 dimensional techniques have become underused. However, this tutorial demonstrates how Projection Master and 2.5 dimensional techniques can become a powerful part of your sculpting workflow.

`sebleg.free.fr/`

ARTIST SPOTLIGHT: STEVE WARNER
GENERATING A BUMP MAP FROM SCULPTED DETAILS

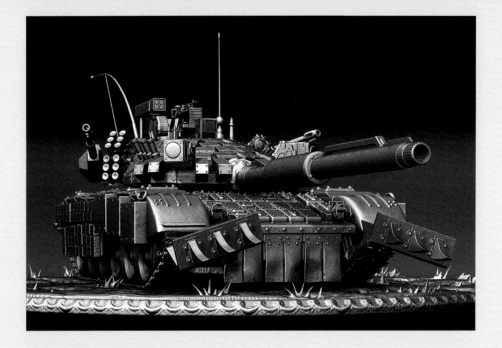

ZBRUSH ALLOWS YOU TO SCULPT an amazing amount of detail onto your objects. However, re-creating all of that detail in a traditional 3D program can be a challenge, especially in a production environment, where you have to keep your poly count and render times under tight control.

I've found that I get the best results from a combination of displacement maps and bump maps. Applying a displacement map to a relatively low-poly object allows me to reproduce the broad form of my sculpted model without significantly increasing my poly count. A bump map can then re-create the fine details.

Most ZBrush users know how to create a displacement map. But fewer seem to know how to create a high-quality bump map. In the following steps, I'll show you the technique I use to derive high-quality bump maps from sculpted details. Before you begin, make sure you save your object. Additionally, make sure you have created the necessary UV maps required for generating a displacement map.

1. Begin by cloning your object. In the Tool palette, click the Clone button. The clone will be placed in your Tool palette. Click the clone to switch to this model.

   The process of extracting a bump is destructive, so it's important to work on a clone and not your actual mesh.

2. Open the Tool → Geometry subpalette and drag the SDiv slider all the way to the right, so that your object is at its highest subdivision level (see Figure 4.91)—for my model, the highest level is 6.

Figure 4.91 *Move the Subdivision slider to the highest level, in this case level 6.*

GENERATING A BUMP MAP FROM SCULPTED DETAILS

3. In the Tool → Geometry subpalette, click the Lower Res button. This drops your subdivision level down one level.

4. In the Tool → Geometry subpalette, click the Del Lower button. This eliminates all lower subdivision levels. You will be left with two subdivision levels. You should be on the lowest subdivision level now.

In order for the following technique to work, it is imperative that you stay on the lowest subdivision level and that you do not switch to the higher level at any point from here on out.

5. Hold down the Shift key. This activates the Smooth brush. Gently brush over your mesh and smooth out all of the fine detail, as shown in the following image. Be careful not to smooth out broad forms. See Figure 4.92. Only smooth out the details that you want to appear in your bump map.

It may seem counterintuitive to smooth out the details that you want to keep, but trust me, it will work.

6. When you are finished smoothing out the fine details, open the Tool → Displacement Map subpalette. Turn on Adaptive mode and Smooth UV. Then click the Create DispMap button (see Figure 4.93).

Figure 4.92 Use the Smooth brush to gently brush over the surface.

When you create a displacement map, ZBrush looks at the currently selected subdivision level and notes any differences between it and the higher levels. It records these differences as black and white values in the displacement map. By smoothing out the details of your mesh, you forced ZBrush to take note of the detailed areas during the displacement map creation.

When the displacement map has been created, you will see the details reappear on your mesh, as you see in Figure 4.94. These details are now coming from the map. However, rather than containing a record of the broad changes and the fine details as is normally the case with a displacement map, it will contain only a record of the fine details. In essence, you've created a perfect bump map.

7. Click the Disp On button in the Tool → Displacement Map subpalette. This will allow you to toggle the map so you can see the effect it is having.

Figure 4.93 Turn on Adaptive and Smooth UV in the Tool → Displacement Map subpalette.

GENERATING A BUMP MAP FROM SCULPTED DETAILS

Figure 4.94 The new map will host all the detail.

8. If you are satisfied with the results, click the Clone Disp button in the Tool → Displacement Map subpalette. This will send the map to the main Alpha palette. You can now export the map as you normally would, exporting it as a TIF file (see Figure 4.95).

Figure 4.96 shows a side-by-side comparison of the sculpted details (left) and the details being re-created via the map (right).

Figure 4.95 Click Clone Disp to create a map that will be sent to the Alpha palette.

GENERATING A BUMP MAP FROM SCULPTED DETAILS

Figure 4.96 *A comparison between the original sculpt (left) and the sculpt with the map (right)*

STEVE WARNER *is an award-winning artist and best-selling author with over 30 years of experience in the computer graphics industry. Steve received his formal education from the University of Arizona, where he earned his bachelor's degree in studio art. Throughout the 1990s, he ran an independent design studio based in Tucson, Arizona. In 2001 he became the art director for CAE at Davis-Monthan Air Force Base, where he oversaw the air-to-air combat simulation work for the A-10 and EC-130 training programs.*

Steve is recognized as an expert in NewTek's LightWave 3D. He has co-authored three books, including the best sellers LightWave 3D 8: 1001 Tips and Tricks *and* Essential LightWave v9. *He is also recognized as an expert in Pixologic's ZBrush, having worked on the Beta team for ZBrush 3.0 and 4.0. His ground-breaking hard-surface sculpting work has been featured on the Pixologic website and in the* Getting Started with ZBrush *guide.*

In 2008, Steve moved to Orlando, Florida, *to work as the 3D modeling instructor at the Digital Animation and Visual Effects School. His extensive knowledge of 3D tools and techniques has benefited hundreds of students now working in the film, television, and gaming industries. In 2010, Steve was promoted to the role of executive director. He oversees the program, faculty, and curriculum development for the school.*

Steve continues to work as a freelance artist. He has contributed to recent projects for Pepsi, Time, *Billboard,* DirecTV, *and* The Wall Street Journal.

www.daveschool.com

five

Adding a Splash of Color

After you complete a sculpt, *your next step is to bring some color to your creation. ZBrush was the first application to allow you to paint directly onto the model while having complete interaction with that mesh. It was the first time you could rotate, zoom, and move a mesh around and then apply color. ZBrush calls this polypainting: painting directly onto the polygons, or, in ZBrush, the vertex points.*

This chapter covers the tools created because of the polypaint capability. Polypainting is the quickest way to paint directly onto a model, but many other tools, such as Spotlight and ZAppLink, give us more freedom. So let's get our tablet pens and remember those days of applying paint to canvas.

A great reference book for basics on PolyPainting is Eric Keller's *Introducing ZBrush4* (John Wiley & Sons, Inc., 2011).

- Understanding the basics of polypainting
- Using AO to colorize
- Using Mask By Cavity to paint out detail
- Painting with UV Master
- Texturing with Projection Master
- Using Photoshop to paint
- Using Spotlight

Understanding the Basics of Polypaint

If you have never textured in ZBrush, I want to briefly cover polypaint basics to lay a foundation for all other techniques discussed in this chapter. Start with this exercise:

1. Open LightBox. Then select the Project menu, double-click the DemoProjects folder, and double-click on the DemoDog.ZPR file to load the dog shown in Figure 5.1. Save your current open project so you do not lose any of your hard work.

2. The dog loads with a brown color. Change the dog's color to white by moving the color picker to white. Also notice that the material for this project is SkinShade4. I strongly recommend always using this material when you paint in ZBrush.

Figure 5.1 Select the Project menu in LightBox and double-click DemoDog.ZPR.

When you change the dog to white, it immediately changes color. However, the dog is not actually filled with a color; it is a blank canvas. So you need to fill the dog (canvas) with a base color.

3. With white still selected, you can fill the dog by clicking the FillObject button in the Color palette (see Figure 5.2).

Now changing color in the color picker will not change the overall color. This is exactly how you want to start with polypainting.

4. Select the Standard brush and turn on only the RGB button at the top of the interface, as shown in Figure 5.3.

With RGB the only selected button, ZBrush will apply only color information to the model. If you want to sculpt, the ZSub button must be on, but we are focused on only polypainting right now.

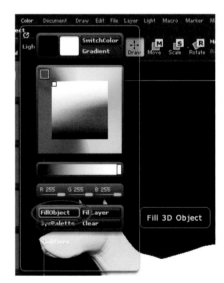

Figure 5.2 Fill any tool with selected color by clicking FillObject in the Color palette.

5. Select red in the color picker. With a small brush size, apply a stroke to the dog. You can see in Figure 5.4 that I did not get the result I wanted.

Figure 5.3 Turn only the RGB button on.

To get a more detailed stroke, you need to divide the dog into polygons. This is the key to polypainting. The more polygons you have, the more detailed you can get with polypaint strokes.

6. Divide the dog to level 5, which is 2.044 million polygons, and apply the stroke again. As you can see in Figure 5.5, the line is much cleaner now.

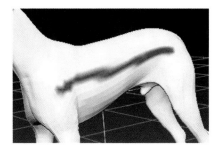

Figure 5.5 *After dividing the dog to level 5, a defined line can be painted.*

Figure 5.4 *Apply a red stroke to the dog.*

These are the basics of polypainting. The detail you get when you apply color depends on the number of polygons your tool has. Try messing around a little more to become more familiar with polypainting.

Using AO to Colorize

Figure 5.6 *Mask Ambient Occlusion button in the Tool → Masking subpalette*

Expanding on the idea that you always want to fill your tool with color before applying polypaint, you will use an ambient occlusion (AO) technique to create a base of color with two values instead of one. Here are the steps:

1. Load the character named Hoody.ZTL in the Chapter 2 Assets folder into ZBrush and then click the Mask Ambient Occlusion button in the Tool → Masking subpalette, shown in Figure 5.6. You can see the results in Figure 5.7.

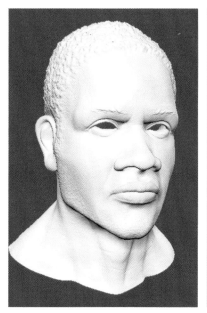

Figure 5.7 *Before the AO (left), and the results after applying AO (right)*

When you use the Mask Ambient Occlusion button, keep your polygon count at or under 1 million polygons. The higher the poly count, the longer ZBrush takes to apply the ambient occlusion. Usually 1 million polygons will have enough form on the sculpt to capture the AO. After you create the mask, you can walk up to the highest subdivision to update the mask.

In the previous figure, a black mask is added where less light falls onto the surface—for example, around the eyes. You can apply the color in the mask to a texture and control it by the main color and secondary color located right underneath the color picker.

2. Change the secondary color to red. Then in the Tool → Texture Map subpalette, click New From Masking to create a texture similar to the one in Figure 5.8. Figure 5.9 shows the texture applied to my tool. (If you are using a different project than the exercise, remember that your mesh must have UVs.)

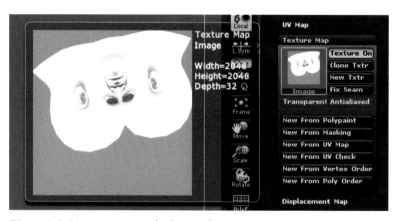

Figure 5.8 New texture applied to tool

You can see in the previous figures that ZBrush applies the Main Color as the main overall color to the texture and the Secondary Color as the masked sections. To apply this texture as polypaint information, you need one more step.

3. Have your tool at the highest subdivision level so you can capture all the detail, and clear your mask on the model. Then in the Tool → PolyPaint subpalette, click the PolyPaint From Texture button (see Figure 5.10) to apply your texture as a base for polypainting.

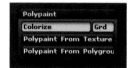

Figure 5.10 The PolyPaint From Texture button will apply any texture as polypaint to your selected tool.

Figure 5.9 AO Texture applied to the tool

Texture Map

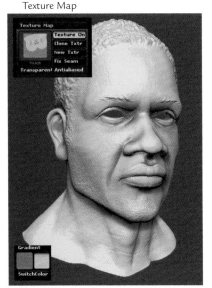

Main & Secondary Color

Texture Map

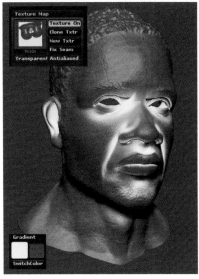

Main & Secondary Color

Texture Map

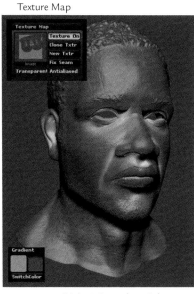

Main & Secondary Color

Figure 5.11 *Three extreme examples of using AO for paint*

In Figure 5.11, you can see a few examples of this technique being used a little differently. In the three images, you see my Main Color and Secondary Color, the texture created, and how the texture appears when applied.

4. Another trick is to change the overall skin tone of a character and add a bit of red color. As shown in Figure 5.12, apply a texture from the AO to the polypainted character. In this example, I dropped my RGB Intensity to 10 before clicking the PolyPaint From Texture button.

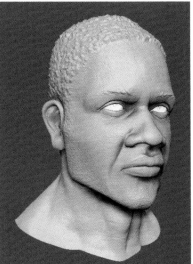

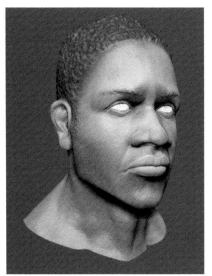

Figure 5.12 *Before I mask by AO (left), the AO as a texture map (middle), and applying the texture with RGB Intensity set to 10 (right)*

5. This is the last tip for AO. Remember that you are using a mask. So invert the mask and then apply the preceding texture to apply only the red color from the texture (see Figure 5.13).

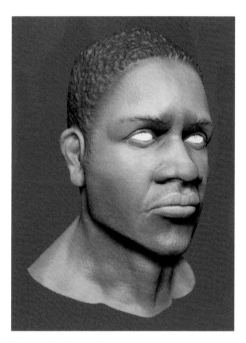

Figure 5.13 *Applying the texture with an inverse masking*

Using Mask By Cavity to Paint Out Detail

Mask By Cavity is a powerful feature; you can add that bit of color change or make a detail pop by applying polypaint in the depressed portion of your sculpt. You can add color in otherwise difficult areas to accentuate the peaks or valleys of a mesh.

Mask By Cavity is in the Tool → Masking subpalette (see Figure 5.14). Next to the button is a slider called Blur that blurs the mask. Below that is an Intensity slider that controls the strength of the mask being applied, and right below Intensity is a Cavity Profile curve that lets you mask your cavities in just about any way.

You want to use this mask to add a little more color to the lips.

1. I went a little extreme just so you could easily see my result, adding a little more pink and red to the lips, as shown in Figure 5.15. Click Mask By Cavity so ZBrush will mask off all cavities. You can then apply any color to the mesh. However, because we used Mask By Cavity, this color change was not applied to the depressed areas of the sculpt.

Figure 5.14 *Mask By Cavity in the Tool → Masking subpalette*

2. Invert the mask to paint in the creased areas. You can see how this will make the color you previously added really pop, as shown in Figure 5.16.

3. Let's have some fun and turn the guy's hair gray so the roots are still black. Use Mask By Cavity in the hair to get results like those shown in Figure 5.17.

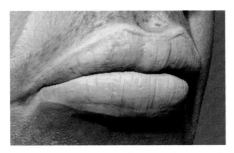

Figure 5.15 Adding a bit of red and pink to the lips with Mask By Cavity

Figure 5.16 Inverting the Mask By Intensity mask to paint into the creases of the tool

As you can see from these two examples, there are many ways to use Mask By Cavity. Don't forget about it the next time you need a small detail to stand out more.

Painting with UV Master

Pixologic offers many plug-ins that could really be their own piece of software, and these plug-ins are free. UV Master is a powerful plug-in that lets you quickly lay out readable UVs for your mesh. If you do not have UV Master installed on your system, you can find it in the download center of the Pixologic site: www.pixologic.com/zbrush/downloadcenter/zplugins/.

After you install UV Master, it will appear in the ZPlugin palette. Let's take the model we've been using and see what kind of UVs are assigned to him. Make sure to take a minute to read the documents for this plug-in to learn more about how UV Master works.

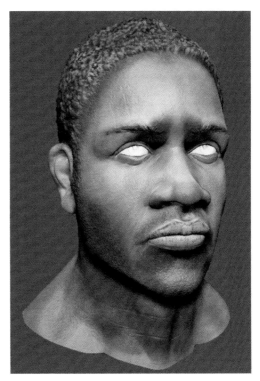

Figure 5.17 Using Mask By Cavity to add gray hair with black roots

1. First, click the Work On Clone button, shown in Figure 5.18.

   Figure 5.19 shows how Work On Clone duplicates the selected tool, drops to the lowest subdivision level, and then deletes all other subdivision levels.

2. We already have a UV layout on this tool, so just click the Flatten button, shown in Figure 5.20, to see the actual UV layout (see Figure 5.21). Also turn on Polyframe mode so you can see the actual UVs.

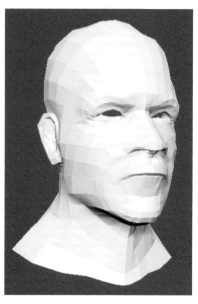

Figure 5.18 *Work On Clone button in UV Master*

Figure 5.19 *The clone mesh made by UV Master after clicking the Work On Clone button*

Figure 5.20 *The Flatten button in UV Master displays the actual UV layout of the selected tool.*

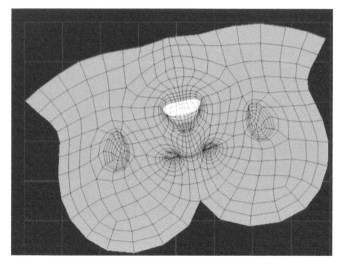

Figure 5.21 *UV layout of my tool*

3. You can now paint directly on the flattened mesh based on the UV layout. Before you start polypainting, though, you need to divide the mesh up to the same SDiv level as the actual sculpted tool, which for this guy is level 6.

Make sure Smt is deactivated; it's next to the Divide button in the Tool → Geometry subpalette, as shown in Figure 5.22. With Smt off, you can divide the mesh without applying smoothing. You want to make sure that when you are finished, the UVs will still match the original UVs on the sculpted mesh.

Figure 5.22 *Geometry subpalette with Smt off and the mesh divided to level 6*

4. In the Texture Map subpalette, turn your texture back on and then apply it to the mesh by clicking PolyPaint From Texture in the PolyPaint subpalette, to get results like Figure 5.23.

5. Now you can polypaint directly on the UV layout. In Figure 5.24, I have started to paint the base colors for a bruised eye.

6. In the Tool → Texture Map subpalette, click the New From Polypaint button to add the black eye to the already selected texture. As Figure 5.25 shows, the black eye is added to the original paint job.

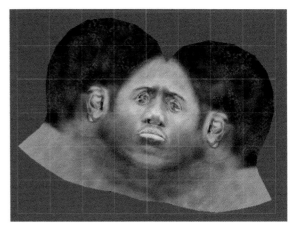

Figure 5.23 *Texture applied to the flattened UV layout*

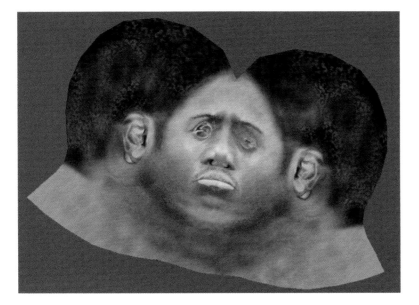

Figure 5.24 *Painting a base bruised eye directly onto the UV layout*

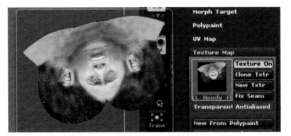

Figure 5.25 *The polypainted bruised eye applied to the original texture by clicking the New From PolyPaint button*

7. Click the Clone Txtr button, and a copy of the texture is sent to the Texture palette (see Figure 5.26).

8. Now select the original sculpt, and in the Tool → Texture Map subpalette, select the texture with the black eye (see Figure 5.27).

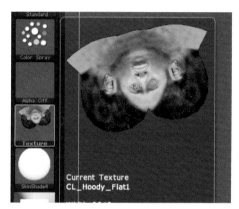

Figure 5.26 *Cloned texture in the Texture palette*

This is a neat trick to paint directly onto your UVs in ZBrush, but let's keep exploring the other painting tools in ZBrush to see what else we have.

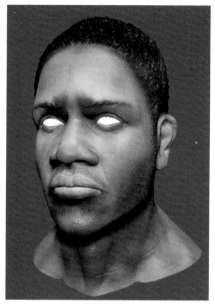

Figure 5.27 *New texture applied to the original sculpted tool*

Texturing with Projection Master

There are two techniques for texturing with Projection Master. The first technique is to project your paint onto the tool, and the second technique is to project the paint to the texture. You will see throughout this book that many professionals still use this valuable tool to pull off some of the coolest tricks.

Let's start with projecting the paint to the tool:

1. With a cube selected, divide up to 1.5 million polygons. Click the Projection Master button or use the shortcut G to open the dialog box you see in Figure 5.28. Because you are only painting, select Colors and keep Fade on by default.

2. Click the Drop Now button. A dialog box opens, asking whether you want the paint information applied to the tool or a texture. Click the Activate Polypainting option.

One great advantage to using Projection Master is the number of ways to apply your stroke to the tool. Figure 5.29 shows 15 ways to apply color information.

3. For this exercise, choose the grid with the star selected in the Texture palette and draw out a stroke (see Figure 5.30).

4. Your stroke may not go exactly where you want it. Turn on Move mode at the top of the UI; a gyro appears that lets you move your stroke into the correct position (see Figure 5.31).

Figure 5.28 *Dialog box of Projection Master*

Figure 5.29 *Multiple stroke options when using Projection Master*

Figure 5.30 *Star stroke applied to cube*

Figure 5.31 *In Move mode, the gyro lets you move the stroke into the correct spot on the cube.*

5. When you are happy with your position, click the Projection Master button or press G to pick up the mesh. The Projection Master dialog box appears (see Figure 5.32). Click the Pickup Now button to apply the paint to the tool as polypaint information, as shown in Figure 5.33.

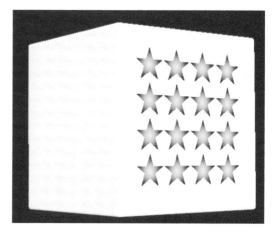

Figure 5.32 *Dialog box when anything is picked up from Projection Master*

Figure 5.33 *Paint applied to the cube as polypaint information*

Now that we applied color as polypaint, let's try using the other technique and apply the paint information to the texture:

1. First create a texture for the cube. Do this by clicking the New Txtr button (see Figure 5.34). The resolution of the texture is controlled by the setting set in the Tool → UV Map subpalette.

2. Follow the same steps as in the preceding exercise to apply the color. This time the color was applied to the texture (see Figure 5.35). I even wrote *Texture* on the cube itself so that would be transferred to the texture.

Figure 5.34 *The New Txtr button in the Texture Map subpalette will create a new texture for the selected subtool.*

Although these examples are basic, the workflow can be powerful. I want to make sure that when you use Projection Master, you understand the two options available for applying paint. It's key to pick the right technique for the right circumstance. This will be the foundation for the next two painting techniques in ZBrush.

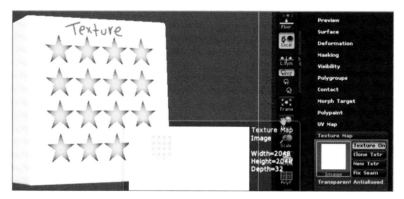

Figure 5.35 *Color information applied to selected texture in the Texture Map subpalette*

Using Photoshop to Paint

If you are using ZBrush, you are probably using Photoshop. Many artists have saved Photoshop brushes over the years or established great techniques they enjoy using in Photoshop. So Pixologic has developed two plug-ins that let you use Photoshop to apply color information to your ZBrush work.

The first plug-in is ZAppLink, and the second is GoZ Photoshop. Each gives different results, but each gets you to your goal of painting your ZBrush models with Photoshop.

Remember, you can download these plug-ins off the Pixologic download center: www.pixologic.com/zbrush/downloadcenter/zplugins/.

Using ZAppLink

I covered Projection Master before ZAppLink to make sure you understand which plug-in to use in the different circumstances you come across. Projection Master can apply paint to a tool by projecting everything as polypaint information or apply paint directly to the texture. ZAppLink and GoZ will do one or the other.

The ZAppLink plug-in applies any of the painting done in Photoshop as a projection to the polypaint. So your polygon count is important once again.

After you install ZAppLink, the button for the plug-in appears in the Document palette. This plug-in comes preinstalled with ZBrush 4R2 (see Figure 5.36).

Follow these steps to use ZAppLink:

1. Load the character head once again. This guy is great for showing these techniques. Open up the ZAppLink Properties so you can store the positions of your tool. ZAppLink Properties is at the bottom of the Document palette.

Figure 5.36 ZAppLink button in the Document palette

Now you can store the positions of your head tool. Here is an example of how this works:

- First move the model to face the camera. This is the front, so when you click the Front button, ZBrush stores the position as Front and automatically stores the Back button as the back of the head.

- Now if you move the head to the right side and click Right, ZBrush stores the position as Right and automatically stores the Left button.

Figure 5.37 shows all views I have stored, including Cust1 for a custom view. Anywhere you can position the tool can be a custom view. Most people will use these two custom views to store a three-quarters view of each side of the face. You can tell which views are stored by the little orange marker on the side of each view.

Figure 5.37 Stored views are highlighted with orange.

2. With views stored, you can now click the ZAppLink button to send everything into Photoshop. After you press this button, a dialog box appears with a check box labeled Enable

Perspective, as shown in Figure 5.38. Select this box only if you already have perspective on in ZBrush. If perspective is off in ZBrush, do not turn this on.

3. Click OK, and ZAppLink launches Photoshop and creates a layer for every view that was stored in ZBrush. Figure 5.39 shows all the layers in Photoshop that are created based on the views stored previously in ZBrush.

Figure 5.38 ZAppLink dialog box. Only turn on Enable Perspective if you already have perspective on in ZBrush.

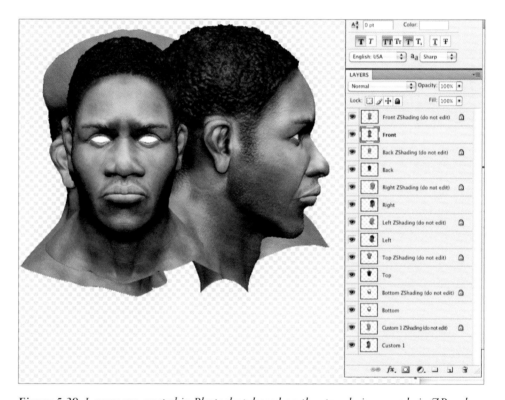

Figure 5.39 Layers are created in Photoshop based on the stored views made in ZBrush.

As you can see, every view has two layers. One layer is just flat color, which is named for the stored view. For example, when only Front is active, you see the diffuse polypaint information (see Figure 5.40). You paint on these flat diffuse layers. When the eye is turned on for the Front ZShading (Do Not Edit) layer (see Figure 5.41), you see the shaded render of your model so you understand where the detail is on the model. Do not paint on these ZShading layers.

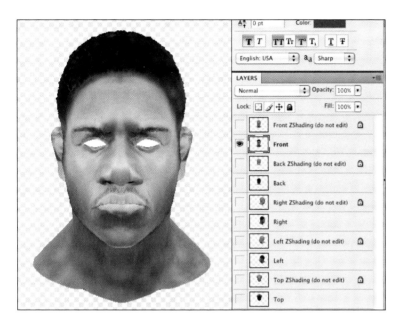

Figure 5.40 *Front view layer gives the polypaint diffuse information. Paint only on these layers.*

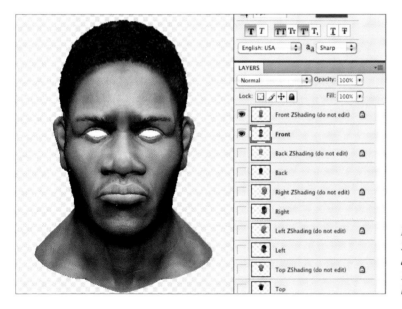

Figure 5.41 *Front ZShading layer gives a render of the detail. Do not paint on these layers.*

4. In Figure 5.42, I wrote the word *Front*; I also added the position name to every other view. Do this on your layers so when you send everything back to ZBrush, you understand what ZBrush does with each of these layers.

5. After you paint on your layers in Photoshop, press Ctrl+S. This saves the file but does not change the name. Do *not* change the name of the file. That will break the link that ZBrush has established with Photoshop. Now you need to switch to ZBrush. When you switch over to ZBrush, you may get a dialog box like the one in Figure 5.43.

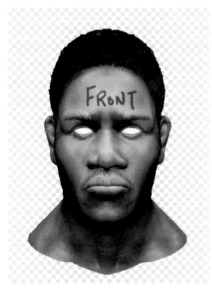

Figure 5.42 *I wrote* Front *on the layer to use as an example of what ZBrush does with the layers.*

Figure 5.43 *This dialog box appears in ZBrush after you have saved the file in Photoshop and switched back to ZBrush.*

What do these options mean exactly? ZBrush is looking for the link to be established. Because I work on a Mac, ZBrush was selected without any changes to the Photoshop file. So ZBrush is asking three questions:

- OK (Unchanged) = Click this if you just want to go back into ZBrush and apply no changes.
- (Re-check) = ZBrush looks at the Photoshop file again to see what changes were made.
- Return To External Editor = Keep the link between ZBrush and Photoshop good and switch back to Photoshop.

6. Because you made changes to the Photoshop file, you want to choose the (Re-check) option so ZBrush will look at the file again. After you click that button, another dialog box appears, as shown in Figure 5.44.

7. Click the Re-enter ZBrush button to bring over the Photoshop layers and project them one layer at a time.

Figure 5.44 *Dialog box indicating there were changes to the Photoshop file*

Figure 5.45 shows the dialog box that appears before any layer is projected onto the model. ZBrush asks whether you want to fade the projection, have it be double-sided (which will project the same color information on both sides of the model), and whether perspective should be enabled. Remember, if perspective was off from the beginning, then keep it off throughout this process.

After you go through your options for each layer, ZBrush projects everything as polypaint information, as shown in Figure 5.46.

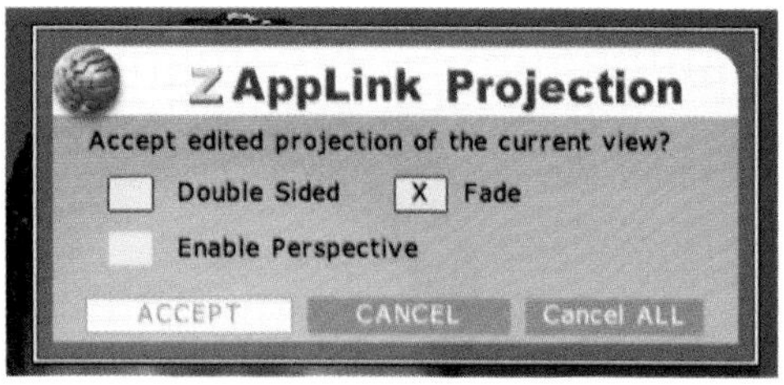

Using GoZ Photoshop

What if you cannot divide up your model any more because of computer restrictions? How do you get your Photoshop painting to project onto the model if you don't have enough polygons to capture the paint detail? This is where GoZ Photoshop comes in handy: you still use the power of Photoshop, but you apply all the paint to the texture, not the polygons.

Make sure the most recent GoZ version is installed on your system. (Visit the Pixologic download center: `www.pixologic` `.com/zbrush/downloadcenter/zplugins/.`) This plug-in works only with Photoshop CS3 and up. Then follow these steps:

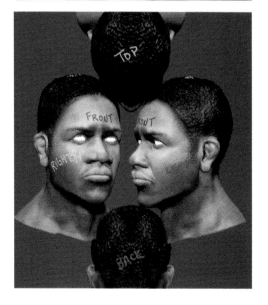

Figure 5.45
Dialog box that appears before any of the layers are projected onto the model

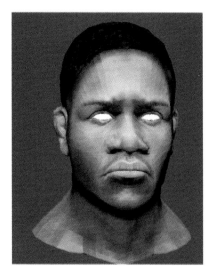

Figure 5.46
Layers from Photoshop projected as polypaint information to the model

1. Start by dropping your model to a lower level, as shown in Figure 5.47. Then turn on the texture, as shown in Figure 5.48. Although the poly count is low, you can see all the detail in the paint because the texture hosts that information.

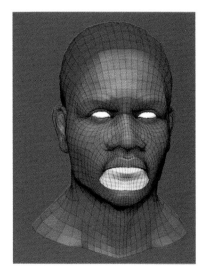

Figure 5.47 The tool at a lower subdivision level will not capture the paint detail.

Figure 5.48 Texture is turned on in the low-resolution mesh to show that paint detail is still high because of the texture hosting the information.

Figure 5.49 GoZ
buttons are at the top
of the Tool palette.

Make sure Photoshop is the current selected GoZ application. Then with the texture on in the Texture Map subpalette and UVs already applied to the mesh, click the GoZ button at the top of the Tool palette (see Figure 5.49).

2. Figure 5.49 shows an R next to the Visible button. Click the R, and a dialog box appears. Figure 5.50 shows that Maya is my current GoZ application. Select Photoshop, if it is not selected already.

Figure 5.50 was taken on the MAC side. If you are using the Windows version of ZBrush, you will also have 3DSMAX as an option for external applications.

Figure 5.50 Dialog box for
choosing the GoZ application

After Photoshop launches, you are placed in Photoshop 3D mode, where you can paint directly onto the model. You can see Photoshop 3D mode in Figure 5.51.

3. In 3D mode, paint directly onto the model, as shown in Figure 5.52, to add the start of a headband.

In this mode, you can paint on the UV layout as well, just as you did with the UV Master plug-in.

4. To view the UV layout, double-click the Hoody_1_TXTR layer (see Figure 5.53). This layer is automatically created when you GoZ everything over from ZBrush. You see a UV layout similar to Figure 5.54.

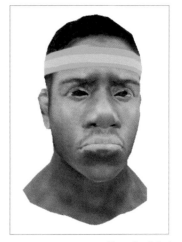

Figure 5.52 Headband added
to the model while in 3D mode

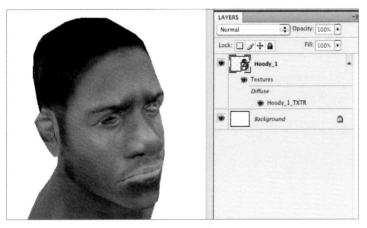

Figure 5.51 3D layer created in Photoshop

Figure 5.53
A TXTR file is
automatically
created so
you can paint
directly onto
the UV layout.

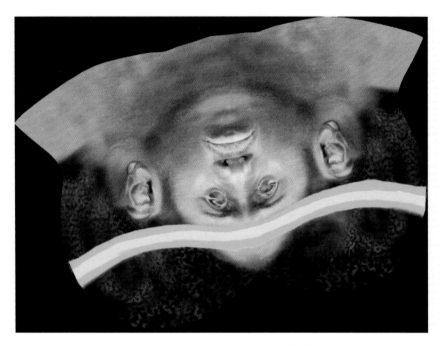

Figure 5.54 *UV layout of the model with texture applied*

5. To see the actual UVs of the model, return to the Photoshop menu called 3D and click Create UV Overlays → Wireframe (see Figure 5.55). A layer for the UVs is automatically created.

   Anything that you do in this mode is applied to the 3D model as soon as you click the Photoshop file.

6. Add a ZMan logo on the headband in UV layout. The logo is automatically added to the 3D model in Photoshop.

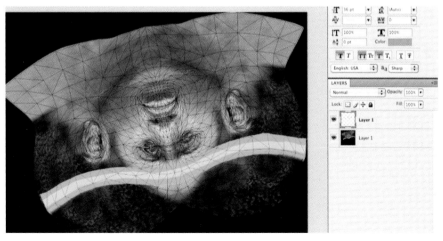

Figure 5.55 *UVs created as a layer when you choose 3D → Create UV Overlays → Wireframe in Photoshop*

7. Turn off the UV overlay layer so that is not applied to the model in 3D mode. Now you need to send this all to ZBrush. Click File → Automate → GoZPlugin in Photoshop to send everything over to ZBrush (see Figure 5.56).

In Figure 5.57, you can see that everything in Photoshop was applied to the texture in ZBrush.

Many artists like implementing Photoshop in their workflow. It's up to you to decide which plug-in works best in your workflow.

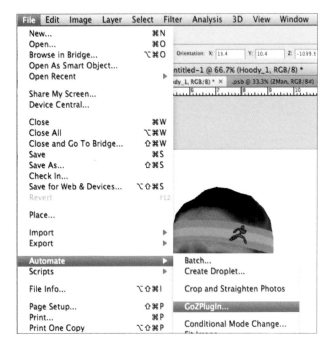

Figure 5.56 GoZPlugin sends everything from Photoshop to ZBrush.

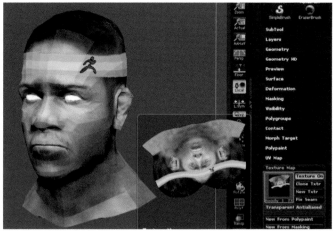

Figure 5.57 Photoshop paint applied to ZBrush texture

Using SpotLight

Spotlight is a powerful feature to use for texturing, but you can also use it for sculpting. This section covers only the texturing part of Spotlight. However, I encourage you to grab some popcorn and watch Spotlight in action at ZBrushCentral and at Pixologic:

www.zbrushcentral.com/showthread.php?t=071829

www.pixologic.com/zclassroom/homeroom/tutorial.php?lesson=spotlight

There are two ways to activate Spotlight. The first way is to double-click twice on any texture or alpha in LightBox, and the image automatically loads into ZBrush, if there is already a texture loaded in Spotlight (see Figure 5.58).

The other way is to click the Add To Spotlight button, shown in Figure 5.59, to add any active texture in the Texture palette. After you click this button, the selected texture is added to your ZBrush document (see Figure 5.60).

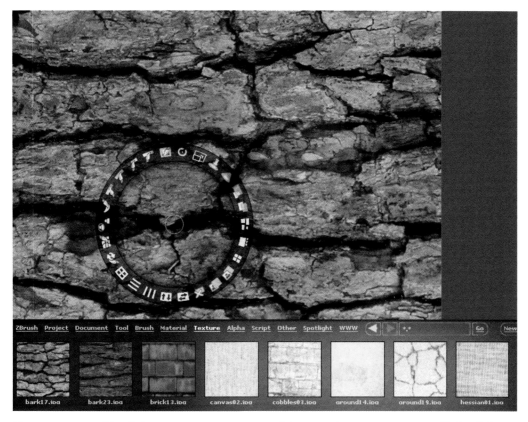

Figure 5.58 *Double-click twice on any texture or alpha in LightBox to automatically load the image on the ZBrush document if there is already a texture loaded into Spotlight.*

Figure 5.59 *The Add To Spotlight icon in the Texture palette activates Spotlight.*

Figure 5.60 *The texture selected in the Texture palette is added to Spotlight.*

The dial in Figure 5.60 represents *Spotlight Edit* mode, where you can use Spotlight to edit any loaded image. When you no longer see the dial, and you see only the textures and the model, as shown in Figure 5.61, you are in *Spotlight Projection* mode. This mode will project the texture onto the model. To get in and out of these two modes, you just have to use the keyboard shortcut Z.

A lot can be covered for the basics of Spotlight, but I would like to move on to using Spotlight to accomplish a couple of techniques.

The following are two key shortcuts when using Spotlight:

- Z turns Spotlight Projection mode on or off.
- Shift+Z closes Spotlight and returns to standard ZBrush mode.

Figure 5.61 *Spotlight Projection mode projects any loaded texture onto the model that is in Edit mode.*

Adjusting Hue

Sometimes you want to match the hue more closely among several textures, such as skin tone, or brick colors, or even two tree bark textures. Matching two tree bark textures is exactly what I want to do for this next technique. You can follow along with textures of your own:

1. Load two textures in LightBox into Spotlight (see Figure 5.62).

   I want to change the hue of the image on the left (the target image) to match the texture on the right (the source image).

2. Select your target texture—for me it's the texture on the left—by clicking directly on the texture. Figure 5.63 shows that the texture on the left is selected, as indicated by the thin red line and the dial over the texture.

3. Select the Hue brush. To match the hue of the two textures, you click the Hue brush and drag it over to the source image. Figure 5.64 shows the results.

This is a quick and simple way to match textures to make them look as if they belong to the same tree. I also like to adjust the intensity of the texture by turning the dial while using the Intensity brush, as you see in Figure 5.65, so the intensity adjustment matches the textures even more closely.

Figure 5.62 Two textures with completely different hues loaded into Spotlight

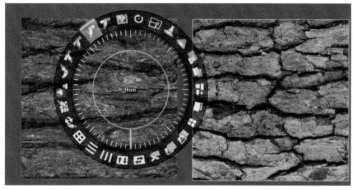

Figure 5.63 The texture on the left is selected, which is indicated by a thin red line around the texture.

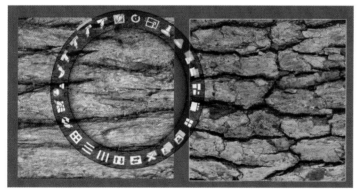

Figure 5.64 The selected texture is now matched to the texture on the right with the Hue brush.

Figure 5.65 The Intensity brush helps adjust the texture to match the other texture even more.

Masking Out a Texture

Spotlight lets you mask out parts of the texture that you do not wish to use when you apply the color to the model. For this example, you will paint the tattoo you see in Figure 5.66 onto your model. Here are the steps:

1. Open the tattoo texture included with `Chapter 5 Assets`; the file is called `Tattoo.psd`.

   You will immediately encounter an issue when you first try to apply the tattoo to the model. You can see in Figure 5.67 that the tattoo and the background white color are both applied.

2. To apply any texture, remember to click Z to come out of Edit Spotlight mode and into Spotlight Projection mode, and use any 3D brush with only RGB on to apply the texture.

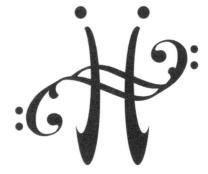

Figure 5.66 The tattoo that you will apply to the head model

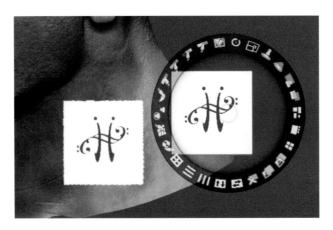

Figure 5.67 Just applying the tattoo as is will apply all color from the texture.

3. With the Paint brush and a green color selected, hold the Ctrl key and then click and drag anywhere in the white area of the texture. All the white turns green, as you can see in Figure 5.68. This example uses green so you have a visual. The color is of no importance.

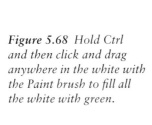

Figure 5.68 Hold Ctrl and then click and drag anywhere in the white with the Paint brush to fill all the white with green.

4. To mask out the green color of the texture, switch to black and then hold Ctrl while you click and drag everywhere that you see green.

ZBrush will see black as transparent so the tattoo can be visible in the texture, as shown in Figure 5.69. To mask out any part of a texture, just switch to black with the Paint brush. Everything black will become transparent.

5. Now apply the texture to the character; you get only the tattoo on his neck, as shown in Figure 5.70.

This is a simple way to use this feature that you will find useful along your pipeline.

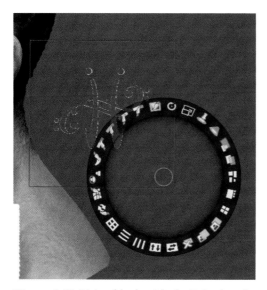 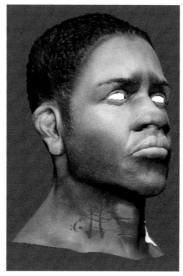

Figure 5.69 *Using black with the Paint brush masks out the texture.*

Figure 5.70 *Tattoo applied using the Paint brush with black to mask out the white part of the texture*

Using the Pin Feature

The Pin feature in Spotlight lets you use one texture multiple times on a tool with a simple brush stroke. Let's use the Pin feature to apply a window on a basic cube with just a few clicks:

1. First create a cube, and apply the image of house siding, siding.jpg, from the Chapter 5 Assets folder to make the cube look like a house. Figure 5.71 shows that the siding is too large for the cube.

Figure 5.71 *House siding is too large for the cube.*

2. Hold the Tile V button in Spotlight and turn the Spotlight dial clockwise to tile the texture so that the siding size will fit better. In Figure 5.72, the siding fits the cube a lot better.

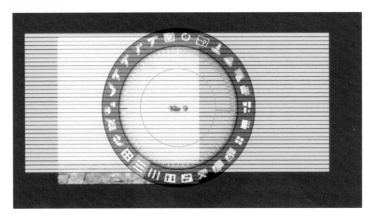

Figure 5.72 Tile V will tile the texture along the vertical axis.

If you hold the Shift key when you click Tile V or Tile H, Spotlight will tile the selected texture along the vertical and horizontal axes at the same time.

Apply this siding to all sides of the cube, as shown in Figure 5.73.

Next you want to apply a window a few times on the cube (see Figure 5.74). The Pin feature lets you accomplish this task.

Figure 5.73 The siding applied to the whole cube

Figure 5.74 Window that you want to apply to the cube

3. Load the window file Window.jpg from the Chapter 5 Assets folder. Before you can apply the window, you need to mask out the rest of the texture that you don't want; use the Paint brush masking feature as you did with the tattoo. After you mask the rest of the texture, you should get results similar to Figure 5.75.

4. Now you want to move the center circle of the Spotlight dial right over the middle of the window. Click and drag anywhere in the center of the orange circle in the middle of the Spotlight dial, and then turn the dial clockwise while holding the Spotlight Radius to activate the Spotlight feature.

Figure 5.75
Window masked alone by using the Paint brush

Figure 5.76 shows that I turned the Spotlight Radius up a little. When you press Z to go into Spotlight Projection mode, you will see the texture only when the brush scrolls over it. There will be an effect like a flashlight or spotlight, similar to Figure 5.77.

5. Now for the Pin feature. Activate the Pin feature, shown in Figure 5.78, and you can enter Spotlight Projection mode and drop the window wherever you like.

Figure 5.76
Turning up the Spotlight Radius activates a Spotlight feature.

The brush will always have the window underneath the icon (see Figure 5.79), so wherever you paint, the window gets painted. You can then paint multiple windows rather quickly. Remember that where the middle of the Spotlight dial is located is the start of the texture.

Hopefully, these basic techniques get you thinking of more tasks you can accomplish with Spotlight. Now let's try to do something a little more complicated, like texturing a face.

Figure 5.77 With the Spotlight feature enabled, the texture is viewable in Spotlight Projection mode only when the brush comes in contact with a texture.

Figure 5.78 The Pin feature is now activated.

Figure 5.79 The Pin feature makes it easy to paint multiple windows of the same texture.

Texturing a Face

Texturing a face has its challenges, but using Spotlight definitely puts you on the right path. This exercise shows how I textured the head tool we used throughout this chapter. To make a more realistic texture, I used pictures of people that I found at the amazing reference site www.3D.sk. If you are not a member of this site, I highly recommend it.

1. First you fill this guy with some color. Figure 5.80 shows the color I chose to fill the head with.

2. Import all your textures into the Texture palette from the www.3D.sk site. Figure 5.81 shows all the new textures loaded into Spotlight. I used a feature called Tile Unified to stack all my textures off to the left of my ZBrush document.

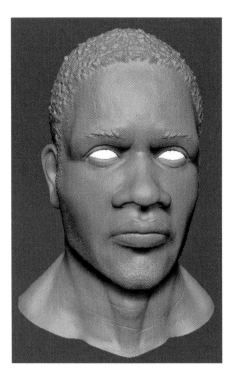

Figure 5.80 *Fill the head with a solid color.*

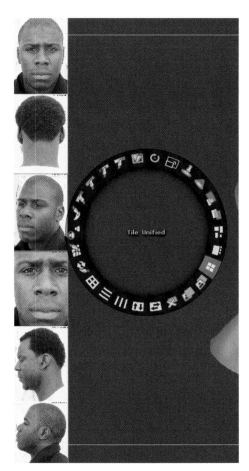

Figure 5.81 *All the textures loaded into Spotlight*

3. Start with the front of the face. In Figure 5.82, the texture is lined up to the tool. Put the Spotlight center right over the eye in the texture and then align the model's eye to that. This way, if you rotate or scale the texture, it happens around the eye.

4. Use the Nudge brush to match the image more precisely to the underlying model of the head. Figure 5.83 shows the Nudge brush lining up the texture of the nose with the model of the head. Remember, ZBrush has x-symmetry capability, so all you need worry about is matching one side of the face.

5. With the front texture in place, enter Spotlight Projection mode by clicking Z and apply the texture. Figure 5.84 shows the front of the face with texture.

Figure 5.83 The Nudge brush helps line up the texture to the tool.

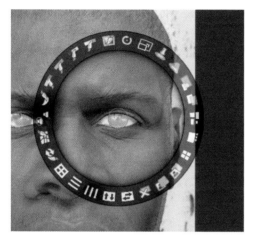

Figure 5.82 Move the Spotlight dial over the eye. This is a great point to line up on the human face.

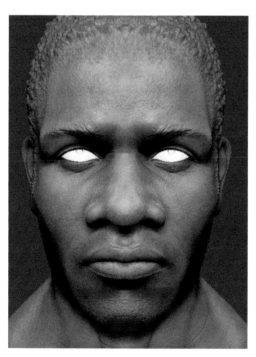

Figure 5.84 Front of the face textured with one texture

6. Switch to the side view and use the ear to line everything up. Figure 5.85 shows how you can use a little Nudge brush to get most of the side of the face to match.

7. With the help of a few more images, finish off the texture of the head. Figure 5.86 shows all the images that were used and my finished result.

Spotlight is such an amazing tool, and you will continue using it throughout this book. I highly recommend playing with Spotlight yourself.

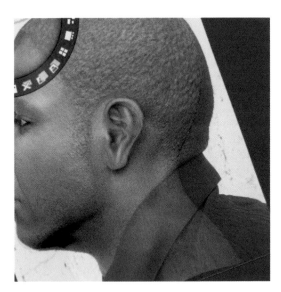

Figure 5.85 *Using the ear to line up the side of the face with the texture*

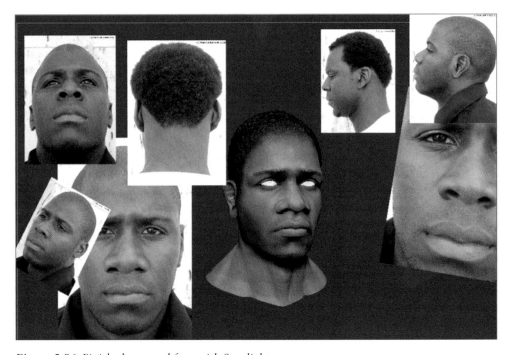

Figure 5.86 *Finished textured face with Spotlight*

ARTIST SPOTLIGHT: MICHAEL DEFEO
CREATING HAIR FOR DIGITAL MAQUETTES

THIS TECHNIQUE lets you create hair for digital maquettes in ZBrush. It's a nice way to create hair that looks more realistic than a solid sculpted mass. Although the results are not supposed to look like real hair or like that of a hair-rendering system such as FiberMesh, they will help provide a good target for what the hair could look like.

You can use this same technique to create all kinds of hair and fur. Experiment and have fun.

1. Insert `Hair.ZTL` from the `Michael Defeo Asset` folder to any of your characters. The image on the right indicates placement of the hair sphere.

2. Use the Move brush to pull the sphere into a basic shape, as shown in the image on left, below. Always make sure to do these changes on lower subdivision levels.

3. Continue to refine the hair on higher subdivision levels by using the Move brush (below right).

CREATING HAIR FOR DIGITAL MAQUETTES

4. Continue to work with large simple forms of the hair.

5. Select the Clay BuildUp brush to create fluid lines; it helps to turn on LazyMouse and set your Roll Distance to **10**, which will stretch the alpha to 10 times the original length.

6. Begin to sculpt medium-sized forms with the ClayBuildUp brush. Make your lines simple and flowing, as shown in these images.

CREATING HAIR FOR DIGITAL MAQUETTES

7. Now add some finer detail. Still using the ClayBuildUp brush, change the alpha for the brush to Alpha 01 and set H Tiles in the Alpha palette to **4**, which repeats the alpha along the horizontal axis to create a more hair-like stroke. The following image shows how your alpha should look.

8. Try to create lines that helix or spiral as they move down the form. This will make the sculpture look more like hair than if you just make straight lines.

9. Now break the silhouette of the hair. Hold Ctrl and draw lines with the MaskPen brush to mask the surface to establish that flow with the base hair forms. Leave space between the lines.

10. Adjust the Thick slider to **0.0005** in the Extract section at the bottom of the SubTool palette and click Accept to create a new subtool from the mask. You can see the result of the extraction in the following image.

CREATING HAIR FOR DIGITAL MAQUETTES

11. Use the Move brush and Move Topological brush to pull the extracted mesh away from the surface, as shown in the next image.

12. Hold the Shift key and use the Smooth brush to thin down the extracted hair strands. Try to taper the lines gradually to the ends.

13. Duplicate the subtool of the extracted hair, move it, and give it the same color as the base hair by clicking FillObject in the Color palette with your base color selected. Use Move to slightly alter the position of each subtool and move Topological brushes.

14. Make some shorter hair to vary the look of the lengths of hair. Same as before, mask the hair using the MaskPen brush.

CREATING HAIR FOR DIGITAL MAQUETTES

15. Extract this masking.

16. Smooth down the short hair created from the preceding steps with the Smooth brush.

17. To create a better hairline, append a cylinder to the tool, and make it thin and long by using the Transpose brush. Then give it a bend with the Move brush. Duplicate that hair several times and merge these four strands to create one subtool.

Scale that tool down and move it into place at the hairline. Once in place, duplicate it and move it to create a deeper layer of hair. Use the SubTool Master plug-in to mirror that to the other side to get results similar to the following image.

18. Add some polypaint color of your hair on the head to soften the hairline. I usually like to adjust the RGB Intensity to **8** so I can build this up slowly. In the next image, you can see the result of adding color and small hairs to the hairline.

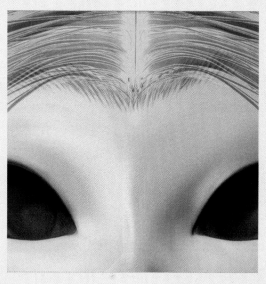

19. Now we want to get some medium-sized strands. Go back to one of the hair subtools and use the Inflate brush to thicken up the strands. Then use HPolish to flatten the areas that look too fat and round. Try to vary the size and number of medium strands.

CREATING HAIR FOR DIGITAL MAQUETTES

20. Finally, use a bit of good ol' SnakeHook brush to finish off the bottom of the base hair sub-tool, as shown in the next image. Don't go too crazy with this.

21. Turn on all the subtools to show the final result of the hair. The following image shows the final result.

CREATING HAIR FOR DIGITAL MAQUETTES

MAKING PEOPLE *feel warm and cuddly about a time when the earth was draped in polar ice sheets is not a problem for top character development artist Michael Defeo, who transformed Peter De Sève's char-acter designs into the celebrated, animated stars of* Ice Age *as well as the sequels* Ice Age 2, Ice Age 3, *and the upcoming* Ice Age 4. *Defeo's knack for transformation also benefited Blue Sky Studios itself; Defeo personally created and supervised the company's modeling and sculpting departments, honing a structured pipeline that would allow the company to overlap films and increase quality and productivity. When* Horton Hears a Who! *was approved for development as an animated feature, Defeo, meltingly hot off his* Ice Age *success, was entrusted with the challenge of transforming Seuss's iconic drawings into living 3D characters. He captured the Seuss spirit so well, he was subsequently commissioned by Illumination Entertainment to do it again for* The Lorax, *scheduled for release in 2012. Recently Michael finished work on* Despicable Me 2 *(2013). Defeo began his career pursuing his passion for special effects and makeup, later making sophisticated stop-motion puppets for commercials, television, theatre, and film. Parlaying this expertise into the world of feature animation, Defeo's versatility and unique use of traditional and digital mediums give life to a wide array of characters, from teddy bears to creatures for the film* Alien Resurrection. *As a comple-ment to his commercial work, Defeo continues to create personal art in terra cotta, bronze, and marble, combining his extensive expertise in state-of-the-art software with traditional materials and classical tech-niques. This creative experimentation gives his work an increasingly deep range of expression and emotion. Defeo's additional credits include the upcoming* Leaf Men, Rio, *and* Hop, *as well as* Robots, Star Trek: Insurrection, A Simple Wish, *and the Academy Award-winning short,* Bunny.

www.michaeldefeo.com

ARTIST SPOTLIGHT: RUDY MASSAR
ROUND CORNERS IN A MASK

HERE'S A REALLY EASY trick to quickly get nice rounded corners in your mask. This can help a lot when creating mechanical parts, a gasket, or anything using ShadowBox or an extrusion from your model.

The amount of blur controls the radius of the corner as well as the resolution of your ZTool. Be careful that you do not blur too much, as you can also break the mask shape. Here are the steps:

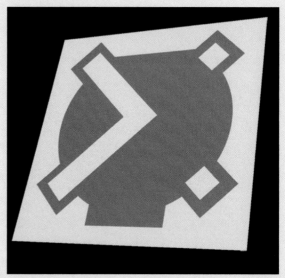

1. Create a mask that has hard angles everywhere, similar to the following image. MaskCircle and MaskRect are used to create something like this.

2. Blur the mask a few times; hold the Ctrl key and click the mask to blur.

3. Sharpen the mask by holding the Ctrl+Alt keys and clicking the mask.

   The more you blur the mask before sharpening, the rounder you will make the corners, as shown in the following image.

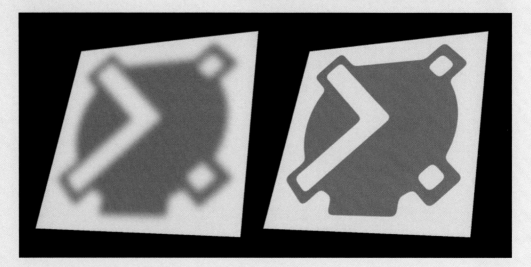

Voila, all the hard angles are now nice and round, even more uniform than they would be if you used the Mask Curve brush.

Be careful not to blur the mask too much, as it will break apart the original mask.

Note that when you are working on a really dense mesh, you might want to drop a few subdivisions first; this will blur the mask more easily and quickly. Before sharpening the mask again, go back to the highest subdivision and perform the sharpen mask effect.

ROUND CORNERS IN A MASK

GoZ Crease from Maya to ZBrush

When using Maya, there is a nice little GoZ feature to crease the edges of your imported model:

1. With GoZ already set up with a connection to Maya, in the Preference → GoZ subpalette, click the Import As SubTool button. This tells ZBrush that every mesh coming from Maya is appended as a subtool to the selected tool.

2. Switch to Maya and block out your mesh. Press the 3 key, and your model will display smoothly in the viewport (similar to subdivision 2 or 3 in ZBrush). Knowing this, you can add edge loops with the Insert Edge Loop tool in Maya to block out your mesh.

While in smooth model view, use Maya's Crease tool from the Mesh Edit menu to begin creasing the edges that you wish to stay crisp.

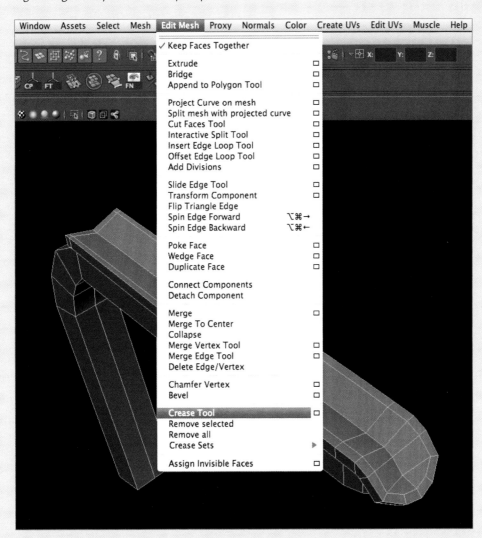

For hard edges, you don't add extra edge loops. Simply use the Crease tool. As shown in the following image, Maya indicates creased edges with thick edges. ZBrush will recognize this

ROUND CORNERS IN A MASK

and adopt the creased edges from Maya. Before hitting the GoZ button on the GoZ shelf, name this model, and ZBrush will adopt the new name.

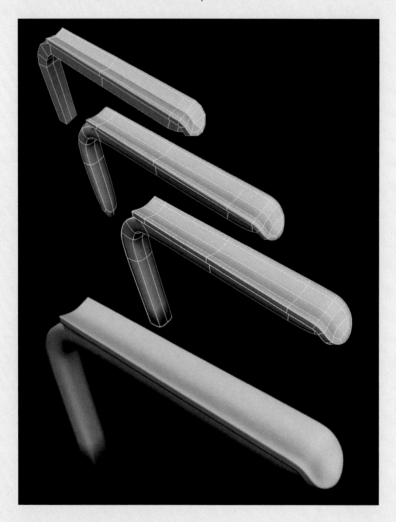

3. Click the GoZ button in Maya, and ZBrush opens automatically. The Maya model is appended to the selected tool and takes the name from Maya.

   Because the ridge of the arm support has a nice rounded edge, you don't want to crease this edge every time you subdivide.

4. Next to the Crease button you see CreaseLvL. In this case, I've set it to 2, which means that the crease will work for only the first two subdivisions. After the second subdivision, it will start smoothing the edges again. The next image shows how my subtool looks in ZBrush with the creases applied on two subdivisions.

   If you would like to remove the indicator that tells ZBrush which edge to crease when subdividing, simply click the UnCrease button while holding Shift. This will remove all the creased edges.

ROUND CORNERS IN A MASK

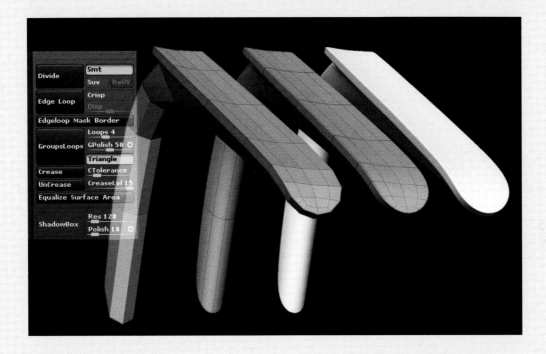

RUDY MASSAR *lives in Rotterdam, the Netherlands. His first experience with 3D was back in 1994, working on a Silicon Graphics Indigo running Wavefront TDI Explore. He teaches at the Willem de Kooning Academy in Rotterdam and has worked as a freelance artist for many years. Rudy's job at Guerrilla started in 2005, where he currently leads the character art team.*

www.rudymassar.com

SPECIAL PROJECT | WORKING WITH SCAN DATA

MANIPULATE SCAN DATA

CAPTURING COLOR FROM SCAN

MAKING BACK MESH OF THE BAI

SCULPTING THE HAIR WITH FIBE

Working with Scan Data

Data from a scan can *sometimes be a very tricky mesh to work with. Often the axis and orientation of scan data is off in some distant space in our 3D applications. This is because when you scan data, the scanning system does not apply any world orientation; the scanner just lines up scans to create a completed mesh. For the project in this chapter, you will be projecting scan data into a topology-ready mesh. You will learn how to manipulate scan data and how to create a ball cap, and will end with creating hair for your character.*

- Starting with scan data
- Understanding how to manipulate scan data
- Capturing color from scan data
- Making the back mesh of the ball cap
- Sculpting the hair with FiberMesh

Starting with Scan Data

Many industries use scan data, including gaming, feature films, and toy manufacturing. Scan data provides a great start, enabling artists to save time on sculpts. Often artists use scan data to begin a likeness sculpt of a famous actor or to work from existing sculptures such as Michelangelo's *David* or to take anything from real life. ZBrush is a great tool to edit scan data because if you add this process to your workflow, you quickly will see how little work you need to do to edit the scan data with ZBrush. Often scan data appears anywhere in space as compared to your topology-ready mesh, as you can see in Figure 6.1.

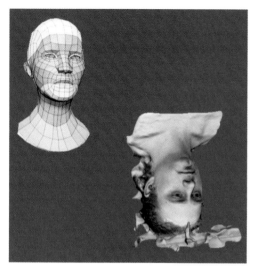

Figure 6.1 Scan data in ZBrush may not line up with your base mesh.

After you create a scan that you want to manipulate, you can import the scan data into ZBrush. I included the scan for this project, RawScan.ZTL, in the Chapter 6 Assets folder on the DVD. I saved the file as a ZTL so you can simply open it as a tool. It is a scan of Joseph Drust, who has also shared tips for this book at the end of Chapter 8, "Special Project—Creating Hockey Skates." I would like to thank Joseph for providing the scan of himself for this chapter.

So you can avoid the process of aligning the scan data with the base mesh, I also included a file in the Chapter 6 Assets folder called Final.ZTL. You can see in Figure 6.2 that the base mesh and scan data are lined up perfectly, so we can work along together in this project. There are four subtools to this tool. One is called BaseMesh, which you will use to project the scan data into. The scan data subtool is called Joseph-rawscan_1. The subtool called Joseph-Final is the final result of the model with the scan data projected into the base mesh. And the last subtool is just the final eyeballs for the model.

Understanding How to Manipulate Scan Data

Although the scan data gives you a great start, you still need to do a lot of cleanup work. In this section, you will focus on how to easily manipulate the data so it can be projected onto a clean piece of geometry:

Figure 6.2 Four subtools lined up for projecting the scan data into the base mesh

1. Begin by loading the Final.ZTL file from the Chapter 6 Assets folder. Then select the subtool called Final, which will be the top subtool.

2. Make sure the Final subtool is at subdivision level 2 so you can get more polygons for projection.

3. Store a morph target by clicking the StoreMT button in the Tool → Morph Target subpalette at this subdivision level. See Figure 6.3. You will be using the Morph brush along the way to push back unwanted details that you will not want to keep after projections.

   Remember that a morph target can be stored for only the currently selected subdivision level, so make sure you are aware of

Figure 6.3 Store a morph target before moving on. The Morph Target subpalette is in the Tool palette.

which subdivision level is currently selected in the Tool → Geometry subpalette before storing a morph target. As you go through this first section of the chapter, you will create and delete morph targets.

Next you need to mask out only the area that you want ZBrush to project into with the scan data. Look at the Final subtool with Polyframe mode on, and you will see two polygroups, as shown in Figure 6.4. One polygroup is green, and the other is blue.

4. Hold down the Ctrl+Shift keys, and with SelectRect as your brush, click the blue polygroup. Then hold Ctrl and click on any open space in the document to mask all. You can see the result in Figure 6.5.

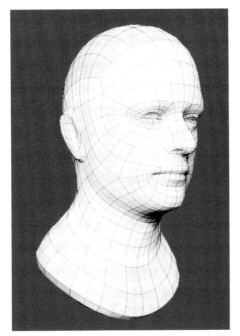

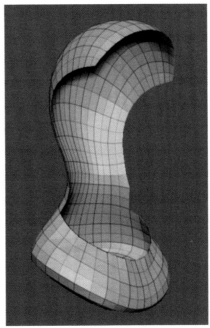

Figure 6.4 The Final subtool has two polygroups that you will use for masking.

Figure 6.5 By showing only the green polygroup, you can completely mask out that part of the face.

5. Next you need to restore the visibility of the whole head. Once again, hold the Ctrl+Shift keys and just click anywhere on an open space of the document to show the whole head again. When you mask the top of the head and the neck, you ensure that the projection does not affect the back and neck of the base mesh. Figure 6.6 shows where you should be at this stage.

Now that you are ready to project into your base mesh, you need to turn on the visibility of the raw scan data subtool. This is a separate subtool called Joseph-rawscan_1.

6. Turn on the visibility of the Joseph-rawscan_1 subtool by clicking the eye icon for this subtool, as shown in Figure 6.7.

You can see in the figure that the green subtool breaking through the scan data is your base mesh. You must now match the base mesh to the detail in the scan data.

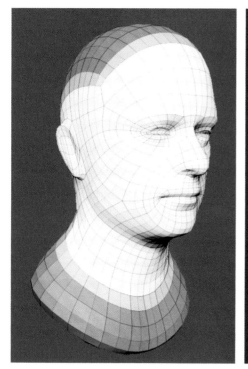

Figure 6.6 *Use the polygroups with masking to get the exact same mask on the front of the face.*

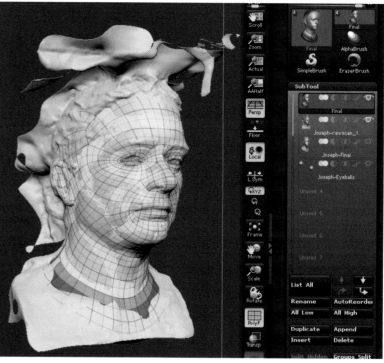

Figure 6.7 *Click the eye icon next to the second subtool, the raw scan data of Joseph.*

7. You can project data from the visible subtools to the selected subtool by clicking the Project All button in the Tool → SubTool subpalette. Go ahead and click that Project All button to get the result in Figure 6.8. Project All projects the detail of Joseph-rawscan_1 into the Final subtool.

8. You can see that you have captured some of the hair in the projection. Switch to the Morph brush and push the hair back to its original state. Figure 6.9 shows where you can push back parts you don't want in the projection.

9. Delete the morph target and clear the mask before subdividing up to the next subdivision level, which should be level 3. If you forget to clear the mask, you'll end up with a mesh that is locally subdivided (that is, has more polygons in one area than another). Subdividing locally is covered in Chapter 1,

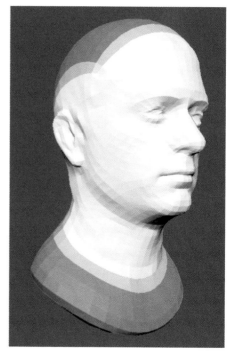

Figure 6.8 *Turn off the scan data subtool to see what you get.*

"Understanding the Basics." It's a useful technique, but you don't want to do it right now.

10. Repeat steps 3–8 on subdivision level 3.

11. Use the Morph brush to push back unwanted details. Figure 6.10 shows the result of the projection at subdivision level 3.

12. Repeat this process with the Morph brush on each subdivision, all the way up to subdivision level 6, to gain complete control of the scan data you want included in the projection and the data you want to exclude. Figure 6.11 shows the data captured for subdivision level 6.

13. Scan data will capture only so much facial detail, so you must go in and sculpt areas that the scan missed. The major areas that lose detail are the eyes, ears, and nostrils—so you must work on those. Figure 6.12 shows the various parts of the model that needed to be touched up.

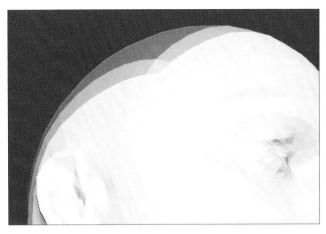

Figure 6.9 Push back parts of the projection you don't want with the Morph brush. In this projection, the Morph brush pushes unwanted hair back to normal.

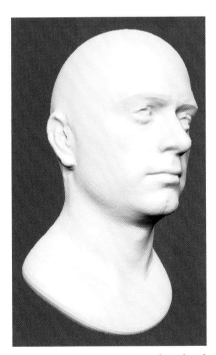

Figure 6.10 Projection result at level 3 subdivision and a little touch-up with the Morph brush

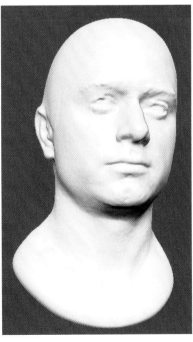

Figure 6.11 Continue to mask, store a morph target, and then project all the way up to level 6 to capture all the scan details.

Figure 6.12 Touching up the sculpt a bit, especially in areas such as the ears, eyes, and nose

Capturing Color from the Scan Data

You aren't finished yet with your scan data. This whole time you have been capturing only the sculptural detail. Our scan data also contains color information. So you need to capture this color information and use it as a texture. Here are the steps:

1. Set the Subdivision to level 6 and click the Divide button in the Tool → Geometry subpalette. This adds a seventh SDiv level, and the model will now contain more than 2 million polygons at this level.

2. If you have a morph target, go ahead and delete it. Then store a morph target at subdivision level 7.

3. Turn on the Joseph-rawscan_1 subtool if it's not already on.

4. Make sure to turn on the little brush icon to tell ZBrush to show the polypaint information that is applied to the model. Figure 6.13 shows the little brush icon turned on in the Final subtool and in the Joseph-rawscan_1 subtool that hosts your color information.

Figure 6.13 You turn scan data and color information on by selecting the brush icon for each subtool.

5. With the Final subtool still selected, make sure to activate only the RGB button at the top of the interface. Select white for your color, and then click the FillObject button in the Color palette. This fills the Final subtool with all white.

6. Click the Project All button again to project the color information of the scan data into the Final subtool.

7. You will get some sculptural changes in your model; click the Switch button in the Morph Target subpalette to get your original sculpt back, but with color information now. Morph targets store only the shape of the mesh and not the color. So you can use Project All to transfer color from one subtool to another and then use a morph target to restore the shape of the mesh. You should get results similar to Figure 6.14.

   Do not be concerned that the color information was not projected onto the eyes, because the eyes are a separate subtool. However, you do want to paint out parts of the hair.

8. Use the Standard brush with only RGB on and with white selected as the color. Figure 6.15 shows white painted over the unwanted parts of the hair.

9. Now let's clean up the ears and nose. Touch up the eyes by using the ZProject brush to paint in the areas of the ear and eyes. Make sure to select the Final subtool with Joseph-rawscan_1 on so ZBrush knows what color information to capture. Figure 6.16 shows how a little touch-up gives us polypaint that is ready to convert into a texture.

Figure 6.14 *Use Project All to capture the color of the scan data.*

10. Next you take this polypaint information and apply it to a texture. Fortunately, this model already has UVs on it, so you just click the New From PolyPaint button in the Tool → Texture Map subpalette to get the result in Figure 6.17. If you did not already have UVs, they would need to be generated before creating the texture.

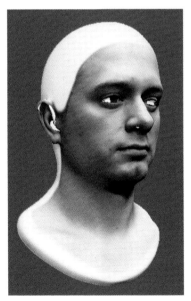

Figure 6.15 *Use the Standard brush with white to polypaint out parts of the color information.*

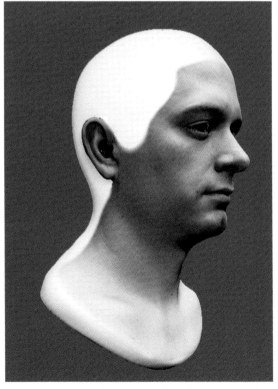

Figure 6.16 *Use the ZProject brush to paint in the details with just a few brush strokes.*

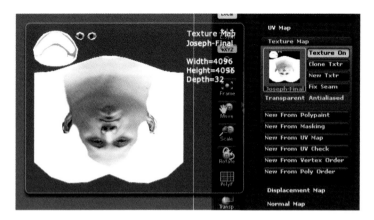

Figure 6.17
Click the New
From PolyPaint
button to create
a texture from
the polypaint
information.

Now you can use your texture to bring more detail into your model.

11. Click the Mask By Intensity button in the Tool → Masking subpalette to use the intensity of the texture color to create a mask. Figure 6.18 shows the mask that is applied to the character. The texture itself is turned off at this point.

12. If there is still a morph target, delete it so we can clear for a new morph target. After you delete the morph target, store another morph target.

13. Under the Tool → Deformation subpalette, click right above the orange bar in the Inflate slider to highlight the number in red. Type **5** and press Enter. ZBrush inflates the details from the mask into the sculpt. Figure 6.19 shows how this little trick can really add a lot of detail into your sculpts.

14. Do a little more skin sculpting, and you will have a finished Joseph Drust head similar to Figure 6.20.

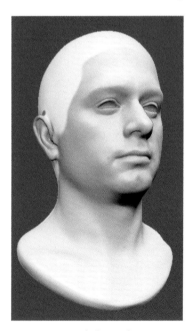

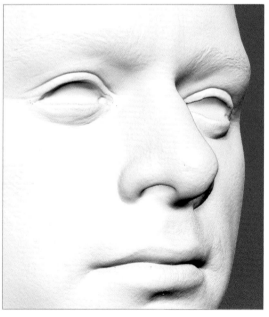

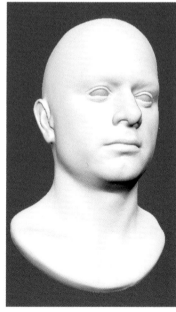

Figure 6.18 Click Mask By
Intensity to use the texture to
mask out your model.

Figure 6.19 You can add subtle detail by using a
texture for masking to be used for a slight inflation
of the model with Inflate deformation.

Figure 6.20 Finished sculpt of
Joseph Drust from scan data

Making the Back Mesh of the Ball Cap

The following example shows how I perfected the baseball cap for the character. The ultimate goal is to create a cap similar to the one in Figure 6.21. But let's focus on how to create the mesh on the back of the hat. This process may seem a little difficult, considering the complexity of the model we want to create. However, the NoiseMaker plug-in will create the look of this meshed fabric with just a few clicks.

Figure 6.21 The completed ball cap

Follow these steps:

1. Load the tool called `BallCap.ZTL` from the `Chapter 6 Assets` folder on the DVD. Figure 6.22 shows that this tool has four subtools. Make sure that the subtool named BackBallCap is selected, as shown in Figure 6.22.

2. With the BackBallCap subtool selected, open the Tool → Surface subpalette. Click the Noise button in the Surface subpalette to open your NoiseMaker window, as shown in Figure 6.23.

3. I have already created UVs for this cap. Click the UV button at the top of the window (see Figure 6.24). This tells ZBrush to assign the noise based on the UV coordinates.

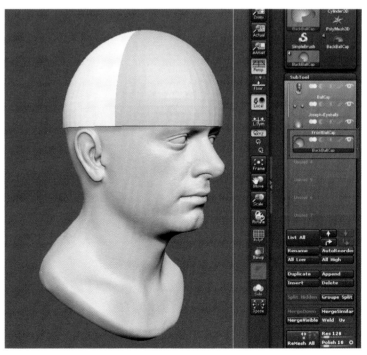

Figure 6.22 Load the `BallCap.ZTL` tool with the BackBallCap subtool selected.

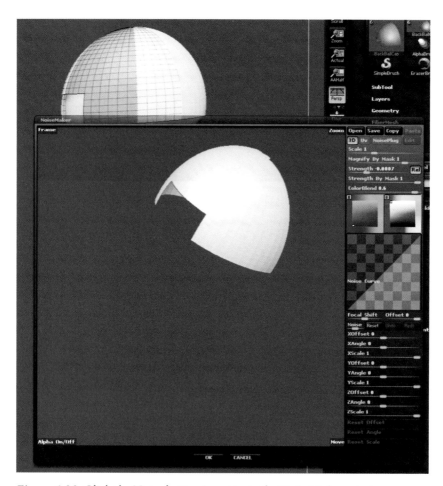

Figure 6.23 *Click the Noise button to activate the NoiseMaker window.*

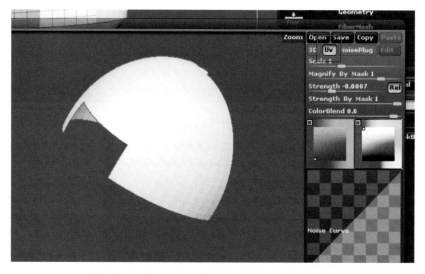

Figure 6.24 *Click the UV button at the top of the NoiseMaker plug-in.*

4. Click the NoisePlug button beside the UV button. This activates the NoiseMaker library of noises (see Figure 6.25).

5. Click the noise called HexTile. Under the Color menu for this noise, move the Tile Color slider all the way to the left and move the Mortar Color slider all the way to the right (see Figure 6.26).

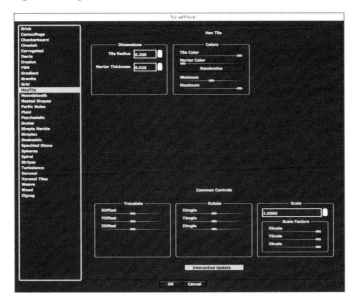

Figure 6.25 NoisePlug activates the library of noises that come with the NoiseMaker.

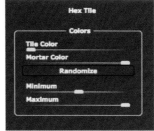

Figure 6.26 Move the Tile Color slider and the Mortar Color slider.

6. Click the OK button at the bottom-right corner of the NoiseMaker library window to apply the HexTile noise to the model. It may look like nothing happened. Your default settings for Scale and Strength need to be adjusted so you can see results.

7. Adjust the Scale to something close to **0.036** and adjust the Strength to something close to **-0.05** (see Figure 6.27). After you make these two adjustments, you should have results similar to Figure 6.27.

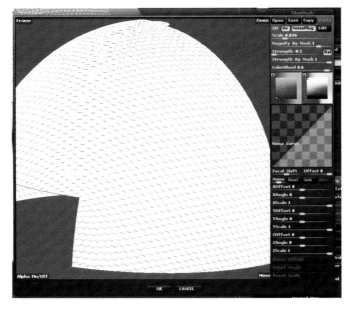

Figure 6.27 Adjust the Scale and Strength sliders to change the result of noises.

8. The Offset slider sits right under the Noise Curve. Set this slider to **-0.4**. This moves the left point of the curve up (see Figure 6.28). After you move the Offset, the mesh look comes alive.

9. Now move the left point of the Noise Curve back down to the bottom-left corner (see Figure 6.29). Do not change your Offset value.

Figure 6.28 Move Offset to -0.4 to move the left point of the Noise Curve up.

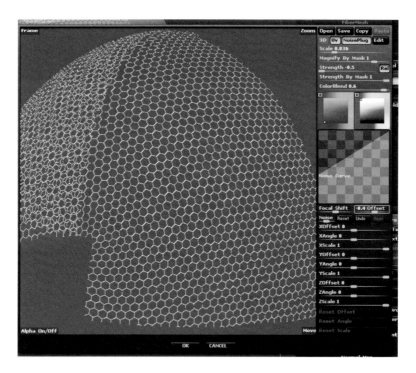

Figure 6.29 Move the left point of the Noise Curve back to the bottom-left corner without changing the Offset value.

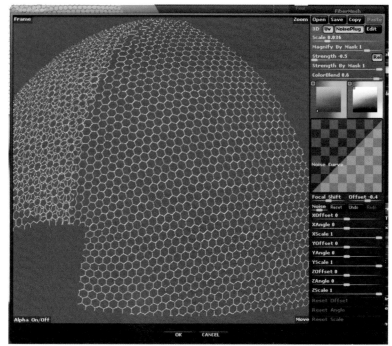

10. Voila! You get the look of a see-through mesh on your ball cap, just like Figure 6.30. This look will also render with accurate shadows.

Figure 6.31 shows what this looks like from the back of the cap.

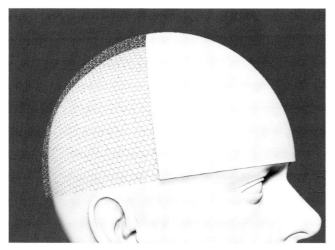

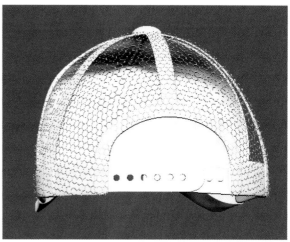

Figure 6.30 *The finished mesh noise applied to the back of the ball cap*

Figure 6.31 *The finished hat from the back*

Sculpting the Hair with FiberMesh

Hair is a difficult subject for ZBrush beginners, and even experts need help with sculpting hair better. There are many ways to sculpt hair in ZBrush, but in this lesson, I will share a quick way to start hair with FiberMesh. This method is a great way to bring a little more life to the character.

Let's begin by loading the tool named Bust.ZTL from the Chapter 6 Assets folder. Everything is complete on this model except for the hair. You'll start by selecting the portion of the model you want to create the hair from:

1. With Bust.ZTL in Edit mode on your document, put the model in Polyframe mode either by pressing Shift+F or by choosing the PolyF button on the right side of the interface.

2. Make sure to have the Bust subtool selected, and set this to the lowest subdivision level by holding Shift+D or by moving the Subdivision slider to level 1 in the Tool → Geometry subpalette.

3. Make sure that the Bust tool is selected and that the eye icon of the Bust is off. This tells ZBrush to display only the selected subtool—the rest will be hidden.

4. With the model in Polyframe mode, you see a green polygroup where hair would go. Hold Ctrl+Shift and click the green polygroup so the only mesh showing is the green polygroup, as shown in Figure 6.32.

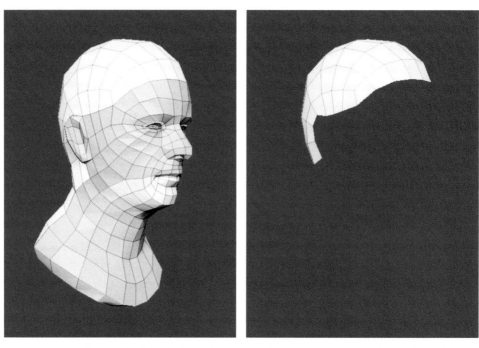

Figure 6.32 *Before Ctrl+Shift-clicking the green polygroup, where hair should be (left), and after hiding everything but the green polygroup (right)*

5. With only the green polygroup showing, hold the Ctrl key and click on the open space of the document to mask off this polygroup.

6. Hold Ctrl+Shift and click on any open space in the document to show the whole bust again. You should have what I do in Figure 6.33.

7. Move up to subdivision level 3 on the selected subtool so you have smaller polygons. This will be important when you use the ByArea slider later in the Tool → FiberMesh subpalette.

8. Open the Tool → FiberMesh subpalette and click the Preview button. This instantly creates hair on the bust's head. This subpalette is divided into two sections. The top half is used when creating fibers, and the bottom half is used for rendering the fibers. Figure 6.34 highlights these two sections.

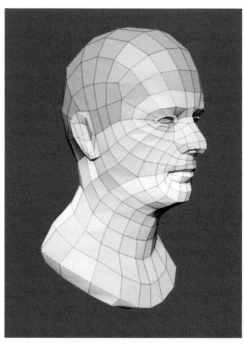

Figure 6.33 *The green polygroup is masked off.*

This is to open and save fibers for future use.

This section is for the creation process. After the Accept button is selected, these settings will all be grayed out.

Turn this on for quicker feedback when editing fibers.

Export fibers as guides to external applications.

Adjust these settings at BPR render time.

Export fibers as a vector displacement for external applications.

Figure 6.34 *The top of the FiberMesh subpalette is for the creation process, and the bottom is for rendering.*

9. You want to create hair that just reaches the ear. Make the following adjustments to the each of the sliders listed to give you a great start to the hair. Keep all other settings at the default.

- MaxFibers = 80 (Controls the number of fibers created.)
- ByArea = 0.4 (Varies fiber size and length by underlying polygon size. This is why you moved up to subdivision level 3. If you were at subdivision level 1, you would create longer, thicker fibers.)
- Length = 220 (Adjusts the length of the fibers.)
- Coverage = 12 (Controls how thick the fibers will be.)
- Gravity = 0.9 (Pulls the fibers toward the bottom of the document. Model position will affect how fibers lie on the mesh.)
- NoV = 0.18 (Controls gravity variation.)
- Twist = 0.08 (Adds twisting to each fiber.)
- Segments = 5 (Controls the number of polygon faces each fiber has.)

At this point, you should have something similar to Figure 6.35.

10. Let's change the color to be more brown. Adjust the Base and Tip color icons close to brown, as shown in Figure 6.36. Or if you want, find a different color that you like.

11. Let's do a quick render by pressing the Shift+R keys. This is a great feature when creating fiber meshes. Even though you have not accepted the fibers yet, you can still take a look at how the hair will render. Figure 6.37 shows results with the SkinShade4 material selected.

12. If you like the results, click the Accept button in the Tool → FiberMesh subpalette. This creates the fibers into a subtool right below the Bust subtool.

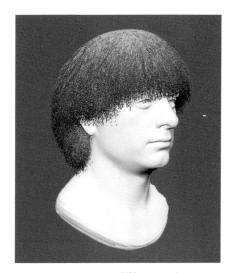

Figure 6.35 *State of fibers with adjustments made*

13. ZBrush asks whether you want to activate Fast Preview. Click No. (If you choose Yes, ZBrush will drop the quality of the fibers so that you can edit more quickly with the Groom brushes. Don't panic if you click Yes. They will not render this way, and you can always turn off Fast Preview.)

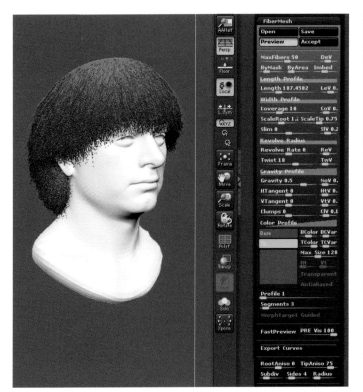

Figure 6.36 *Adjust the Base and Tip color icons to make the fibers brown.*

Figure 6.37 *Complete a BPR render.*

14. Select the Fiber subtool that ZBrush creates when you click Accept. You want to make some minor adjustments to the hair. Select the GroomBrush1.

15. Change the Draw Size to about **103**.

16. In the Alpha → Modify subpalette, move the H Tiles to **12**. This makes this brush act more like a comb.

17. Now move the head around, combing the hair a little (see Figure 6.38).

18. You have been using a material that is not really meant for hair. Let's select the Hair material.

19. In the Material → Modifiers subpalette, move the Ambient slider to **40**.

20. In the Tool → FiberMesh subpalette, move the RootAnisotropic slider to **80**. The more you turn up this slider and the TipAnisotropic slider, the more of a shine you get in the hair at the BPR render. Figure 6.39 shows the BPR render up to this point.

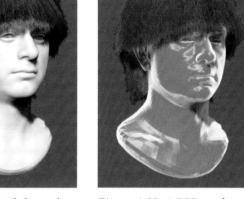

Figure 6.38 Comb the hair with GroomBrush1 (left), and the results after a BPR render (right)

Figure 6.39 A BPR render with the Hair material selected

21. The Hair material is being applied to all subtools, and you obviously do not want this. So let's assign the Hair subtool to this material by activating the M at the top of the interface. Click the FillObject button in the Color palette to fill the hair with this material.

22. Select the SkinShade4 material so all other subtools will be displayed with this material.

23. Activate all subtools by making sure all eye icons are activated for every subtool.

    You may notice that when everything is turned on, your hair breaks through the cap, just as in Figure 6.40.

24. Select the Move brush to make some adjustments to the hair.

Figure 6.40 With all subtools turned on, the hair clips the cap.

25. In the Brush → FiberMesh subpalette, make the following adjustments to select sliders:

- Preserve Length = **100** (With this set all the way up, you tell ZBrush that this brush will edit fibers and not to change their lengths at all.)

- Forward Propagation = **1** (The brush will adjust the whole fiber from the root out, keeping the tip more in the current position.)

- Front Collision Tolerance = **0** (This maintains the fibers over any underlying surface. Because you want to push the fibers under the cap, you need this setting off.)

Make all the adjustments so that the hair is behind the cap, as it is in Figure 6.41.

26. Make the following adjustments to two sliders in the Render → BPR Shadows subpalette:

- Rays = **40**
- Angle = **50**

Then do a BPR render to see what you have by pressing the Shift+R keys. You should have something close to Figure 6.42.

FiberMesh is a very powerful tool that will allow you to create hair, trees, grass, fur, and so much more. I encourage you to play a little with this feature to really see the various results you can get. Don't forget to visit Pixologic's ZClassroom at www.pixologic.com/zclassroom to see more ways that FiberMesh can be used, and make sure to have fun with it.

Figure 6.41 Push all the hair behind the cap.

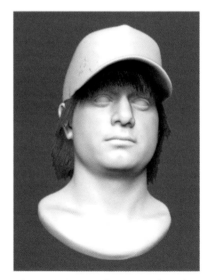

Figure 6.42 Final BPR render of the model

ARTIST SPOTLIGHT: MIKE JENSEN

CREATING MECHANICAL STAMP BRUSHES

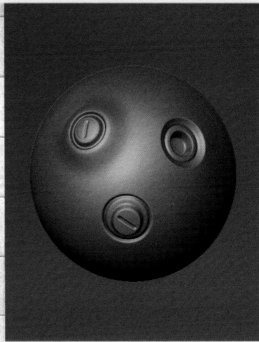

INSTEAD OF INDIVIDUALLY creating mechanical details for your characters, it's often easier and quicker to create stamp brushes, as shown in the following images.

To create a mechanical stamp brush, follow these steps:

1. From the Tool palette, select the Plane3D tool (number 38).

2. Turn the Plane3D tool into a PolyMesh3D by clicking Make PolyMesh3D.

3. When you have your polymesh plane, go to the Geometry subpalette and turn off Smt (smoothing). Now divide the mesh several times; in the image below, the mesh was divided five times.

CREATING MECHANICAL STAMP BRUSHES

4. When you have a high polymesh, choose Activate Symmetry in the Transform palette, turn off >X< and turn on >Z<, and click (R) to activate radial symmetry.

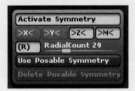

5. Now you're ready to create a cylindrical detail. Use a combination of brushes to create the stamp you'd like. I often use the Clay brush, Standard brush, and DamStandard brush for things like this. The following image shows an example.

6. To get a correct stamp alpha, the document must be square. In the Document palette, turn off the Pro button and change the Width and Height to **512**, and click Resize. For stamps, a resolution higher than 512 isn't needed.

7. If your model is in Edit mode, you must first clear the document by pressing Ctrl+N. Then redraw the plane out and put it back into Edit mode by pressing T. Turn off Perspective, lock the view to the top view (by rotating and holding Shift), and frame the object by pressing the F key. When your model is centered, zoom in until the edges of your detail are almost (but not quite) touching the edge of the document (see the following image).

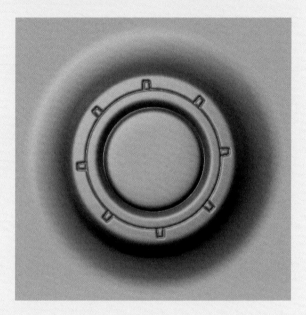

8. On the left of the interface, you'll see an icon for an easy access to all of the alphas. When you click on this icon, click the GrabDoc button at the bottom of the pop-up palette.

CREATING MECHANICAL STAMP BRUSHES

When you click the GrabDoc button, ZBrush takes the depth information of the document and creates an alpha from it.

9. It's time to make the brush. On the left side of the interface, click the Brush icon so the Brush Selection window pops up. Make sure you have the Standard brush selected, and then click the Clone button as shown in the following image. This creates a duplicate brush that you can edit.

10. To make the brush act like a stamp, you need to change the type of stroke. Under the Brush icon is the Strokes icon. Open it, and select DragDot. This lets you drag your stamp across the model for easy placement.

11. To finish the stamp, you need to modify the Focal Shift and Z Intensity of the brush. Press the O key to bring up a slider to quickly change the focal shift. Change this number to something close to **-100** to make sure that the alpha isn't affected by too much of a falloff (see the following image).

12. Now press U to change the Z Intensity. In the example brush shown in the image, I found that the correct intensity is **40**. Experiment with this number to see what gives you the best results.

CREATING MECHANICAL STAMP BRUSHES

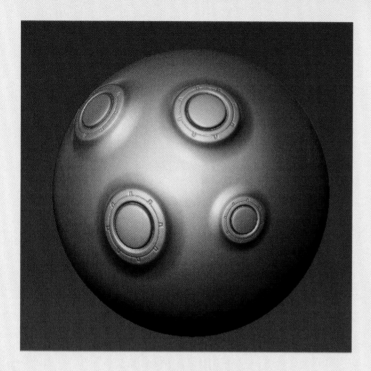

13. Test your stamp several times and play around with the values. I use a polysphere to do most of my testing, as shown in the image on the left.

If you're creating a stamp that carves into the mesh rather than builds upon it, try using the MidValue slider in the Alpha palette. Playing with this will allow you to make stamps that either cut into the mesh completely, or both add and subtract from the mesh.

MIKE JENSEN *is a freelance character artist living in Seattle, Washington. He specializes in creating mechanical and hard-surface characters. He has created several training packages on ZBrush, including the book* Zen of ZBrush *and the Eat3D DVD* ZBrush Hard Surface Techniques. *Mike is currently finishing up his art degree at the University of Washington. During his non-art free time, he enjoys playing strategy games such as chess, swimming laps (specifically struggling not to drown), and spending time with his family.*

http://mikejensen.daportfolio.com

ARTIST SPOTLIGHT: BRYAN WYNIA
USING ZBRUSH FOR CHARACTER CONCEPTS

WHEN I START A NEW CHARACTER sculpt, I usually start with the ZProject DynaMesh032 found in LightBox. This tool helps me freely concept a character without having to worry about the underlying geometry.

1. Load DynaMesh032. Start with a lower poly count so you can focus on the big picture and not get caught up in any details in the early stages.

2. As you begin to manipulate the mesh, notice that the polygons become stretched and hard to work with. At this point, use the DynaMesh function to create a more optimized sculpting surface: hold the Ctrl key and drag a small rectangle on the canvas. You can see in the following image how re-DynaMesh will redistribute the polygons of your mesh.

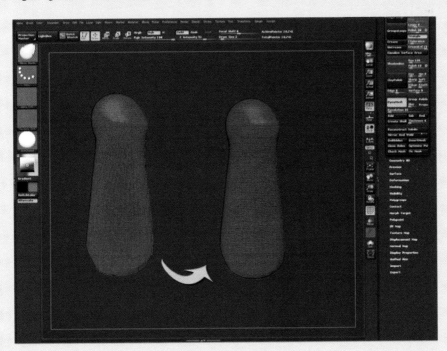

USING ZBRUSH FOR CHARACTER CONCEPTS

3. Use the Move Elastic brush to quickly create large shapes and the silhouette of the character. You'll use the DynaMesh function as you work to keep the polygons evenly distributed throughout the mesh, just as you see in the following image.

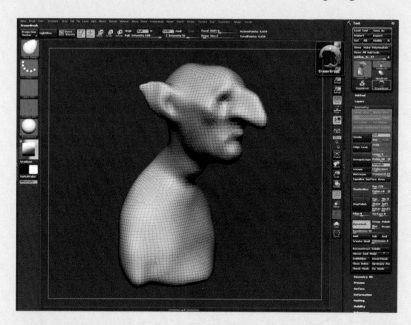

4. With the major shapes of the character established, add a few subdivision levels. I find myself using the ClayBuildup, Move, and DamStandard brushes in this stage of sculpting. These brushes are great for creating natural organic forms (see the following image).

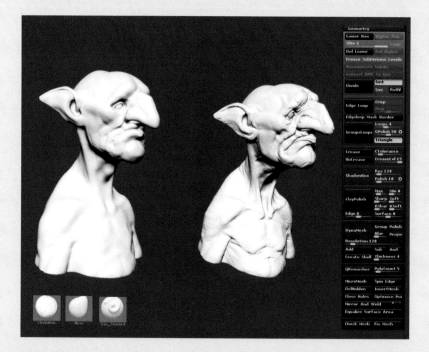

USING ZBRUSH FOR CHARACTER CONCEPTS

5. Use masks and the Extract feature at the bottom of the Tool → SubTool subpalette to create clothing and accessories, just as in the following image. Try to create your extracts at a low subdivision level to keep your total poly count at a manageable level. A great manageable level is anything under 100,000. You will need to click the Accept button once you find the extraction you are looking for to make it a SubTool.

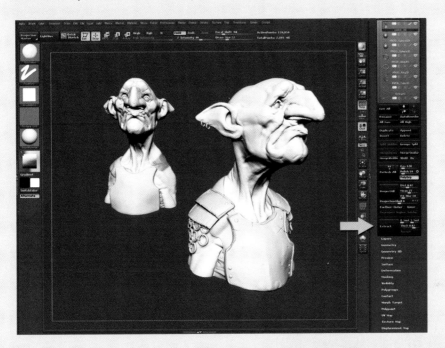

6. To create a quick and simple skin texture, use the Standard brush with the Spray setting and a simple directional alpha. You can then use a more specific alpha to create areas of interest, as shown in the image at right.

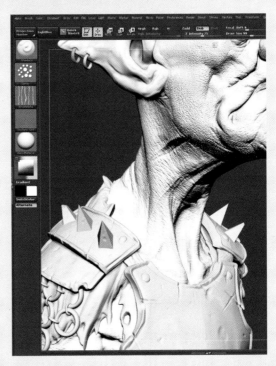

USING ZBRUSH FOR CHARACTER CONCEPTS

7. To finish off the sculpt, use the LightCap system with the wax material preview to present the character. I find that adding some color to the rim light is a nice way to introduce a bit of color and mood, as shown in the following image.

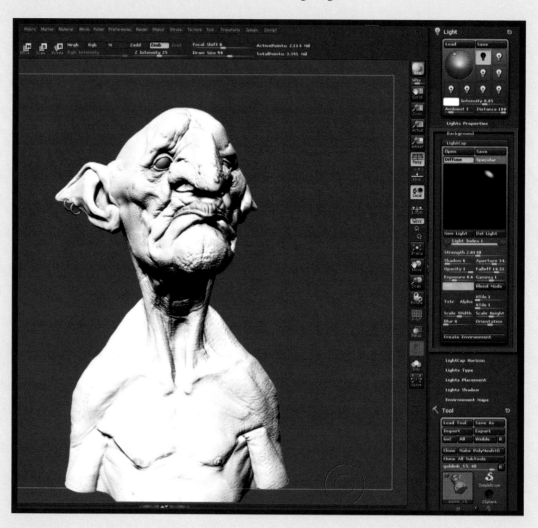

USING ZBRUSH FOR CHARACTER CONCEPTS

BRYAN WYNIA *is a senior character artist at Sony Santa Monica. Previously he worked at Naughty Dog, where he contributed to the video games* Uncharted 2: Among Thieves *and* Uncharted 3: Drake's Deception. *He also works as a freelance character designer and sculptor. His clients include The Aaron Sims Company, Gentle Giant Studios, Electric Tiki Design, and Masked Avenger Studios.*

His work has been featured in Famous Monsters of Filmland, Imagine FX, 3D Artist, *and* 3D World. *Bryan is also a beta tester for Pixologic and was a presenter at SIGGRAPH 2010 and 2011 on behalf of Pixologic. Bryan has taught classes and workshops at the Concept Design Academy, Gnomon School of Visual Effects, and Art Center College of Design.*

bryanwynia.blogspot.com

seven

Posing—Bringing Movement to Your Work

After you create a cool *character, you need to bring that creation to life. This chapter covers how to create dynamic character poses for rendering out an image. This is often a part of sculpting that people have trouble accomplishing or put off for as long as possible. But if you have a great sculpt, there is nothing cooler than putting that sculpt in a really dramatic pose.*

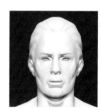

Two major features in ZBrush allow you to pose a character. I find that using a ZSphere rig works well for moving the limbs to establish the overall pose. Then I like to use the Transpose line to add subtle changes that finish the pose.

- Setting up a ZSphere rig with a single subtool
- Rigging a single subtool with sculpted detail
- Using a rig with Transpose Master
- Creating multiple poses with layers
- Assigning multiple poses to the timeline
- Exporting blend shapes from ZBrush to Maya

Setting Up a ZSphere Rig with a Single Subtool

In this first section, you will start with the simple task of building a rig for a full human character that has no subtools. Now, I'm not going to leave you hanging, with just the following words and images to teach you how to build a rig; make sure to watch the video for this section. The video, `Rig_Step1.mov`, is in the Videos folder of Chapter 7. Then follow these steps:

1. Load a project that is already installed in ZBrush. Open LightBox, and under the Project menu, double-click the DemoProjects icon. Click the project called `SuperAverageMan.ZPR`, as shown in Figure 7.1, and then double-click this project to load it into ZBrush.

2. Now you need to build the rig. In the Tool palette, select the ZSphere. This automatically swaps the SuperAverageMan for a ZSphere in the ZBrush document (see Figure 7.2).

3. While the ZSphere is on the canvas, open the Rigging subpalette of the Tool palette, and click the Select Mesh button. As you can see in Figure 7.3, the tool selection fly-out window opens. Click SuperAverageMan.

   This places the SuperAverageMan into the document with the ZSphere. Figure 7.4 shows that the SuperAverageMan is also in Ghost Transparency mode.

4. You don't want Ghost Transparency on because you will not be able to snap ZSpheres to the mesh in the next step. So turn it off by first turning on the Transparency button on the right of the interface. The Ghost button right below it also turns on. Turn the Ghost button off so that your SuperAverageMan is no longer in Ghost Transparency mode (see Figure 7.5).

5. Click the X key to activate x-Symmetry mode. If you are not sure symmetry is on, go to the Transform palette and make sure the Activate Symmetry button is on along with the X button.

6. Switch to Scale mode at the top of the interface to scale down your ZSphere to fit into the SuperAverageMan—the ZSphere will act as a pelvic bone (see Figure 7.6). Use Move mode to place the ZSphere into the position of a pelvic bone.

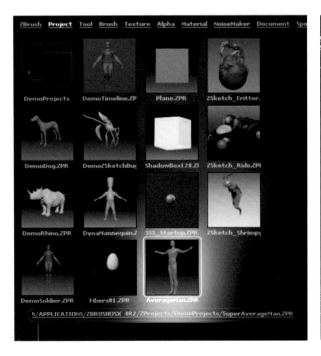

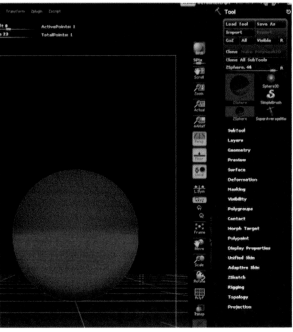

Figure 7.1 *Load the* `SuperAverageMan.ZPR` *project into ZBrush.*

Figure 7.2 *Select the ZSphere in the Tool palette.*

7. Now you are ready to start drawing out a rig. The ZSphere should still be selected; if not, switch to Move mode and click the ZSphere to select it. (See Figure 7.7 for a selected ZSphere, which is indicated by a middle red circle.)

8. Switch to Draw mode and click on either side of the ZSphere to start the leg bone (see Figure 7.8).

Figure 7.3 *Click the Select Mesh button in the Rigging subpalette to select SuperAverageMan.*

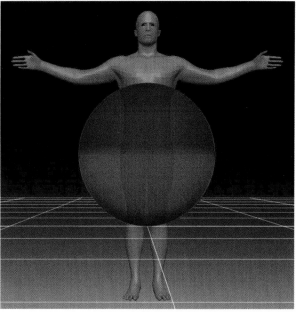

Figure 7.4 *SuperAverageMan added to the ZSphere with Ghost Transparency turned on*

Figure 7.5 *Turn off Ghost to see the SuperAverageMan clearly.*

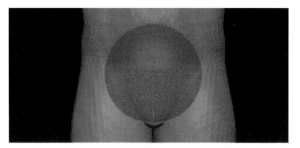

Figure 7.7 Make sure to select the ZSphere by using Move mode.

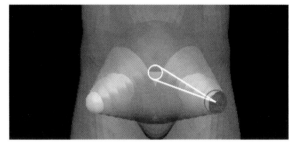

Figure 7.6 Use the Scale and Move modes to position the ZSphere to act as a pelvic bone.

Figure 7.8 Click on the mesh on either side of the ZSphere to begin drawing out the leg bone.

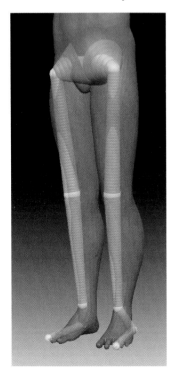

Figure 7.9 Continue to draw out ZSpheres down the leg.

9. Now, making sure that the last drawn-out ZSphere is selected, continue to draw by clicking on the mesh, down the leg. Add a ZSphere at the knee, then at the ankle, and then at the heel, and finish off at the toes (see Figure 7.9).

To make it easy on yourself when selecting which ZSphere to draw from, I recommend switching to Move mode to select a ZSphere. Then switch back to Draw mode to draw out where the next ZSphere needs to be.

---

10. Turn your SuperAverageMan to the side. You may notice that the ZSpheres you have just drawn out are not sitting inside the model. This is an easy fix. Just switch to Move mode again and position the ZSpheres so your model matches Figure 7.10.

11. Let's continue up the body. In Move mode, select the pelvic bone ZSphere again (switch modes with the shortcuts W = Move and Q = Draw).

    Now in Draw mode, draw out the upper body (see Figure 7.11).

12. As with the lower legs, you need to switch to Move mode to position the ZSpheres into the correct spot (see Figure 7.12).

13. Switch back to Move mode to select the ZSphere at the chest. Switch to Draw mode and finish off the top of the body (see Figure 7.13). You can also see that I have already positioned the final ZSpheres.

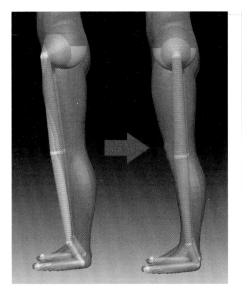

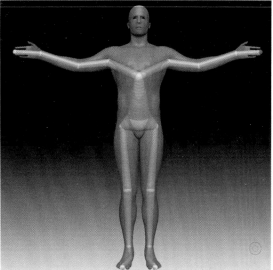

Figure 7.10 Use Move mode to position the ZSpheres into place. The left image shows the original ZSpheres' positions, and the right shows where I moved them.

Figure 7.11 Draw out the upper rig.

14. Add two sets of rib joints (see Figure 7.14). Click anywhere between the pelvic bone ZSphere and chest ZSphere to add another ZSphere between them.

15. Place ZSpheres on either side of the elbow, hip, and knee joints (see Figure 7.15). This will give a better bend at the joints.

16. Finally, add a ZSphere at the front crotch and two at the buttocks of the character so you can have individual movement there (see Figure 7.16).

17. In the Tool → Rigging subpalette, turn on the Bind Mesh button.

You are now free to pose away. Switch to Rotate mode and click any ZSphere chain that is between any ZSpheres to pose your character. Don't forget to click the ZSphere itself instead of the chain to make a more central rotation. Switch to Move mode to use built-in IK (Inverse Kinematics) with a ZSphere. Then turn off Symmetry so you can make some crazy poses (see Figure 7.17).

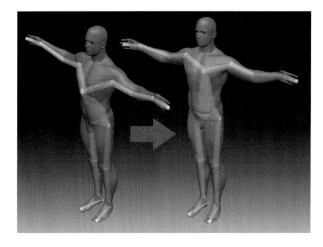

Figure 7.12 Switch to Move mode to position the ZSpheres.

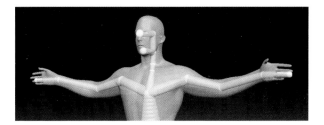

Figure 7.13 Finish the upper torso.

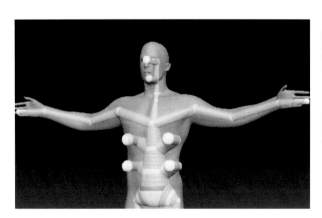

Figure 7.14 *Add two sets of ribs to the rig.*

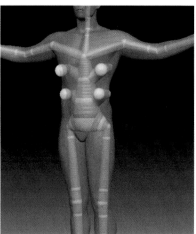

Figure 7.15 *Add ZSpheres on either side of joints to create a better bend when posing.*

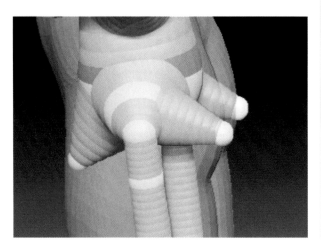

Figure 7.16 *Add one ZSphere at the front and two at the back for precise movement.*

Figure 7.17 *With a rig completed, you can pose the character in any way.*

To see a preview of the mesh after the pose, click the preview in the Tool → Adaptive Skin subpalette or use the shortcut A. To make a tool, click the Make Adaptive Skin button, and ZBrush will create this preview as an actual mesh.

Rigging a Single Subtool with Sculpted Detail

Now let's look at how you handle a mesh with details sculpted into the surface. I would like to thank Caroline Delen for allowing me to use her sculpt in this section.

Figure 7.18 shows the sculpted detail and five subdivision levels on the model. You can view a video of the whole process in the Chapter 7 Videos folder. The video is called SingleSubToolwithDetail.mov.

1. Load the Julie.ZTL tool from the Chapter 7 Assets folder. Drop the sculpted step to the lowest level and create a rig, as you did in the preceding section. Figure 7.19 shows the rig I built for the model. Notice the extra ZSpheres added to her back and chest.

2. Before you begin posing, you need to complete some key steps so the sculpted detail is transferred to the pose. First turn Bind Mesh on in the Tool → Rigging subpalette.

3. In the Tool → Adaptive Skin subpalette, set the Density slider to match the same subdivision level of the mesh. Here it is set to **5** because the model has five subdivision levels.

4. Hold Shift and click the Preview button in the Tool → Rigging subpalette. This puts your mesh into a Preview mode with the sculpted detail coming in (see Figure 7.20).

5. While in Preview mode, you *must* click on the mesh at least once. ZBrush needs an interaction with the model to verify the sculpted detail on the highest subdivision level so that the detail will transfer when posed.

6. Now you are free to pose the tool. Let's take the model out of Preview mode and pose her. Figure 7.21 shows the pose and all the sculpted detail that has been transferred.

Using a Rig with Transpose Master

Now let's look at how to pose a character when you have several subtools with several subdivision levels. Another video in the Chapter 7 Videos folder, Rig_Step2.mov, can help you with this process.

To pose a character with several subtools, you will use the ZBrush plug-in Transpose Master. This is automatically installed with ZBrush 4R2, and you can get updates on the Pixologic website at www.pixologic.com/zbrush/downloadcenter/zplugins/. Follow these steps:

1. Open LightBox again with the Project menu selected and in the DemoProjects folder open the DemoSoldier.ZPR project. Double-click this project to load it into ZBrush (see Figure 7.22).

2. From the ZPlugin palette, open the Transpose Master subpalette and click the ZSphere Rig button (see Figure 7.23).

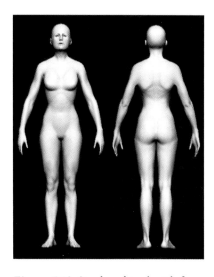

Figure 7.18 *Single subtool with five levels of sculpted subdivisions*

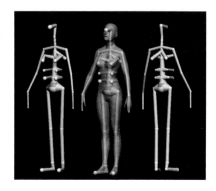

Figure 7.19 *Rig of the woman*

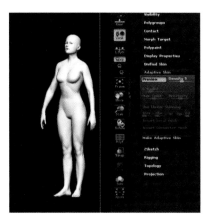

Figure 7.20 *Shift-click the Preview button.*

Figure 7.21 *Posed character with sculpted detail transferred*

Figure 7.22 *Load the* `DemoSoldier.ZPR` *project in the* `DemoProjects` *folder of the Project menu.*

Figure 7.23 *Click the ZSphere Rig button.*

3. Click the TPoseMesh button. All 11 subtools of the DemoSoldier automatically drop to level 1 and merge as one with a ZSphere at the center (see Figure 7.24). This process also actually creates a new tool.

4. Turn off Ghost Transparency. Then build the rig as you did in the prior section, "Setting Up a ZSphere Rig with a Single Subtool" (see Figure 7.25).

5. I saved this as a project so you can load it into your own ZBrush 4R2 program. However, you must load the project through the SubTool Master plug-in: click the Load TM Prj button. The project, `Step2.ZPR`, is in the `Assets` folder of Chapter 7.

6. Look closely at the extra ZSpheres I added to control things such as the backpack, shoulder straps, shoulder guard, and so on. You can see all of these added ZSpheres in Figure 7.26.

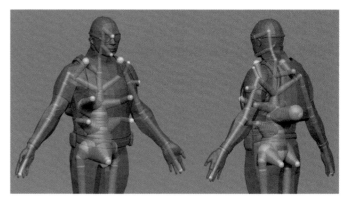

Figure 7.24 *The TPoseMesh button merges all subtools into one with a ZSphere at the middle.*

Figure 7.25 *Completed rig in TPoseMesh*

Figure 7.26 *Add some ZSpheres for more control on certain subtools.*

7. Click the Bind Mesh button in the Tool → Rigging subpalette and begin posing (see Figure 7.27).

8. To transfer this pose to the tool with all of the subtools and sculpted detail, click TPose → SubT button.

When the process is complete, the pose is transferred to the tool with all the detail, as shown in Figure 7.28. This process could take some time, depending on the model and your computer system. Just sit back and let ZBrush do all the magic.

9. Some of the subtools intersect with each other; this will happen from time to time. This usually occurs because your subtools do not have the exact same subdivisions, so they all have different polygon counts. Just adjust your subtools a little (see Figure 7.29). I like to use the Move brush to make these adjustments.

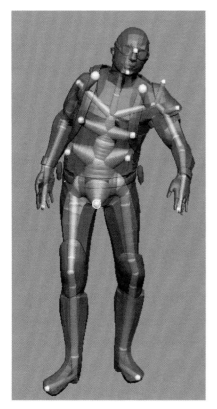  

Figure 7.27 Posed DemoSoldier using the Transpose Master plug-in

Figure 7.28 The pose is transferred to the multiple subtool mesh with subdivision levels.

Figure 7.29 Touch up the pose by adjusting subtools.

You can see how easy it is to pose a multiple-subtool mesh with detail on all of the subtools and bring your creations to life.

Creating Multiple Poses with Layers

So you have gone from a single-subtool to a multiple-subtool posed mesh. Sometimes it takes a few poses to figure out which pose fits the action you want to illustrate. Now I want to show you how to use Transpose Master with SubTool Master to create more than one pose very quickly:

1. Load the Step2.ZPR project through the Transpose Master by clicking Load TM Prj.

2. A TPose#1_DemoSoldier_1 tool and a DemoSoldier_1 tool appear in the Tool palette. The TPose mesh is the one selected automatically in the project. In the ZPlugin palette, open the Transpose Master plug-in (see Figure 7.30).

3. Make sure the ZSphere and Layer buttons are activated in Transpose Master. Click StoreTM Rig. This copies the rig that I have built for this model into memory.

4. Click DemoSoldier_1 and click the TPoseMesh button. Again, this merges all of the subtools into one and drops in a ZSphere.

5. Under the Transpose Master plug-in, click PasteTM Rig. This replaces the single ZSphere with the rig that you copied in step 3.

6. Activate the Bind Mesh button in the Tool → Rigging subpalette.

7. Under Tool → Layers, create a new layer. This creates a layer called Pose_TMask_Layer. You will store your first pose on this layer to be sent back to your DemoSoldier_1 with the multiple subtools.

8. After you complete a pose, click the TPose → SubT button. The pose is sent to the DemoSoldier_1 tool, but the pose is applied to a layer because you activated the Layer button in Transpose Master. Figure 7.31 shows how my crazy pose was sent to the tool and applied to the layer.

9. In the Subtool palette, select each subtool and set the value for the layer to 0.

10. Now you're ready to create a new pose. Just click the TPose#13_Demo soldier (you may have a different name) that you made when the TPoseMesh button was clicked in step 4. This is the version of the figure that you posed in step 4 (see Figure 7.32).

11. By default, this mesh will automatically be put into Preview mode in the Tool → Adaptive Skin subpalette.

12. Press the A hot key on the keyboard to bring back your ZSphere rigged version.

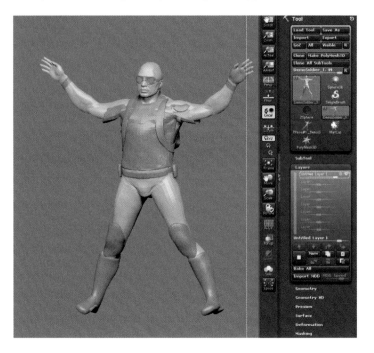

Figure 7.30 Click StoreTM Rig to copy the ZSphere rig.

Figure 7.31 The pose is transferred to DemoSoldier_1 and applied to the layer.

13. As you know, you created a layer for this first pose in the Tool → Layer subpalette. Move the Pose_TMask_Layer to **0** so that your DemoSoldier is back to a neutral pose.

14. Create a second layer to store another pose on the rigged mesh. Create a second pose now. After you have the pose you're looking for, click the TPose → SubT button to send this second pose to DemoSoldier_1. This pose is automatically applied to the second layer of every subtool (see Figure 7.33).

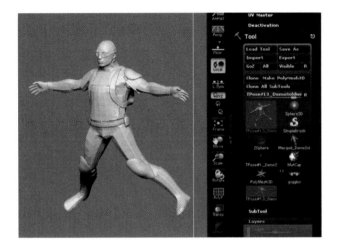

Figure 7.32 *Click the mesh created with the rig.*

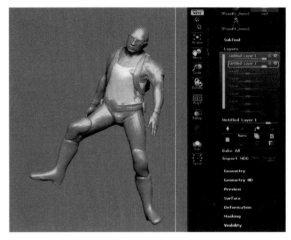

Figure 7.33 *The second pose is stored on a new layer.*

Now just continue this process to keep creating new poses until you find the one you want.

Assigning Multiple Poses to the Timeline

Let's put your poses into motion by adding each layer to the timeline. Then you can watch a movie of the character going from one pose to another. I saved the multiple-posed character as a project in the Chapter 7 Assets folder. The file is named TimelinePose.ZPR.

I also created a video of me walking through the process of storing the poses on a timeline. This video is called TimelinePose.mov in the Chapter 7 Videos folder.

1. Choose Movie → TimeLine and then click the Show button (see Figure 7.34). The timeline appears above the ZBrush document.

2. Select the first layer of the DemoSoldier subtool. Click the Name button in the Tool → Layers subpalette and rename this **Pose1**. Rename every subtool with this layer-naming convention. See Figure 7.35.

3. With Pose1 selected in the Layer subpalette, the timeline also shows that Pose1 is selected (see Figure 7.36). Set Pose1 at **1** on the timeline and then click the front of the timeline to create a keyframe. If you see the word *Camera* next to the timeline, you do not currently have the layer selected, and any keyframes added to the timeline will be applied to the camera position.

Figure 7.34
Turn on the timeline in the Movie palette.

Figure 7.35
Create two layers, naming the first one Pose1 and the second one Pose2.

4. Now move the Pose1 layer to 0 and create another keyframe further down the timeline (see Figure 7.37). These two keyframes will not cause the DemoSoldier body to move out of Pose1 into no pose.

Figure 7.36 *Click at the beginning of the timeline to create a keyframe.*

Figure 7.37 *Create another keyframe with Pose1 layer at 0.*

5. Switch to the Pose2 layer, which will be set to 0. Figure 7.38 shows that the timeline also updates to Pose2. Notice the gray keyframes; these show where the keyframes were placed for Pose1.

6. Switch the body to the other pose and place a keyframe at the second gray keyframe (see Figure 7.39)

Figure 7.38 *Switch to Pose2 to update the timeline. All keyframes that are placed will affect the Pose2 layer.*

Figure 7.39 *Place a keyframe where the second keyframe lies.*

7. Turn the Pose2 layer to 1, and then create a new keyframe on the timeline (see Figure 7.40).

8. When you cycle through the timeline, your character will switch from one pose to the other.

9. Click on the ZBrush document. The timeline now reads *Camera*. Click once at the beginning of the timeline, and a second time anywhere else, to set what you want the camera to do when playing back the video.

10. Complete this action for every subtool so that the whole character will move smoothly. You can watch a movie of my character going through the poses in the `Chapter 7 Videos` folder. This video is called `MultiplePoses.mov`.

Figure 7.40 *Create another keyframe on the timeline with Pose2 set at 1.*

If you had more poses, you could continue this process down the timeline. You also could change the transition speed between each pose by just moving the keyframes closer along the timeline.

Exporting Blend Shapes from ZBrush to Maya

ZBrush is often used to create blend shapes for characters' facial expressions. A few of the Artist Spotlights cover this subject in more detail, such as Marco Menco's Artist Spotlight at the end of this chapter. I would like to walk you through a simpler approach using the layer system again and the preinstalled ZBrush plug-in, Maya Blend Shapes. Here are the steps:

1. Select `DemoHead.ZTL` in LightBox from the Tool menu. Make sure it is in Edit mode on the ZBrush document. Now let's give this guy some expressions.

2. Create a new layer in the Tool ＞ Layers subpalette and name the layer Eyes Closed.

3. Add several more layers on the head, as shown in Figure 7.41. Notice that each expression is on its own layer.

Figure 7.41 Apply one expression per layer.

4. Before sending these layers over to Maya, test them with the timeline feature. Turn on the timeline again if it's not already on by clicking Show in the Movie → TimeLine subpalette.

5. Activate the camera track by clicking any open space on the ZBrush document, and then add two keyframes by clicking the timeline twice. See Figure 7.42.

6. Select the first layer of your DemoHead (in this example, this is Eyes Closed). If you wish to use my DemoHead, I have saved it in the `Chapter 7 Assets` folder as `DemoHead_Expressions.ZTL`.

7. With the Eyes Closed layer set to **0**, create a keyframe at the beginning of the timeline. With the layer set to 0, the eyes will be open. You can see in Figure 7.43 where I am at this point.

8. Now adjust the Eyes Closed layer to **1**. This closes the eyes. Click another spot on the timeline to indicate where you want the eyes to be closed. Figure 7.44 shows where I am at this stage.

9. Repeat this process for every layer of expressions. When you are finished, move along the timeline to see how your expressions are working.

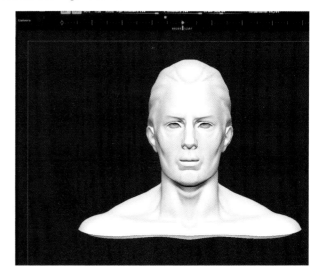

Figure 7.42 Make two keyframes on the camera timeline before beginning to add keyframes for the layers.

If you do not like the looks of your expressions, you can turn that layer to **1** and click to the left of the eyeball to put the layer back into REC mode. Make your changes and then click to the right of REC to turn your eyeball back on. These changes will also be updated on the timeline.

When you are happy with your expressions, export them to Maya, which is easy with the Maya Blend Shapes plug-in for ZBrush.

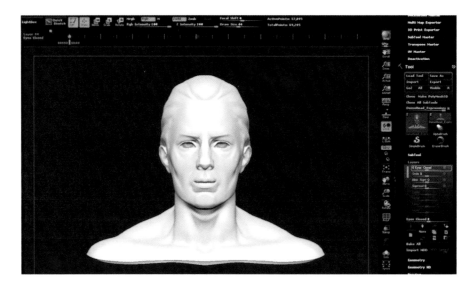

Figure 7.43 *Create a keyframe at the beginning of the timeline with the Eyes Closed layer set to 0.*

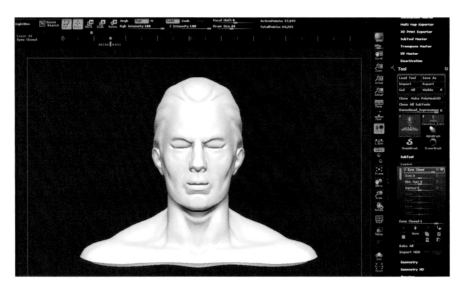

Figure 7.44 *Turn the Eyes Closed layer to 1 and create another keyframe on the timeline.*

10. Turn on All in the Maya Blend Shapes plug-in. This tells ZBrush to export all subtools into Maya.

11. With the DemoHead still selected, click the Export Blend Shapes button (see Figure 7.45).

Figure 7.46 shows that all layers import into Maya as blend shapes with the same names as the layers in ZBrush.

Figure 7.45 Click the Export Blend Shapes button to send your layers into Maya as blend shapes.

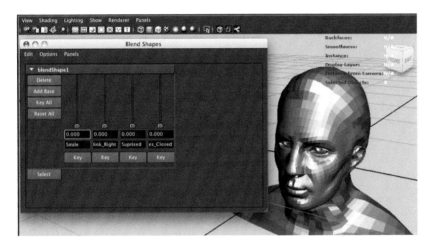

Figure 7.46 ZBrush layers imported into Maya as blend shapes

With all the layers coming over to Maya as blend shapes, you can see how easily you can create a really cool workflow, going back and forth between both applications to create a realistic animation.

ARTIST SPOTLIGHT: GEERT MELIS

FAST MESH-GENERATING WITH MESH EXTRACT AND MASKING WITH THE CLIP BRUSHES

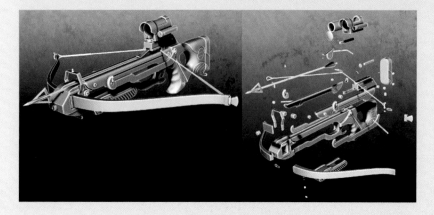

I DO ALL MY MODELING in ZBrush, from low-poly base meshes to finished high-res sculpts. This allows me to fully concentrate on concept creation without having to readjust to different working environments and workflow paradigms of other software.

I would like to show a few of the workflows that I use to create my hard-surface objects within ZBrush. The following models have a fairly simple shape in order to emphasize the techniques and workflow that, when mastered, you can use to create shapes ranging from a simple table to the most complex spacecraft.

One of the fastest ways to generate a mesh is to extract one from a plane or from an existing mesh. In the next example, I will show how to use this technique in combination with a reference image. The following image is an example of what I created using this technique.

1. Select the Plane3D primitive in the tool palette in Edit mode and then click the MakePolyMesh3D button.

2. Choose Tool → Geometry and click Divide four times, or use the shortcut Ctrl+D, so the plane has five subdivision levels.

3. Choose Texture → Import to load a reference image of your choice. For this example, I loaded a gun image.

4. Press the +/- button you see in the following image to load the texture into Spotlight (Texture → +/- button).

5. Use the Spotlight dial to adjust the position, size, and opacity of the image, as shown in the following image. Press Z to hide the Spotlight dial to switch into Spotlight Projection mode.

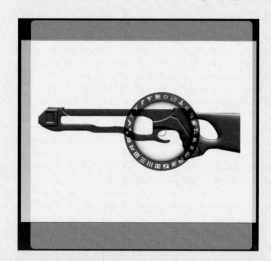

FAST MESH-GENERATING WITH MESH EXTRACT AND MASKING WITH THE CLIP BRUSHES

6. With the Standard brush selected, and with only RGB on at the top of the interface, draw your reference image on the plane by stroking over the image.

7. Using the reference image as a guide, use the masking brushes to mask off the shape you need. I used the MaskRect brush in the following image.

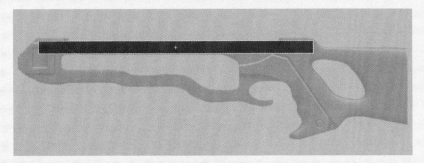

Continue to use the masking brushes to mask the rest of the gun off.

8. In the Tool → SubTool subpalette, click Extract. This creates a new mesh based on the mask, as shown in the following image.

If needed, you can adjust the edge smoothness (E Smt), the surface smoothness (S Smt), and the thickness (Thick) before clicking Extract. After you see what you like, click the Accept button to create a subtool from the mask. Experiment with the slider settings to see their effect when extracting.

A technique I use a lot is to mask parts and then use the clipping brushes to create some detail.

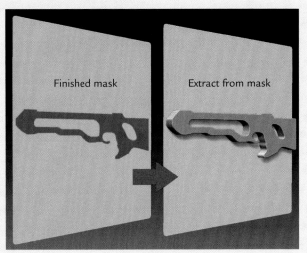

Finished mask

Extract from mask

FAST MESH-GENERATING WITH MESH EXTRACT AND MASKING WITH THE CLIP BRUSHES

9. Using one or more of the masking brushes, draw and invert if needed to get the shape you want (see the following image). Switch to a side view and use the ClipCurve brush to control both the depth and shape of the carved form.

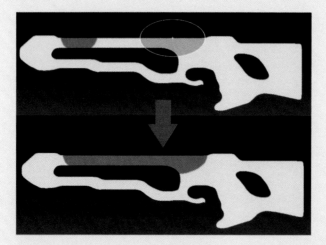

10. Invert the mask and then switch to a side view; use the ClipCurve brush to control both the depth and shape of the carved form.

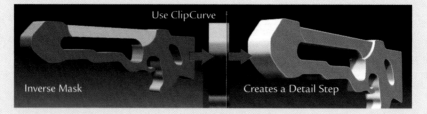

11. Create another mask like the following image.

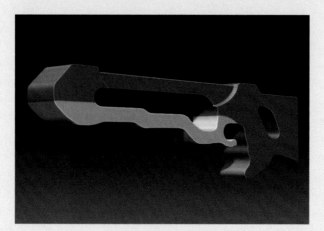

FAST MESH-GENERATING WITH MESH EXTRACT AND MASKING WITH THE CLIP BRUSHES

12. Turn your view to the front and draw out a unique curve with the ClipCurve brush, as shown on the left of the following image. Your result will be something like the right side of the following image.

The following image shows the changes to the gun.

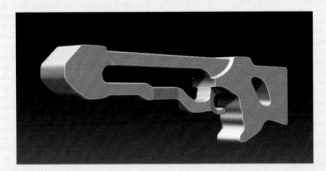

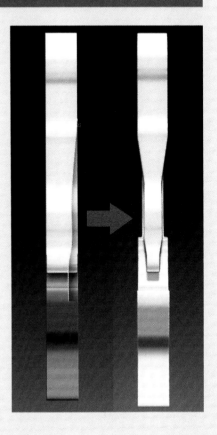

13. Continue the process of masking and extracting to create more pieces just like the following image. When you have enough pieces, use the ClipCurve brush to refine the gun. This technique of extracting is great because the new mesh created will follow the underlying surface perfectly.

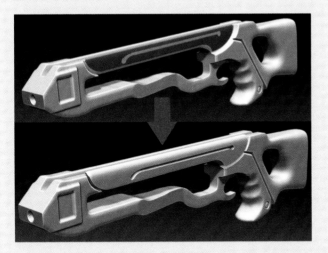

There's More

Geert has completed two more techniques that appear on the DVD in the `Geert Melis` folder. Enjoy the rest of his tips, and I encourage you to continue keeping an eye on Geert's thread to see all the great hard-edge techniques he does with ZBrush.

GEERT MELIS *lives and works in Belgium. He studied at the Royal Academy of Fine Arts in Antwerp and is employed as an art teacher and ZBrush Certified Instructor at De Kunsthumaniora—Antwerp. He was a beta tester for Pixologic on the PaintStop and UV Master plug-ins, ZBrush 3.5, ZBrush 4, and ZBrush 4R2.*

The development of his personal project The Thin Veil of Reality *can be followed in his Etcher_Sketcher thread at ZBrushCentral,* www.zbrushcentral.com/showthread.php?78703-Etcher_Sketcher. *It contains more than 100 sheets filled with tips and tricks on drawing and sculpting the human figure, concept drawing and sculpting, and working with ZBrush and PaintStop.*

www.geertmelis.com

ARTIST SPOTLIGHT: MARCO MENCO

USING LAYERS AND PROJECT ALL TO WORK WITH FACIAL EXPRESSIONS

The power of using the ZBrush layer system is that it lets you break up your model details into layers and lets you store the different morph targets of your model. You can exploit this feature by using it interactively to generate a library of facial expressions. I say *interactively* because you can store your morph in the layer and see your mesh deforming in real time by using the slider for each respective layer (see the following image).

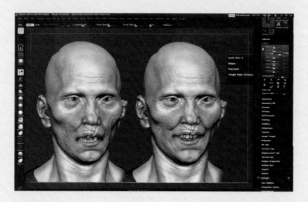

1. Before you start to work on facial shapes, make sure you have all the subtools you need. For the head model that you are working on, you need the following:
   - Your head model
   - A duplicate of your head model
   - Teeth/tongue (whatever mouth pieces you have)
   - Eyeballs

   As the title suggests, I use Project All quite a bit during the whole process, and that means that I interact between subtools.

2. Create a layer and then rename it right away so that you always know what you are focusing on while working. I rename the layer with the name of the muscle that I plan to work with, or with the name of the facial expression I want to store. Usually I use something such as *muscle-base* for the name of the layer on facial expressions because it allows me to collect a more varied range of targets that I'm going to combine in order to achieve specific expressions.
   - To create a layer, click Tool → Layers → Plus button.
   - To rename the layer, click Tool → Layer → Name.
   - Make sure the layer is in Recording mode. Click the full circle on the same line of the layer you're working on.

3. Now you begin the process of sculpting. You want to work on the *zygomatic major* (this will be the name of the layer) muscle of the cheek. Use the Move Topological brush, and make the brush size big enough to have a nice falloff on the movement of the skin. Then go to Subdivision level 1 in the Geometry subpalette (this also helps for a nice falloff). Now start moving the geometry from the fleshy part of the face along the length of the muscle to the cheek bone, where the muscle inserts. Keeping the wireframe visible helps you see what part of the mesh is moving and how (see the following image).

USING LAYERS AND PROJECT ALL TO WORK WITH FACIAL EXPRESSIONS

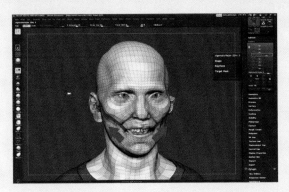

4. Now you can start moving up to the higher subdivisions and use the Nudge brush to refine the act of skin sliding. After you do the initial blocking of the shape in lower subdivisions, duplicate the head geometry and give the duplicated head a vibrant color. I like red.

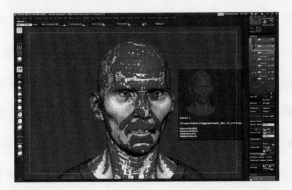

5. At this point, it's going to be clear where you've lost volumes or if you accidentally changed the morphology of the skull. You need to reproject those volumes where the bones are. So hide all subtools but the two heads: the one that you're working on and its duplicate.

   You're still working on lower subdivisions, so you avoid projecting high-frequency details onto areas that have now moved. At the end of the process, you want to achieve a nice skin-sliding-over-bones effect. That means you need the high-frequency details to remain untouched and the UV to remain intact.

6. Select the MaskPen brush by holding down the Ctrl key and then paint-mask over the cheek bones. Click Tool → Masking → BlurMask until the mask is nice

and blurred, and then invert the mask by clicking Tool → Masking → Inverse, so that anything you do now affects only the areas that are not masked. Once you have this set up, choose Tool → SubTool and click ProjectAll.

7. Tweaking the distance or the blur usually helps to achieve better results. However, in general, if you didn't move the geo too far from the duplicate mesh, you won't need to tweak anything (see the following image).

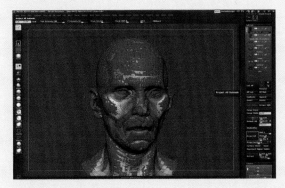

8. Now you can start to play with the Layer slider that you have been sculpting on to see how the skin moves. If the movement doesn't look realistic enough, go to the higher subdivisions and play a bit with the Nudge brush and keep sliding the skin more where it's needed.

   You can hide the duplicate head and make all the other subtools visible so that you see whether you're crashing into some of them while the expression is happening. Keep sliding the layer and refining the movement until you're happy with it, as I did in the next image.

USING LAYERS AND PROJECT ALL TO WORK WITH FACIAL EXPRESSIONS

9. Now you can think about the details that the skin movement is supposed to create on a human face. So switch between one subdivision and another as necessary to sculpt wrinkles and bulge details by using the DamStandard and Inflate brushes in ZBrush's main Brush palette (see the following image).

10. Sculpt a library of expressions for each layer. That is, keep repeating the preceding process until you cover the range of movements that face muscles can make. Then you can pick and choose several layer sliders to get the expression you want, as shown in the following image.

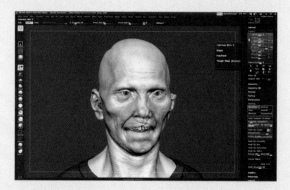

11. Now you really need to give the shapes a run by starting to pull the sliders around and then trying to combine them to see whether you can achieve believable expressions (see the following image). Try spinning the head around and looking at it from different angles so that you can see whether the combination makes the skull lose its volumes.

12. Most of the time when you combine the layers, areas will crash into the other subtools, such as the teeth. This is due to the nature of the layer, which has a linear interpolation. Create a new layer called **lipsTweak**. This is basically a layer that works as an in-between for other layers. Now when you turn on one or more combinations of shapes, you also pull that tweaks layer to fill the loss of volume that happened because of the linear interpolation. As shown in the following image, for instance, I used the lipsTweak layer to avoid having the lower lip crash into the teeth subtool.

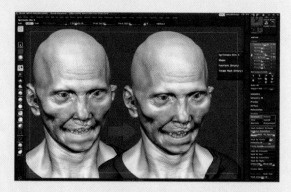

13. The specific head you're working on has a fairly flat face, so you can avoid making many layer tweaks. You can more easily avoid geometry colliding into other subtools if most of your muscle movement happens on the same plane of the face. For instance, if you were working with the face of a wolf, or a creature with a longer muzzle, or a more three-dimensional face, you would have to create many more layers for tweaks.

USING LAYERS AND PROJECT ALL TO WORK WITH FACIAL EXPRESSIONS

14. So far you've worked in symmetry. However, when it becomes necessary, you can start to split the layers into left- and right-side layers of face movement. You could have created layers with individual movement (such as right eye closed, left eye closed) instead of having the eyes closed since the beginning. I chose not to work with this approach because of speed. The face can stay asymmetrical even if you work with Symmetry on, as long as you turn Symmetry off when you add major asymmetrical details.

15. To split the layers into left and right sides, simply store a morph target of the default post: click Tool → MorphTarget → StoreMT.

16. Duplicate the layer you want to split and rename it according to the side that will define the shape—for example, **browsSideUpLEFT**. Now you can simply use the Morph brush and paint out one part of the face. Duplicate the original, symmetrical layer again and rename it **browsSideUpRIGHT**. Then use the Morph brush on the right side and paint out the other side of the face. The following image shows how I used one layer to create two separate layers for the brow. Keep doing this for all the shapes you need to split.

Where I work currently at Image Engine Design, we have a script that will separate the two sides of the symmetrical shapes automatically in Maya by using one attribute map.

17. The last thing you have left to do is to create expressions! In the next image, you can see all the expressions I have started to create with the ZBrush layer system.

MARCO MENCO *grew up in a big Italian family at the center of the Adriatic coast of Italy. He spent his youth admiring artists such as Gustave Dore and the Italian Renaissance masters.*

Between school and work, he has always focused on improving his artistic skills. His experience includes illustration, comic drawing, 3D modeling and texturing, and concept designing for film and television. In the past, he also has worked as a traditional sculptor for theater scenographies.

When he finally decided to be an artist for life, Marco entered the Academy of Fine Arts and in 2007 obtained his bachelor's degree. The time he spent on preparing his final thesis was really important for him because it allowed him to finally accomplish several personal pieces of artwork. Of course, his passion for Gustave Dore led him to work on a series of concept illustrations based on Dante's The Divine Comedy: Inferno. *Marco is still in the process of reinventing Dante's* Inferno, *which he decided would be his lifelong project.*

After completing the Academy in 2007, Marco moved to Vancouver, British Columbia, where he works as a senior creature artist at Image Engine Design.

At the moment, his attention is captured by facial expressions and edge flow for high-performance geometries. The most recent project he worked on was The Thing, *the prequel, for which he modeled and sculpted most of the complex creatures present in the sequences. He also created libraries of facial expressions and contributed to the development of animated displacement maps for enhancing facial details for the Image Engine pipeline.*

marcomenco.com

SPECIAL PROJECT | HOCKEY SKATES

CREATE LACES

CREATE A STITCH B

USING DECIMATION MA
TO REDUCE POLY CC

Special Project—Creating Hockey Skates

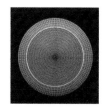

ZBrush is often seen as *a program that creates only characters or creatures, but the fact is that many artists are using ZBrush to create products, environments, toys, medical illustrations, and so much more. Pixologic has some great examples on their website at* `www.pixologic.com/zbrush/industry/`.

For this project, I wanted to show that you can create something that is not a character. The hockey skates were completely created in ZBrush with a few simple techniques. With just a few clicks, you will learn how easy it is to create some of the complex pieces of the skates.

- Creating the laces

- Using a custom Stitch brush

- Using Decimation Master to reduce poly count

Creating the Laces

Creating laces could seem extremely complex, especially when it comes to creating the knots. Often you have more than one way to create something in ZBrush, and laces are no exception. In this section, you will learn two ways to create the laces: using the CurveTube brush and using ZSpheres.

Using the CurveTube Brush

Let's start by using a brush to create the laces. Before you start any project like this, it's best to get some references. For this project, I am sharing my very own hockey skates for the reference image. In Figure 8.1, you can see how the laces lie on the boot of the skate. While creating the skates in ZBrush, I also would often pick up the physical skates. So you want as many reference images as possible before starting any project.

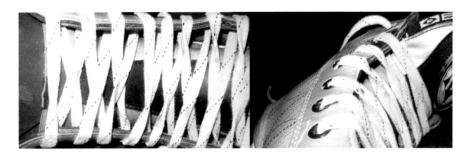

Figure 8.1 Reference images of the hockey skates

I have also created a video for this section called `LacesCurveTube.mov` in the `Chapter 8 Videos` folder.

1. Load `LaceEyeLets.ZTL` (see Figure 8.2) from the `Chapter 8 Assets` folder into ZBrush. Make sure the laces are in Edit mode.

2. Select the CurveTube brush.

3. At the start of my laces, you can see that the first part of the laces sits over the first grommets. Figure 8.3 shows that I drew out a curve from one eyelet to the other. Also note the Draw Size of 23, which will be important.

The Draw Size controls the size of the tube that is drawn out by the brush. If you change the Draw Size to something like **12** and click the curve again, the tube's size is automatically adjusted, as you can see in Figure 8.4.

This is one of the great advantages of using the CurveTube brush: you can update the curve at any point. In fact, Figure 8.5 shows how, when you scroll over the curve, the cursor changes to a turquoise color. This indicates that you can continue moving the points of the curve around until you get the tube into place. This turquoise curve size is controlled by Stroke → Curve Edit Radius.

Adjust the curve a little to get the location of the tube to fit better.

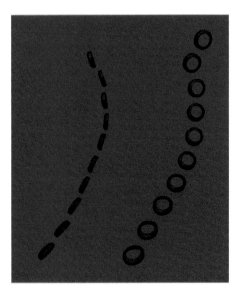

Figure 8.3 Draw from one eyelet to another so that the laces sit over the eyelet.

Figure 8.2 `LaceEyeLets.ZTL` *loaded into ZBrush*

Figure 8.4 Adjust the Draw Size to change the size of the tube.

4. Click the Delete button in the Stroke palette to make more adjustments. This deletes the curve for good.

5. Switch to the Move brush and make the first part of the lace look as if it is coming out of the eyelet (see Figure 8.6).

6. Switch to the TrimDynamic brush to flatten the lace, to give it the look of the real lace in the reference images. Figure 8.7 shows the result of using TrimDynamic to flatten both sides of the lace.

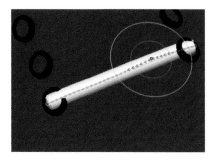  

Figure 8.5 The turquoise cursor indicates that the curve can be adjusted.   *Figure 8.6 Use the Move brush to adjust the lace into place.*   *Figure 8.7 Use the TrimDynamic brush to flatten both sides of the lace.*

7. Because the first lace heads into the first set of eyelets, the next part of the lace needs to be under the eyelets (see Figure 8.8). Again, use the CurveTube brush to draw out the laces. In my example, I set Draw Size at 12 because this was the size I liked for the first part.

> By default, the CurveTube brush will have Bend on in the Stroke palette. This allows you to move certain points of the curve. To move the whole curve at once, deactivate the Bend button.

8. Draw out the laces so they come out of the second set of eyelets to the third set. In Figure 8.9, these laces come out and over the top of the second set of eyelets. Don't forget to switch to the TrimDynamic brush to flatten the laces.

9. Continue these steps all the way up the eyelets until you have results similar to Figure 8.10.

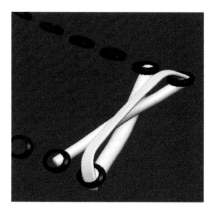  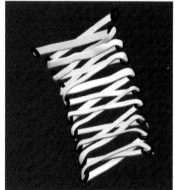

Figure 8.8 Draw out the laces under the eyelets.   *Figure 8.9 Draw out the laces from the second set of eyelets to the third set.*   *Figure 8.10 Finished laces with the CurveTube brush*

Using ZSpheres

Let's take a look at how to build laces with ZSpheres. This approach can be a little bit quicker than using the CurveTube brush. A video for this section, LacesZSpheres.mov, can be found in the Chapter 8 Movies folder. Here are the steps:

1. Load the LaceEyeLets.ZTL file from the Chapter 8 Assets folder. Place this tool in Edit mode on the ZBrush canvas.

2. Append a ZSphere as a subtool.

3. The ZSphere will be a little too large for what you want to do, so switch to Scale mode at the top of the interface and resize the ZSphere.

4. Make sure you are in x-symmetry mode. Switch to Move mode and place the ZSphere at the front of the eyelets. Figure 8.11 shows the size and movement of the ZSphere.

5. With the ZSphere selected, click the first set of eyelets (see Figure 8.12). When you click and drag, make sure to hold the Shift key right after you start dragging so that the ZSphere is the exact same size as the original. The advantage of this technique is that the ZSpheres will click to a vertex on the eyelet, so you can easily work your way up the eyelets with little adjustments.

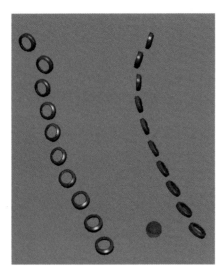

Figure 8.11 Position the ZSphere to the front of the eyelets and adjust the size.

Figure 8.12 Draw out ZSpheres to the first eyelet.

6. With Draw mode selected, click above the ZSphere you just drew out to add a ZSphere. Pull the ZSphere so that the ZSpheres go through the eyelets (see Figure 8.13). Remember to hold the Shift key so the ZSpheres all stay the same size. Switch to Move mode to move the ZSpheres into place.

7. Deactivate Symmetry mode.

8. Switch to Move mode and click one of the bottom ZSpheres to select it.

9. Switch to Draw mode and click the next eyelet diagonally across from your selected ZSphere. Remember to hold the Shift key. Figure 8.14 shows the position of this ZSphere.

10. Draw another ZSphere on top of that ZSphere, so you can have the lace go through the eyelet, just as in Figure 8.15.

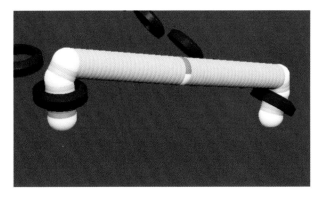

Figure 8.13 *Add a ZSphere above the last one and add another to the bottom.*

Figure 8.14 *Click the eyelet diagonally across from the selected ZSphere.*

11. Now repeat for the other side.

12. Add some ZSpheres in the middle of the chain (see Figure 8.16) to make it look like the ZSpheres sit on top of each other.

13. Continue this process all the way up the eyelets until you have results similar to Figure 8.17.

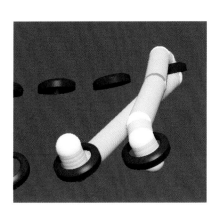

Figure 8.15 *Draw another ZSphere on top of the recent ZSphere.*

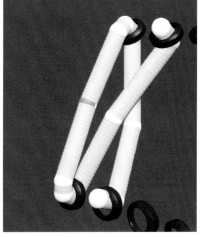

Figure 8.16 *Click in the middle of each chain to add a ZSphere for adjustment.*

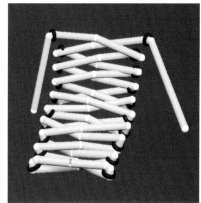

Figure 8.17 *Finished ZSpheres up the eyelets*

14. Click the Preview button in the Tool → Adaptive Skin subpalette or use the shortcut A. This puts the ZSpheres into a mesh preview mode.

15. Click the Make Adaptive Skin button in the Tool → Adaptive Skin subpalette.

16. Append the new subtool that is created when you click Make Adaptive Skin to the eyelets you have been working on. This new subtool will be called Skin_ZSphere.

17. Turn off the eye for the ZSphere subtool. Figure 8.18 shows our progress.

18. Select the TrimDynamic brush again to flatten the laces.

19. Turn on Polyframe mode at the right of the interface or use the shortcut Shift+F. You can more easily select certain portions by holding Ctrl+Shift and clicking the poly-group colors of the laces you want to work on (see Figure 8.19).

20. With the TrimDynamic brush still selected, start to flatten down the lace (see Figure 8.20).

21. Continue this process all the way up the laces so that you have results like those shown in Figure 8.21.

These are great techniques with distinct advantages that showcase the various ways you can create something in ZBrush. Play with both techniques and see which one is best for you.

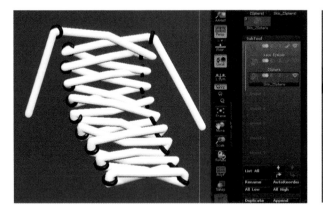

Figure 8.18 *Append Skin_ZSphere to the eyelets and turn off the ZSphere subtool.*

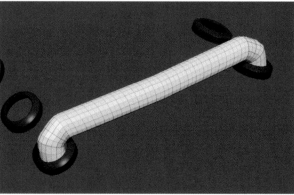

Figure 8.19 *Hold Ctrl+Shift and click a portion of the laces' polygroups so you can sculpt on that portion only.*

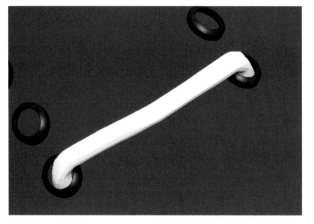

Figure 8.20 *Use TrimDynamic to flatten down the laces.*

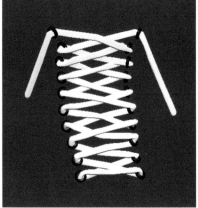

Figure 8.21 *Finished laces using the ZSpheres*

Using a Custom Stitch Brush

Making an element as detailed as stitches that hold the skate together can be a vigorous job if you try to sculpt out all of the stitches. ZBrush makes this task a lot easier by enabling you to create a brush that will represent stitches.

Creating the Model Used for the Alpha

You want to create a single stitch that you can use as an alpha. So you will use ZBrush's 2.5D technology. Let's first start by creating the model that will be used as an alpha:

1. Select the Sphereinder3D brush in Edit mode in the ZBrush document.

2. Under Tool → Initialized, adjust the TRadius to 50 and click the Make PolyMesh button in the Tool palette (see Figure 8.22).

3. Turn off Perspective.

4. Turn on PolyFrame so that you can see the geometry.

5. Turn the mesh to the side. Hold Ctrl+Shift and hide one part of the mesh by using the SelectRect brush (see Figure 8.23).

6. Choose Tool → Geometry, and click the DelHidden button to delete the hidden geometry.

7. Switch the mesh so that you are looking from above.

8. Hold Ctrl+Shift and switch the SelectRect brush's stroke to Circle and then turn on the Square and Center buttons in the Stroke palette.

9. Put the cursor at the center point of the mesh, which ZBrush will snap to. Hold Ctrl+Shift to start drawing out the circle. After you draw the circle, hold only the Alt key to turn the circle red.

10. When you let go, you hide the center portion of the mesh (see Figure 8.24).

11. Choose Tool → Geometry and then click the DelHidden button to delete the hidden geometry.

12. Turn the mesh more to a three-quarter view.

13. Next you will try a technique that Zack Petroc shares in this book at the end of Chapter 2, "Special Project—Creating Accessories for a Bust." Click the StoreMT button in the Tool → Morph Target subpalette.

14. Under the Transform palette, click the little camera icon or use the shortcut Shift+S to take a snapshot of the mesh to the document.

15. Choose Tool → Deformation and then turn the Inflate slider up as many times as you want until you get the desired thickness (see Figure 8.25).

16. In the Tool → Morph Target subpalette, click the Create Diff Mesh button so that ZBrush creates a new tool called MorphDiff_PM3D_Sphereinder3D_1.

Figure 8.22 Adjustments made to the initialized states create a great starting point for the stitches.

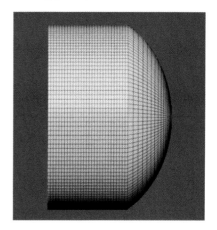

Figure 8.23 Use SelectRect to hide part of the mesh.

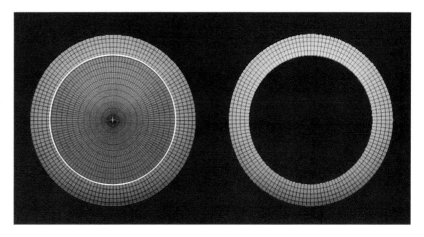

Figure 8.24 Hide the middle portion of the mesh by switching the SelectRect stroke to a circle.

17. Select this new tool.

18. Clear the document by pressing Ctrl+N or click the Clear button in the Color palette. Figure 8.26 shows the result.

19. Turn the mesh back to the side.

20. Hold Ctrl+Shift and change the SelectRect stroke back to the Rectangle.

21. Turn off the Square and Center buttons in the Stroke palette.

22. Select only the bottom portion of the mesh (see Figure 8.27).

23. In the Tool → Deformation subpalette, turn up the Inflate slider to 100 just once.

24. Bring the whole mesh back into view by holding Ctrl+Shift and then click in an open area (see Figure 8.28).

Figure 8.25 Use Inflate deformation to add thickness to the piece.

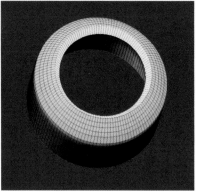

Figure 8.26 The finished piece from the Sphereinder3D brush

Figure 8.27 Select the bottom half of the mesh.

Figure 8.28 By inflating a portion of the mesh, a nice extrusion will be at the bottom of the mesh.

Creating the Alpha from the Model

Now that we have the model that will be our stitch, we need to turn this into an alpha. This is something that I am always doing with ZBrush to create my custom alphas.

1. Continuing from the first part of the tutorial, in the Document palette, turn off the Pro button and set the width to 400 and height to 600 (see Figure 8.29).

Figure 8.29 Set the document size with the Pro button off.

2. Click the Resize button. ZBrush asks whether you want to resize the document now. Click Yes, and the mesh is dropped to the document and stretched.

3. Clear the document by pressing Ctrl+N or by clicking the Clear button in the Color palette.

4. Redraw out the mesh again and put it in Edit mode on the document.

5. Move the mesh to the top of the document. Switch to Move mode and draw out the transpose line so it's straight down.

6. Hold Ctrl and click the middle circle.

7. Start moving the transpose line down. Notice that this duplicates the mesh, so you have another one to position.

8. Hold the Shift key while moving so that the meshes are on the same line, as shown in Figure 8.30.

9. Select the CurveTube brush again.

10. Switch the mesh to the side and draw from one piece to the other (see Figure 8.31).

11. In the Stroke palette, turn off the Bend button in the CurveMode section.

12. Switch to the top view of the mesh and move the tube into place (see Figure 8.32).

Remember, to adjust the overall size of the tube, just adjust the Draw Size and then click the tube again. ZBrush automatically changes the size of the tube to fit into your two rings. You may also need to click either end of the tube to move it into place.

---

13. Hold Alt+Shift and click outside the document. This moves the mesh into the middle and fits the mesh to touch the top and bottom of the document.

14. Move the mesh away from the document borders just a bit to avoid being cut off by the document. The mesh will be positioned like the example in Figure 8.33.

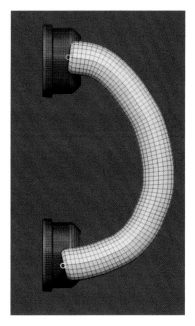
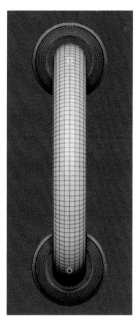
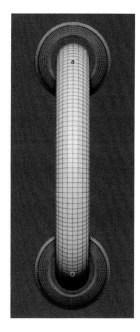

Figure 8.30 Duplicate the mesh and move it down to the bottom portion of the document.

Figure 8.31 Use the CurveTube brush to draw out a tube that goes from one mesh to the other.

Figure 8.32 Move the tube into place so that it sits perfectly between the two mesh rings.

Figure 8.33 Move the mesh away from the document borders.

15. In the Alpha palette on the left side of the interface, click the GrabDoc button so that ZBrush grabs the document and creates a depth map of the single stitch you just created (see Figure 8.34).

16. Open up LightBox now and switch to the Brush menu.

17. Find the folder icon labeled Stitch and double-click this icon to open the folder.

18. Double-click the Stitch1 brush (see Figure 8.35) to load it into the Brush palette.

19. Click the Alpha icon at the left of the interface and select the single-stitch alpha you just made.

Congrats—you just made your own Stitch brush. The brush can be saved by clicking Save As in the Brush palette. Figure 8.36 shows the final brush.

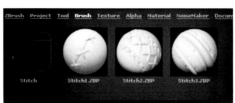

Figure 8.34 Click the GrabDoc button in the Alpha palette to create a depth map alpha.

Figure 8.35 Load the Stitch1 brush from the LightBox Brush menu.

Figure 8.36 Final Stitch brush

Figure 8.37 Results of the new Stitch brush when changing the Draw Size

Save the brush in ZBrush4R2/ZData/BrushPresets; you can now access the brush from the fly-out window that pops up when you press B. If you want to save the brush into LightBox, save it to ZBrush4R2/ZBrushes.

Figure 8.37 shows the results you can get with this new brush just by changing the Draw Size.

With just a few clicks, you created a really cool Stitch brush. I saved the brush I made as PaulStitchBrush.ZBP in the Chapter 8 Assets folder; hope you enjoy it.

Using Decimation Master to Reduce Poly Count

Chapter 1, "Understanding the Basics," covered how to use Make 3D in ZBrush. I made the logo for these skates with this technique. To repeat this technique on this logo, import G_Logo.PSD into the Alpha palette from the Chapter 8 Assets folder on the DVD.

So let's play with some of the settings in Make 3D. Here is a quick overview again of what each slider and button does in this subpalette:

> **MRes** is the mesh resolution. The higher you set this, the better quality you get, but you also have a higher polygon count.
>
> **MDep** is the mesh depth. The lower this number, the thinner the mesh will be when you create it.
>
> **MSm** is the smoothness of the mesh.
>
> **Dbls** stands for *double-sided*. With this button, the mesh will have a back and front.

Here are the steps to produce a logo that will retain the shape with fewer polygons by using the Decimation Master:

1. Let's create the logo with the following settings.
   - MRes = 400
   - MDep = 15
   - MSm = 5
   - Dbls = **On**

Figure 8.38 Logo created instantly when Make 3D is clicked

2. Click the Make 3D button to get the result in Figure 8.38.

3. Turn off Perspective.

4. Turn on the Floor Grid.

5. Turn on Symmetry but switch it from X- to Z-symmetry in the Transform palette.

6. By default, the mesh will have a mask on from Make 3D; you just won't see it. Clear the mask on the logo by holding Ctrl and clicking and dragging anywhere in an open area.

7. While holding Ctrl+Shift, select the ClipCurve brush.

8. Rotate the view of the logo to view it from the side, as shown in Figure 8.39.

9. Hold Ctrl+Shift and draw out a perfectly straight line, with the gradient side facing away from the green line on the Floor Grid. Make sure the curved line position is relatively close to the green line, just as in Figure 8.40. The result will be similar to Figure 8.41.

To wrap the logo to fit the skate, I used the MatchMaker brush again. I covered this in Chapter 2. Revisit this chapter for a recap on how to match logos to underlying surfaces.

In some cases when using Make 3D, your polygon count could get really high. To avoid wasting polygons on something that will never deform, like this logo, you can use the Decimation Master

Figure 8.39 Turn the logo to look at the side.

Figure 8.40 Draw out the curve close to the green line of the floor grid with the gradient side facing away.

plug-in to drop the number of polygons but maintain the logo shape. If you have followed along exactly, your logo is at 63,514 polygons. That isn't really that much, but I would still like to show what you can do when you are working with 1 million polygons or more.

10. Open the Decimation Master plug-in from the ZPlugins palette (see Figure 8.42).

11. In the Decimation Master plug-in, click the Pre-Process Current button. Depending on your machine, it will take ZBrush about three seconds to process. ZBrush has just decimated this logo from 0 to 100 percent into a temp file.

12. Set the percent of decimation at **20** and click Decimate Current. This decimates the mesh and drops the ActivePoints count of the mesh to 12,702 (from 63,514).

The Decimation Master will turn the quad mesh into triangles. ZBrush does not actually count polygon faces, but vertex points, so with the ActivePoints at the top of the interface, ZBrush counts the vertex points (see Figure 8.43). Because the mesh is converted into triangles, you have to double this ActivePoints number to know how many triangles are in the mesh. For this example, the total triangle count is 25,404.

In Figure 8.44, you can see that even at 5 percent, the logo is still holding the form at 3,175 ActivePoints.

This was a fun project for me because I play ice hockey. I hope you enjoyed learning as much as I enjoyed creating the piece.

Figure 8.41 *Result after using ClipCurve brush*

Figure 8.42
Open Decimation
Master in the
ZPlugins palette.

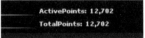

Figure 8.43 *The ActivePoints count of any selected subtool, and TotalPoints indicating the poly count of all subtools*

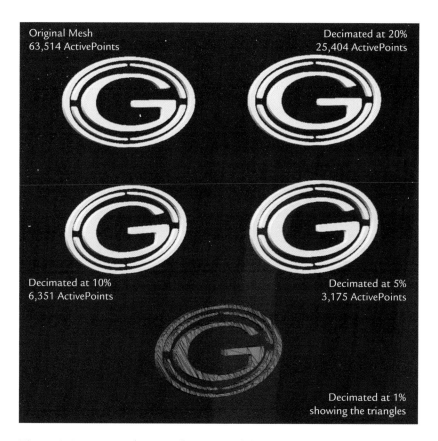

Figure 8.44 *Various decimated versions of the logo*

ARTIST SPOTLIGHT: JOSEPH DRUST

USING SURFACE NOISE TO GENERATE CLOTHING HOLES

SURFACE NOISE IN ZBRUSH not only creates great surface deformation but also can be used with RGB to create randomized tears in clothing. As you can see in the following image, I used Surface Noise to create holes in my cowl.

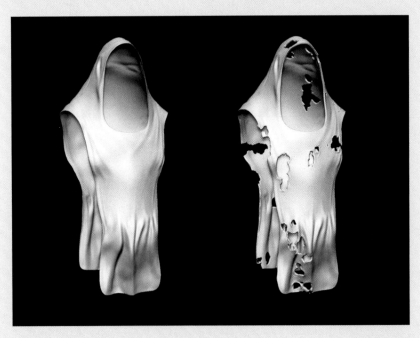

1. Start by applying Surface Noise to a mesh (Tool → Surface → Noise).
2. Change Strength to **.001**, change the scale to 217 and set ColorBlend to **-1** so that it is near the black color selector.

The mesh should take on the color of the surface noise, but not the surface deformation because the Strength is set very low. You can see the results in the following image.

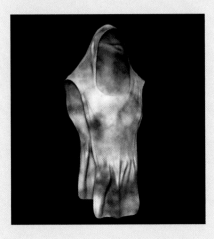

USING SURFACE NOISE TO GENERATE CLOTHING HOLES

3. Click the MaskByNoise button in the Tool → Surface subpalette.

The mesh should now have a mask that closely resembles the applied surface noise.

4. Sharpen the mask until crisp dark spots appear by clicking the SharpenMask button in the Tool → Masking subpalette.

You can see in the next image how sharp I made the mask when clicking SharpenMask.

5. Click HidePt in the Tool → Visibility subpalette. This hides the parts of the mesh that are masked off. At this point, the geometry is not deleted from the mesh, just hidden.

Now you need to delete the hidden geometry. First, you will need to perform a little trick so as not to lose any sculpting detail you may have created.

6. Mask off the entire mesh at the highest subdivision level.

7. After you have the entire mesh masked out, walk to the lowest level of subdivision.

8. Click the DelHidden button near the bottom of the Tool → Geometry subpalette.

Now that you have deleted the hidden geometry once, you walk back up to the highest subdivision level. Use the Move brush and other 3D brushes to give you something similar to the following image.

Voila! You have easily added holes in the clothing.

Using UV Master and Alphas to Quickly Generate Cloth Details

Adding folds to fabric helps create the illusion of realistic cloth. However, most cloth has a textile surface pattern that adds even more realism. Adding these textile details can be quite time-consuming when using dragged alphas

USING SURFACE NOISE TO GENERATE CLOTHING HOLES

across large surfaces of cloth, belts, and straps. One method to quickly generate precise textile details is to use the UVWs of the model with UV Master along with the Alpha tiling options in ZBrush. As you can see in the following image, I used this technique to create the textile surface of this cowl.

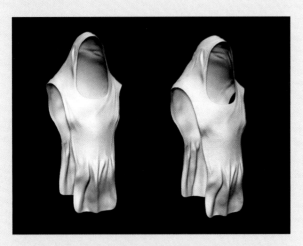

1. Load the model you want to apply the textile surface detailing to and go to the lowest subdivision level. If you already have UVW mapping coordinates that you would like to use on your model instead of generating new ones, skip to step 5.

2. Break up your model into polygroups, as in the following image, roughly where clothing seams would exist. These polygroups will help establish UVW islands in the UVW mapping.

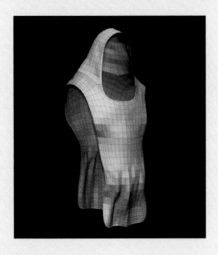

3. Go to the UV Master plug-in inside of ZBrush (ZPlugin → UV Master). You can download UV Master off the Pixologic website at www.pixologic.com/zbrush/downloadcenter/zplugins/.

4. Turn on Symmetry and Polygroups. Then click Unwrap.

UV Master quickly generates UVW mapping coordinates on your model. To see how the UVWs look, choose UV Check Tool → Texture Map → UV Check. The UVWs should be displayed in the Texture window of the Texture Map tab.

5. Now the model should contain good UVWs. Go to the highest subdivision and make sure the active point count is around 1 million or so. The polygon density of the mesh will determine the quality of the masking when it is applied to the model. A higher polygon count will equal a higher mask quality.

USING SURFACE NOISE TO GENERATE CLOTHING HOLES

6. In the Alpha palette, click Import to import a cloth textile that is tileable and that you would like to apply to the model. I loaded a custom alpha, as seen in the following image.

7. With the alpha loaded, choose Tool → Masking → Mask By Alpha and click Mask By Alpha.

8. After the mask is applied, it should be visible on the model. With the current UVWs loaded on the model, the textile detail may appear to be a little too large.

9. To adjust the size of the alpha, go back to the Alpha palette and change the H Tiles and the V Tiles settings to **4**. This should give results similar to the following image.

10. Use Mask By Alpha again on the model (Tool → Masking → Mask By Alpha subpalette).

Keep adjusting the H Tile and V Tile numbers in the Alpha palette and keep using Mask By Alpha until you achieve the

USING SURFACE NOISE TO GENERATE CLOTHING HOLES

desired textile surface. In the following image, an H Tile and V Tile of 3 gave the textile detail size I wanted.

11. With the masking applied to the mesh, go to the Tool → Deformation subpalette and set Inflate to **4**.

12. Clear the mask off the model. The model should now have an even surface textile detail across the entire mesh, as shown in the following image.

Cover up any visible seams with other subtools or sculpt in some mesh seams. Using this technique along with Surface Noise to generate clothing holes can help bring a realistic feel to the clothing, belts, and straps of your models, just as I did in the following image.

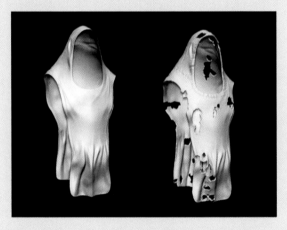

With these two techniques, you will be able to create realistic clothing for any character and take your work to the next level.

USING SURFACE NOISE TO GENERATE CLOTHING HOLES

JOSEPH DRUST *is an artist residing near the small town of Pittsboro, North Carolina. He graduated from the Savannah College of Art and Design with a Bachelor of Fine Arts in Game Design. Joseph has over 10 years of experience working in the video game industry as a character artist with a focus on modeling and sculpting. He has created character assets for games including* Ghost Recon, Ghost Recon Advanced Warfighter, Splinter Cell: Pandora Tomorrow, Ben 10: Alien Force, *and* Earth Defense Force: Insect Armageddon.

Presently, Joseph is a senior character artist with Ubisoft (Red Storm Entertainment) in Cary, North Carolina. His work includes character sculpting for Ubisoft's next-gen game titles. Joseph is also a beta team member for Pixologic's ZBrush and a certified ZBrush instructor. In his free time, Joseph kitbashes Kidrobot's Munny vinyl figures, fishes from his kayak on the local rivers, chases his young son Leo, plays with his Sharpador (Sharpei-Labrador) Kuma, and moonlights doing graphic design and technical support for his wife, Marie's, business.

www.piggyson.com

ARTIST SPOTLIGHT: CHRISTOPHER BRÄNDSTRÖM

USING ZBRUSH PLUG-INS TO CREATE READY-TO-USE GAME CONTENT

THERE ARE A VAST NUMBER of ways to create content and textures for games. Most companies have a pipeline of in-house and third-party software at their disposal—some free, but most quite expensive. I will show you a simple way to create and export a low-poly model with some of the major textures needed to get your model ready to be used within a game, using only ZBrush. You can see the finished model together with a Xpose view of all the seven subtools in the image below.

The model was created from scratch within ZBrush, using only ShadowBox. Because I don't really care how high or low the lowest SDiv is at the moment, I created a fairly high-poly base mesh using ShadowBox. I focused only on the look of the end result and what's easiest to work with. Nothing in between.

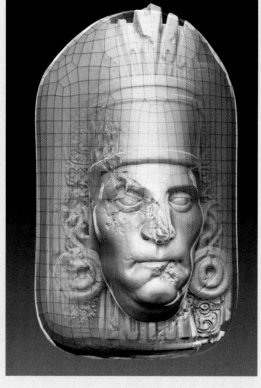

As shown in the image above at right, we want to create one solid mesh for everything instead of seven different ones. This will be the starting point for the mesh for the actual game: one mesh is easier to handle. We also want to conserve memory, which is critical when working with games. That is, we want to keep the poly count of the model low to avoid having many hidden polygons and higher geometry memory to load into the game. Plan your model well in the beginning or it will be difficult to deal with in the end.

1. In the Tool → SubTool subpalette (right), I have all of my eye icons on so that all the subtools are visible. This tells ZBrush that I want the new geometry to be projected onto these subtools.

2. In the same subpalette, deselect the X on the ReMesh All button, which is selected by default. This ensures that the new geometry will not have two identical sides, because the model itself isn't entirely the same on each side.

3. Deactivate the PolyGrp button beside the ReMesh All button so that polygroups will not be created when ZBrush creates the new model from all the subtools.

4. Click the ReMesh All button to create a new mesh that considers all your subtools for size and volume.

USING ZBRUSH PLUG-INS TO CREATE READY-TO-USE GAME CONTENT

The following image shows the progression of the newly generated geometry projected onto the old geometry through six subdivisions. You start with a low-res mesh because you get more accurate projections through each subdivision, and it takes less time for your computer to calculate the projection. The next steps will walk you through this process to get the same result that I got with my model.

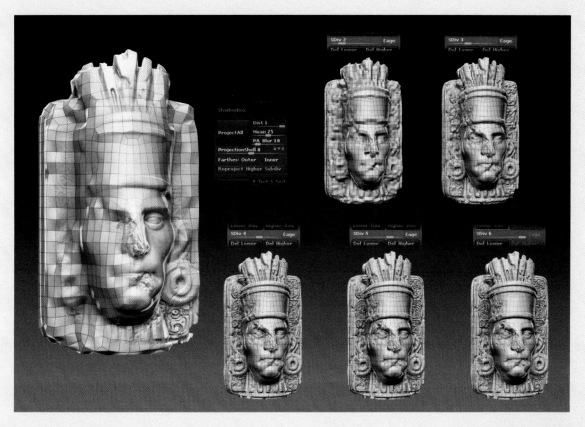

5. With the new geometry as one solid piece instead of seven, we want to get all the detail from the old model onto the new one. Select the subtool you just created from ReMesh All to project the other subtools with the sculpt detail into the ReMesh model. (I named the new ReMesh All subtool Skin-Statue.) Activate the eye icon for the other subtools so they're visible while the Skin-Statue is the selected subtool.

6. Under the Tool → SubTool subpalette, choose ProjectAll. Leave all settings on their default values. This will project the new geometry onto the old one, making it look more like my old model and not just a blob. You do not need to change the default values because the new geometry is similar, but also very different in shape from the old model.

On the next projection, we must change the Dist value because the new model is starting to get the shape of the old one.

7. Change the value on the Dist slider to **0.5**. The distance between the old model and the new geometry isn't as far as it was, so leaving the value too high might cause ugly projections, making polygons fly all over the place.

8. Divide the model once more, making the highest SDiv value **2**. Press the ProjectAll button to project the seven subtools onto the Skin-Statue.

9. Repeat the prior two steps four more times, each time lowering the Dist value by a factor of about /2. The highest level (SDiv 6) should have a Dist value of 0.03125.

USING ZBRUSH PLUG-INS TO CREATE READY-TO-USE GAME CONTENT

Using the Decimation Master Plug-In

The following image shows how the newly created and projected model becomes the in-game model using the Decimation Master plug-in.

This is a very fast and simple way to create the in-game model:

1. Select the highest SDiv-level, in this case SDiv 6. Open your Decimation Master plug-in from the ZPlugin → Decimation Master subpalette.

2. Because we don't have any UVs at this stage or any open holes in the model, under 1-Options, leave Freeze Borders and Keep UVs deselected.

3. Under 2-Pre-Process, click the Pre-Process Current button. Because there is one subtool, that'll be the only one to process. This might take some time, depending on the size of your model. But you need to do this only once.

4. After the preprocessing is done, under 3-Decimate, choose the number of polygons for the model. In this case, leave it at 6,000 Polygons and click the Decimate Current button.

You can see my Decimation Master settings in the following image. Now we have a low-poly and triangulated model to use. If you were not satisfied with the result, you could simply increase or decrease the polygon count, click Decimate Current, and get the new result instantly without having to use Pre-Process Current again.

USING ZBRUSH PLUG-INS TO CREATE READY-TO-USE GAME CONTENT

Creating UVs with UV Master

The next image shows the process for creating a UV map on the newly created in-game model.

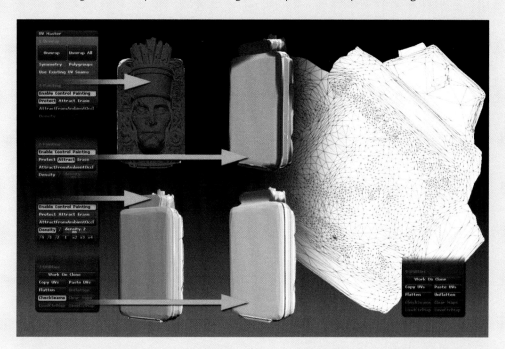

1. Before we create any new UV map, we need to divide and project the old model detail onto the game model, which is the decimated model with triangles. ZBrush has high-res geometry for the maps so we can do the next step. So before that happens I'll just go through the process of creating the UV with the UV Master plug-in.

   If you do these steps on a regular basis, look into creating a script within ZBrush that records and later repeats all the steps you've just done with the press of a button. Check out some of the threads in the ZBrushCentral forum to help you out, or visit the basic information on ZScripting at `www.pixologic.com/docs/index.php/ZScript_Basics`.

2. After you have divided and reprojected the detail from the old model into the in-game decimated model, it's time to create the UVs by using the UV Master-plug-in. You can then find UV Master in the ZPlugin → UV Master subpalette.

3. Under 3-Utilities in the UV Master palette, choose Work On Clone. If you don't do this, ZBrush will give a warning that your model has several subdivisions.

4. Under 2-Painting, select the Enable Control Painting button. This gives you the option to paint where you want the UV seams to be on the model because we will be UVing the entire model. The red color shows areas where seams will not be created, and the blue indicates where seams end up.

5. Select the Density button and with a cyan color, paint on the model where you want high-pixel density or low density. In the example, I painted the back of the model with a /2 density to show the effect. This means the back of the model will have half the pixel density of the front.

USING ZBRUSH PLUG-INS TO CREATE READY-TO-USE GAME CONTENT

6. Select the Unwrap button in the top-left corner of the UV Master palette. ZBrush tells you when the model is processed so you can look at the UVs. You do that by selecting the Flatten button under 3-Utilities to see the flattened model. Select UnFlatten to turn it back. Select the CheckSeams button if you want to see exactly where the UV seams are located on your model.

7. Because we previously chose to work on a clone of the model, we now need to get the new UVs back to the old model. Select the Copy UVs button and then select the original model, making sure it's still on the lowest SDiv level, and select Paste UVs to give the original model the new UV.

   Now that we have a low-res model with high-res information and a UV, we must generate the textures for my model: do that by following the instructions in the following image.

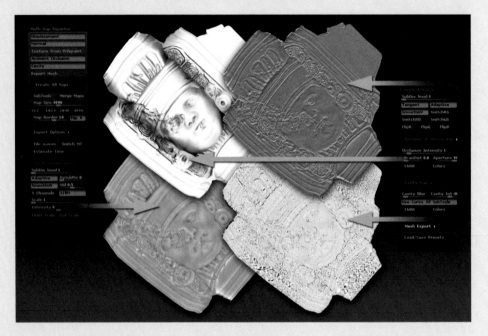

8. The Multi Map Exporter can be found under the ZPlugin → Multi Map Exporter subpalette.

9. In this tutorial, we need four textures: Displacement, Normal, Ambient Occlusion, and a Cavity map. We use Displacement in case the engine supports it and the model could use a shader that supports displacement. We also might want a displacement to enhance the Diffuse texture we will create later.

   The reason I do not create a texture from polypaint is simply because I want to show what you can generate without going through the texturing process. Because the model is for a game, I'll try not to create too many unique textures. In the end, I'll end up using a rock texture I can tile and reuse on other models.

10. Set up the maps you want by selecting the Displacement, Normal, Ambient Occlusion, and Cavity buttons at the top of the Multi Map Exporter palette. Choose the map size by clicking the 4096 button. Go for the high-res textures—at worst, you must scale down the texture rather than redo all these settings again to make it larger. Set the Map Border slider to **10** and click the Flip V button. Expand the settings by selecting the Export Options button.

USING ZBRUSH PLUG-INS TO CREATE READY-TO-USE GAME CONTENT

11. Open the Displacement Map tab to set up the displacement map. Set the SubDiv level slider to **1**, and select Adaptive and SmoothUV. Activate the 32Bit button so you have all the information in the map that you need.

12. Open the Normal Map tab and press the Tangent, Adaptive, and SmoothUV buttons. Depending on the game engine you're working with (for example, the Unreal 3 engine), you may want to select the Flip G button because that's how they calculate their normals, and you may want to show the model in 3ds Max. For Maya, leave that button untouched. An easy way to flip that channel afterward is to open Photoshop, open your normal map, select the Green channel of the map, and invert it.

13. Leave the default settings under the Ambient Occlusion tab as they are; increase the Cavity Int slider to about **40**.

14. Select the Create All Maps button at the top of the palette, type in names for the textures (ZBrush automatically creates suffixes), and then select Save and voila! All textures are saved. Save the mesh by choosing the Export Mesh button at the top and leave all the default settings as they are.

The next image shows the final 6000-poly in-game model with all the textures I generated using ZBrush. I added the model to a game engine, applied all textures including the normal maps, and added a tileable rock texture because that is the most likely texture I'll use to preserve memory in my game. The shader on the model also has a nice rim light, thanks to a Fresnel effect within the game shader.

So that's a fairly easy way to create game content using only ZBrush. If you would like more explanation on all the settings and features in the plug-ins, simply check the documentation for the plug-in at **www.pixologic.com**.

CHRISTOPHER BRÄNDSTRÖM *was born and raised in the cold, northern parts of Sweden 29 years ago. He started with 3D around 2001 and has worked in the game industry for nearly 10 years, creating 12 games, including* Battlefield: Bad Company, Battlefield: Bad Company 2, Battlefield 1943, Mirror's Edge, *and* Need for Speed. *But it wasn't until 2010 that he started working full time with commercials at Framestore in London. In 2011, Christopher started working for Framestore's art department as a senior modeler, character designer, and concept artist for movies such as* World War Z *and* 47 Ronin.

www.badrobots.se

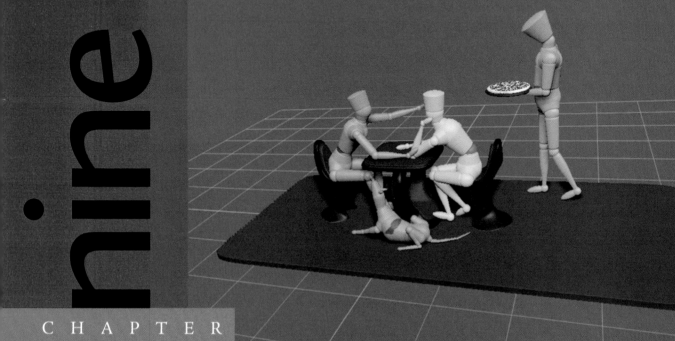

nine

Rendering—Bringing Life to Your Image

It's time to put the *finishing touches on your work, which brings us to the final chapter on rendering. Getting a good render is tough, and it takes some time to figure out the perfect settings.*

This chapter will set you on the right path to creating some really great renders with the BPR render system in ZBrush. The goal of these techniques is for you to have a basic understanding of the render system so you can create your own results. I encourage you to take these tips and expand them further for your own sculpts and projects.

- Rendering a more realistic eye
- Adjusting the shadow settings
- Creating an SSS material
- Using the filter system with BPR

Rendering a More Realistic Eye

I feel strongly that when I see a great image, the eyes are what always pull me in. The eyes can tell a story to the viewer, so I want to touch on how you can use the ZBrush BPR system to create realistic-looking eyes. You can adopt a few of the tricks in this technique for any render, not just for eyes. So let's get down to it.

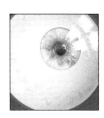

In Figure 9.1, you can see my final render of an eye. I have included this eye and all of my settings as a reference in the Chapter 9 Assets folder as a project. This file is called EyeBall.ZPR. There are two subtools in this eye project. The first subtool is called Eye Ball, and the second is called Reflect. Let's get down to re-creating this project.

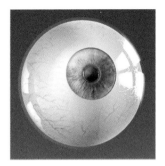

Figure 9.1 Final render of my eyeball

Creating the LightCaps

To make this tutorial a little bit easier to walk through, I have saved a tool of my eye in the Chapter 9 Assets folder so you can re-create the rendering of the final image. The LightCap system is a really quick way to create some dynamic lighting, but we will start out simple for this exercise.

1. Load StartEye.ZTL into ZBrush. You want to start with this tool, not with the project EyeBall.ZPR, because the project will contain all rendering options, materials, and anything else saved in the project. I want you to be able to duplicate the same render, so you want a completely new scene.

   When you first load the tool, the eye will have MatCap Red Wax assigned to the eyeball, and only the StartEye subtool will be visible (see Figure 9.2).

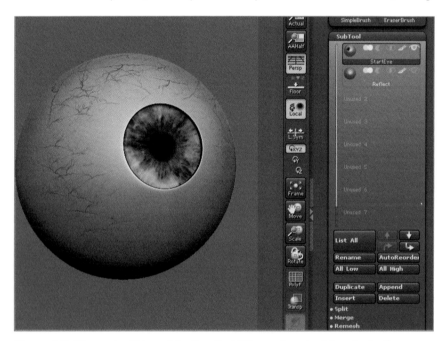

Figure 9.2 The tool will have MatCap Red Wax assigned with only the first subtool selected.

2. Select the SkinShade4 material. You will use this material to set up a DoubleShader later.

3. In the Light → LightCap subpalette, click the New Light button. This creates a light in the scene that will instantly be applied to the eye.

The LightCap system can be used in two aspects. The first is as a light creation system. You must select a standard material to take advantage of using the LightCap system this way, and the standard lights will still be used with any light created in the LightCap sub-palette. LightCap can also be used to create a MatCap material. When you wish to use LightCap to create this type of material, you must select MatCap.

---

4. Make the following adjustments and move the light into the position you see in Figure 9.3:
   - Strength = 0.9
   - Aperture = 168
   - Falloff = 3.6

5. Create another light and move this light into the position you see in Figure 9.4, which is highlighted by the red dot. Also make the following adjustments to this light:
   - Strength = 20
   - Aperture = 60

6. Set the Opacity slider to 0 on the second light. You will notice that the light turns off. Because you are making this light for reflections, you don't want it to affect the Diffuse lighting of the scene; this is why you set Opacity to 0.

7. Switch to the Specular channel at the top of the Light → LightCap subpalette and make the following adjustments, shown in Figure 9.5, to this light:
   - Select the square alpha 28 in the Alpha icon.
   - HTile = 2
   - VTile = 2
   - Scale Width = 0.7
   - Scale Height = 2.1

8. Click New Light again to create the third and final light. In Figure 9.6, you can see the position of this light.

9. Make the following adjustments to this third light:
   - Strength = 1.4
   - Select the square alpha 28 in the Alpha icon.
   - Scale Width = 1.6
   - Scale Height = 0.7

10. Select light 1 again and set the Opacity of this light to 0 in the Specular channel. You can also select the light by clicking on either arrow in Light Index slider.

11. Switch back to the Diffuse channel and make sure that the Opacity and Shadow sliders are set to 0 for lights 2 and 3.

   Now that you have lights, you need to tweak the material to help you get closer to the final render.

Adjusting the Materials

Rendering has several key components that you have to set up to accomplish a quality render. You just finished setting up your lights;

Figure 9.3 *Create a new light in the LightCap system.*

Figure 9.4 *Create a second light and make the adjustments.*

Figure 9.5 *Adjust this light to be a specular light.*

Figure 9.6 *Create a third light by clicking New Light.*

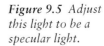

now you need to tweak the materials. With the SkinShade4 material selected, you will start by tweaking the settings for this material first.

1. In the Material → Modifiers subpalette, make the following adjustments to the SkinShade4 material:
   - Ambient = 5
   - Diffuse = 42
   - Reflectivity = 15
   - Color Bump = 1
   - At the bottom of the subpalette, click the Txtr00 icon and select Texture 01, which displays a scene of a desert. See Figure 9.7.

You are now going to use this SkinShade4 material to create a DoubleShader that will be assigned to the eye.

2. With the SkinShade4 material still selected, click the CopySH button at the top of the Material → Modifiers subpalette. This copies the SkinShade4 material (see Figure 9.8).

3. Click the DoubleShade1 material.

4. With S1 selected (see Figure 9.9), click the PasteSH button to paste the SkinShade4 material copied in step 2. S1 stands for Shader 1.

Figure 9.10 Adjust S2 (Shader2) settings.

Figure 9.7 Select Texture 01 to be applied to the SkinShade4 material.

Figure 9.8 Click the CopySH button in the Material → Modifiers subpalette.

Figure 9.9 Click the PasteSH button to paste the SkinShade4 material into the DoubleShade1 S1.

5. Click S2 (Shader2) and click PasteSH to paste the SkinShade4 material again, but this time into the second shader.

6. Make the following adjustments to this S2 shader, as shown in Figure 9.10:
   - Ambient = 100
   - Diffuse = 0
   - Specular =100
   - Reflectivity = 0
   - Color Bump = 0
   - High Dynamic Range = 1
   - Colorize Specular = 100
   - Colorize Ambient = 100
   - In the Spec icon, select a blue color.
   - In the Ambi icon, select a red color.
   - Turn off the texture in the Txtr00 icon.

7. If you look at your eye now, it will be pretty washed out. You need to mix Shader2 with the first shader. To do this, open the Material → Mixer subpalette and make the following adjustments:

- Fresnel = 100
- F Exp = 4

You should now have something like Figure 9.11.

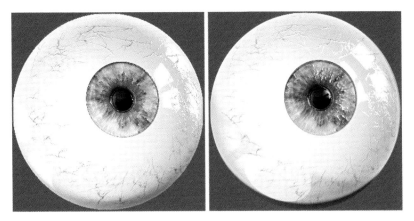

Figure 9.11 Results you should have so far: the eye not rendered (left), and after a BPR render (right)

Figure 9.12 Adjust the BPR Shadow settings to improve the shadows.

8. The shadows are not quite what we are looking for because of the default settings in the Render → BPR Shadows subpalette. Make the following adjustments, as shown in Figure 9.12:

- GStrength = 0.6
- Rays = 38
- Angle = 30
- Blur = 6

You should now have a render that is similar to Figure 9.13.

Because you have a material that is working, you need to assign it to the eyeball. Make sure to have only M (which stands for *material*) selected at the top of the interface, as shown in Figure 9.14.

9. Click the FillObject button in the Color palette. This fills the material on only the eyeball.

Figure 9.14 Select only the M at the top of the interface.

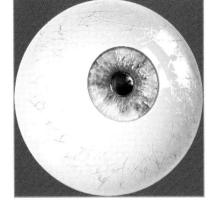

Figure 9.13 Finished BPR render with shadow adjustments

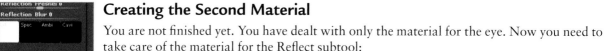

Creating the Second Material

You are not finished yet. You have dealt with only the material for the eye. Now you need to take care of the material for the Reflect subtool:

1. Select the Reflect subtool so you can start to build the material. You will notice that the eye is no longer visible.

2. Select the BasicMaterial from the Material palette and make the following adjustments:
   - Ambient = 14
   - Diffuse = 41
   - Specular = 45
   - Colorize Diffuse = 100
   - Change Dif icon color to yellow, as shown in Figure 9.15.

Figure 9.15 Select a light-yellow color for the Dif portion of the material.

3. With just the M still selected at the top of the interface, click the FillObject button in the Color palette to fill the subtool with this material.

4. This Reflect subtool is meant to provide a transparent glassy look that you see on eyes. To do this, turn on the BPR Transparent Shading button via Tool → Display Properties → BPR Settings.

Figure 9.16 Change NFactor to 1 in the Render → BPR Transparency subpalette.

5. Adjust the BPR Visibility setting to **30**. This controls the amount of transparency that the Reflect subtool has at render time. Turn the BPR Shadow slider to 0 in this subpalette as well. This tells ZBrush that this subtool will not cast shadows.

6. Choose Render → Render Properties, and turn on the Transparent button.

7. Choose Render → Render Properties, and turn on the SmoothNormals button.

8. In the Render → BPR Transparency subpalette, adjust NFactor to 1 and ByColor to **0.5**, just as you see in Figure 9.16.

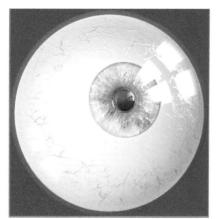

Figure 9.17 Final BPR render result of the eye

That's everything; press Shift+R to complete a BPR render. Figure 9.17 shows my final result from this technique. You have gone through several settings here. I encourage you to try playing with several of these settings to get your own result.

Adjusting the Shadow Settings

Shadows are a key component in bringing more realism to your renders. I'm often asked about the settings used to create good shadows with the BPR render system. This section covers those settings so you have a better understanding of how to produce particular shadow results. After you learn what these settings can do for you, you can apply them to the BPR Ao and BPR SSS subpalettes. You will find the same sliders in all three of the subpalettes. Follow these steps to explore the shadow settings:

1. Let's start by loading a project. In the Project menu of LightBox, open the Mannequin folder and double-click Mnqn_Scene1.ZPR, shown in Figure 9.18.

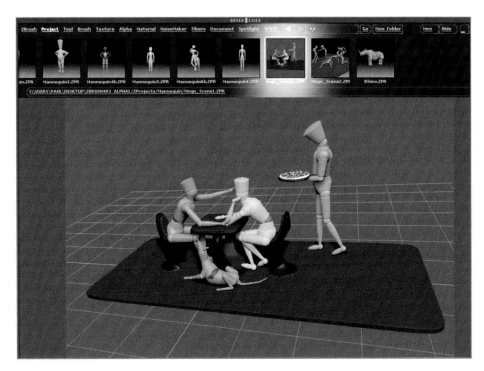

Figure 9.18 Load `Mnqn_Scene1.ZPR` *from the LightBox Project menu.*

You can see the default BPR Shadow settings in Figure 9.19. These settings will give the shadows a sharp look. Press Shift+R or click the BPR button to render out this scene.

2. Let's try making some adjustments so you understand exactly what these settings are doing to shadows. First, let's change the direction of the light. In the Light palette, move the light to the top-right corner, as shown in Figure 9.20.

Before you start playing with all the shadow settings, I want to give a quick overview of each slider:

FStrength controls how strong the shadows will be on the floor when the floor grid is activated.

GStrength is a global setting to control the strength of all the shadows. This works with the Material → Environment Shadow slider. This slider is covered further later in this chapter.

Rays tells ZBrush the number of light rays that each light will cast. This works with the Angle slider.

Angle moves each ray cast in degrees based on this slider.

Res controls the pixel resolution of the shadows being cast. I usually like to start this around twice the size of the biggest document resolution.

Blur blurs the shadows by pixels.

VDepth offsets the shadow's position by pixels.

Figure 9.19 The default settings of the project will create sharp shadows.

Figure 9.20 Move the default light to the upper-right corner.

LDepth offsets the light position in pixels. Moving the slider in the negative direction moves the light closer to the camera. Moving this slider in the positive direction moves the light farther away from the camera.

Spd sets a subpixel depth calculation, which gives shadows greater accuracy.

Gamma controls how much gray value transition appears where the shadows fall on the surface and where the shadows do not fall on the surface.

Falloff controls how fast shadows taper off.

Max Dist controls the shadow not being completely cast when turned up but will cast with a slight gradual change. An example of this can be found in Figure 9.26 later in this chapter.

DistFalloff controls how fast the gradual change occurs when using the Max Dist slider.

3. Press Shift+R again to BPR render. You can see in Figure 9.21 that when the render is done with the default settings, the shadows are pretty harsh. Let's see what we can do to soften them up.

4. To soften the shadows, move the Rays slider to **30** and Angle to **30**. Press Shift+R again to render out the scene. You can see how much these two sliders affect your shadows; the shadows are more spread out in Figure 9.22.

5. Set GStrength to **0.75** so all the shadows are less intense.

6. Set Rays to **20** and Angle to **5**. You can see in Figure 9.23 that we get a sharp shadow now with softer edges.

7. Move the Blur to **12**. This causes the shadows to blur by 12 pixels, as you can see in Figure 9.24.

Figure 9.21 *Press Shift+R to complete a BPR render. These shadows will be harsh.*

Figure 9.22 *Adjust the Rays and Angle sliders to 30 for a more spread-out shadow.*

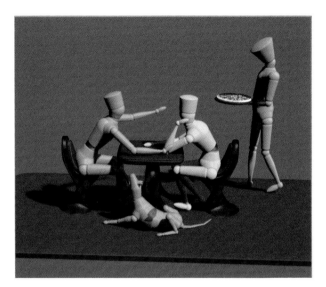

Figure 9.23 *Adjust Rays to 20 and Angle to 5 for harsh shadows with soft edges.*

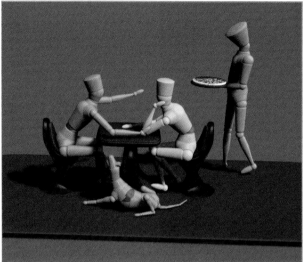

Figure 9.24 *Adjust the Blur slider to 12 to blur all shadows by 12.*

8. Every model in ZBrush will have a material assigned to it. For this model, we have the SkinShade4 selected. In the Material → Environment subpalette, set the Shadow slider to **50**. This causes the shadows to be at 50 percent strength on the material. But as you may remember, in step 5 we set GStrength, which stands for global strength, to 0.75. So let's turn the GStrength back up to **1** and complete the BPR render to get results similar to those in Figure 9.25.

So what have you learned here? Let's recap:

- To create harsh shadows, set the Rays slider to a reasonable level and set the Angle slider to something below **5**.

- For a harsh shadow with a soft edge, set Rays to something around **20** and Angle higher than **10**.

- If you want to blur the shadows, just turn up the Blur slider to pixel-blur the shadows.

- The strength of shadows is controlled by two sliders:

  - GStrength is a global slider to affect all shadows on every material.

  - The Material → Environment Shadow slider controls shadow strength individually on a material-by-material basis.

Figure 9.25 *Set the Material → Environment Shadow slider to 50 and the GStrength slider back to 1.*

The last settings I want to cover are Max Dist and DistFalloff. You can see in Figure 9.26 how these two settings control whether the shadow is cast at 100 percent strength or whether it slowly tapers off. When you turn up Max Dist, more of the shadow is cast, but the closer you get to 0.1, the less of the shadow will be cast. When DistFalloff is lower, the gradient of shadow cast off will be slower. You can use these two sliders to produce some really unique shadows.

In all four images of Figure 9.26, I also had VDepth set to -4.

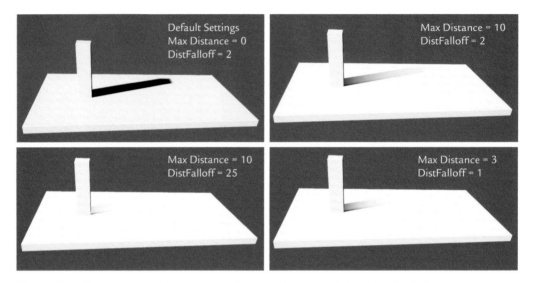

Figure 9.26 *Four images with changes to the Max Dist and DistFalloff with VDepth at -4*

There you have it. You now have a better understanding of shadows. Let's put some of this technique to the test and create a four-shader material that will also have an SSS render in the material.

Creating an SSS Material

You must consider several factors when you want to create a material with a realistic SSS quality. SSS stands for *subsurface scattering*, which occurs when light penetrates the surface of an object, is scattered by interacting with the material, and exits the surface at different points. Even though I am about to lay out the steps for creating this material, the model that you use for rendering will have a major effect on the outcome. For example, does your model have polypaint or no polypaint, and what is the person's skin color? These factors will really alter the outcome of the render.

Two more factors will also affect the render's outcome: the lighting and how the materials will be blended. Your ultimate goal is to create something that is similar to what you can see in Figure 9.27, which originates from a Pixologic post at www.zbrushcentral.com/showthread.php?164247.

Let's walk through the steps to create the material needed for an SSS result. I have combined the eye from this chapter with the scan data of Joseph Drust's head from Chapter 6. You will start with the lighting that I set up for the eyes and expand from there. Load the SSS_Project.ZPR file from the Chapter 9 Assets folder.

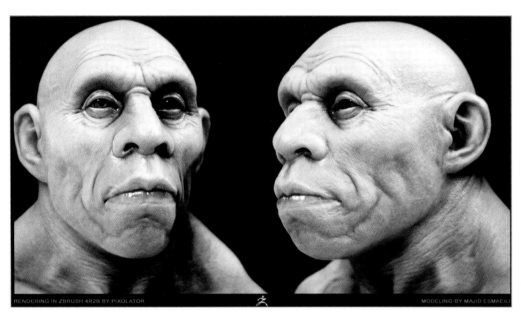

Figure 9.27 The final render from the Pixologic site. The sculpt was completed by Majid Esmaeili, and the final render was completed by Pixologic.

Adjusting the Lights

Because you already have polypaint on this model, you will adjust your main lights. Remember that you created three lights in the LightCap system when you made the eye. These three lights will affect the render along with the standard lights. You will keep the lights in the LightCap system but change the lights in the main Light palette.

Figure 9.28 Adjust the main light in the Light palette.

1. In the Light palette, move the light to the position you see in Figure 9.28. Turn Ambient to 0 and choose a light-blue color with an Intensity of **0.85**.

2. Create a second light by double-clicking the second light icon.

3. Select a blue that is slightly darker than the light blue you chose earlier, and adjust the Intensity to **0.625**.

4. You want to make this light a rim light, so click once on the orange dot to do so. Then move the dot to the upper right, as shown in Figure 9.29.

    This is a great start. You have a total of five lights in the scene: three in LightCap and two in the main light system. We may need to revisit the lights, but first let's get going on the material.

Figure 9.29 Create a second light as a rim light.

Building the Material

Building a material may be daunting, but it's really simple if you break it down to one shader at a time. This is the main goal of this tip. I really want you to take this tip and expand on it to create your very own four-shader materials.

As you can see in Figure 9.30, our model is pretty shiny right now. He almost looks like a piece of metal. You need to change this look, so let's build a four-shader material.

1. Select the SkinShade4 material and click the CopySH button shown in Figure 9.31. This copies all of S1, or Shader 1, of the SkinShade4 material.

2. Select the QuadShaders material. This material has four shaders that will allow us to paste different shaders in each channel. With just M activated at the top of the interface, fill this material on the model by clicking FillObject in the Color palette.

3. With S1 selected in the QuadShaders material, click PasteSH to paste the SkinShade4 S1, or Shader 1, channel you copied in step 2 to this material. In Figure 9.32, you can see that S1, S2, S3, and S4 can all be selected and that all four shaders are activated because every icon number has an open circle indicator.

4. With this material on the model, you will notice that he is washed out (see the left image of Figure 9.33). Turn off S2, S3, and S4 of the QuadShader by clicking the open circles. This will make each open circle closed, which indicates that the shaders are not activated. Notice in the right image of Figure 9.33 how the model is less washed-out now.

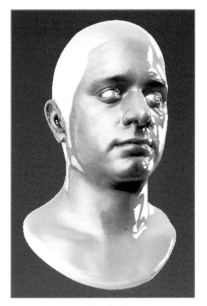

Figure 9.30 After light adjustments, the model will look pretty shiny.

Figure 9.31 Click the CopySH button to copy Shader 1 of SkinShade4 material.

Figure 9.32 Paste the copied shader from the SkinShade4 material into S1 of the QuadShaders.

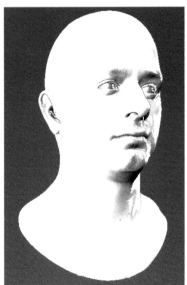
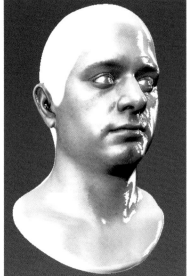

Figure 9.33 With all four shaders on, the model is washed out (left). When the S2, S3, and S4 are turned off, the model is less washed out (right).

5. You want to use this shader as the material that controls mostly diffuse. Make the following adjustments to this shader:
   - Ambient = 41
   - Diffuse = 66
   - Specular = 4
   - Colorize Specular = 0
   - High Dynamic Range = 1
   - AnisotropicDiffuse = 0.2031
   - AnisotropicSpecular = 0
   - Maintain Specular = 1
   - PhongBlinn = 1

6. You also need to adjust the DiffuseCurve and SpecularCurve. Adjust the curves to be something close to Figure 9.34.

7. At the bottom of this material, I also adjusted the Dif color to be more pink. The exact code for this color is Red = **240**, Green = **99**, Blue = **126**. You can plug in these numbers in the Color palette and then drag-click the Dif icon color swatch to the Main Color swatch (see Figure 9.35).

8. With S1, or Shader 1 done, let's move on to S2. Select the HSV Colorizer material.

9. Select S2 of this material and click the CopySH button to copy the shader.

10. Select the QuadShaders material you have been working on and activate the S2 shader by clicking the closed circle to make it open again.

11. Click the PasteSH button to paste this shader into the QuadShader. You should have something similar to Figure 9.36.

12. You will be using this shader to add a little bit of red color to the skin, as shown in Figure 9.37. Make the following adjustments to this shader:
    - Color Blend = 0
    - Saturation = 1
    - Intensity = 0.2582
    - Colorize Shaded Color = 0.24
    - Additive Color swatch to Red = 254
    - BlendColor swatch to Red = 227

Figure 9.34 Match the DiffuseCurve and SpecularCurve.

Figure 9.35 Adjust the Dif color swatch to a more pink color.

Figure 9.36 Paste the HSV Colorizer in S2 of the QuadShader.

Before you move on to the next step, I want to make sure that you completely understand how important this next step is. When you are making a material with multiple shaders, ZBrush has a very powerful feature in the Material palette called Mixer. This tells ZBrush how to mix the select shader with all other shaders before it. If you do not change any of the Mixer settings, you are not taking full advantage of the BPR render system. So without further ado, I give you the Mixer subpalette.

Figure 9.37 Make adjustments to the HSV Colorizer to give a red undertone color to the model.

Figure 9.38 Make adjustments to the Mixer subpalette of S2.

13. Open the Material → Mixer subpalette and make the following adjustments to this shader's mixer, as shown in Figure 9.38:
    - Fresnel = -94
    - F Exp = 0.7828
    - Change the blend mode to Exclusion
    - Turn on Black if it's not already on
    - MaxOpacity = 66
    - PreviewOpacity = 1

14. You are on your way. On to S3, or Shader 3. Select the S1 shader again in the QuadShader you are building and click the CopySH button again. Remember, this copies the selected shader.

15. Click the S3 button again and click the PasteSH button to paste S1 into this channel. Also remember that you need to turn this shader on by clicking the closed circle.

16. You want to use this shader as your Specular channel, so you need to make some adjustments again to this S3 to drive your specularity. Make the following adjustments:
    - Ambient = 46
    - Diffuse = 7
    - Specular = 100
    - High Dynamic Range = 1.1
    - AnisotropicDiffuse = 0.1004
    - Also make adjustments to the SpecularCurve to make the specularity tighter, as shown in Figure 9.39.

17. Remember, before you move on to S4, or Shader 4, you need to tell ZBrush how to mix this shader with the other two in front of it. Make the following adjustments to the Material → Mixer subpalette for this shader (see Figure 9.40):
    - Fresnel = 94
    - F Exp = 1.0495
    - Change Blend mode to Screen.
    - If it's not already on, turn Black on.
    - In the Color swatch, click and drag the cursor to select a brown color similar to the one in Figure 9.40. Mine was Red = 81, Green = 49, Blue = 36.
    - By Sat = 25
    - Sat Exp = 17

In the preceding settings, I mentioned that Black should be turned on. This is key because you tell ZBrush to blend the selected shader with no other shader information from the previous shaders. Instead it will blend as if the previous shaders were black.

Figure 9.39 Adjust the SpecularCurve of the S3 shader.

18. One more shader to go. Select the S2 shader again in your QuadShaders. Click the CopySH button to copy this shader.

19. Select the S4 shader and click the PasteSH button to paste the HSV Colorizer into S4. You are going to use this as your SSS shader.

20. Make the following adjustments to the S4 HSV Colorizer shader, as shown in Figure 9.41:

    • Color Blend = 0.5272
    • Intensity = 0.5202
    • Colorize shaded color = 0.3606

21. Now don't forget about that Mixer sub-palette. This is where you will inform ZBrush that you would like this shader to be an SSS channel. Open the Material → Mixer subpalette and make the following adjustments, as shown in Figure 9.42:

    • Fresnel = -87
    • F Exp = 0.3389
    • SSS = 100
    • S Exp = 1.1676
    • Change the Blend mode to Exclusion.
    • MaxOpacity = 50
    • PreviewOpacity = 1

22. In the Material → Environment subpalette, turn the Shadow and Ao sliders to 0. This ensures that the S4 shader will not cast shadows or ambient occlusion.

23. Before you complete a BPR render, turn on the SSS button in the Render → Render Properties subpalette. Then complete a render by pressing Shift+R or by clicking the BPR button. Figure 9.43 shows my results for a BPR render.

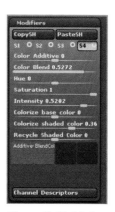

Figure 9.40 Make adjustments to the Mixer subpalette of S3.

Figure 9.41 Make adjustments to S4 HSV Colorizer.

Figure 9.42 Adjust the Mixer of S4 to make it an SSS channel.

Making Adjustments to the Render

I'm sure you have the same issue as I do with the model: it has way too much specularity. Let's make some changes to get a better render. Remember, lights are a key component to rendering, so let's start there:

1. In the Light palette, adjust the intensity of the second light to **1**.

2. Open the Light → LightCap subpalette. Make sure to have the Specular button activated. Select light 1 and adjust the Strength from 20 to **0.681**. This change to Strength will draw back a lot of the specularity.

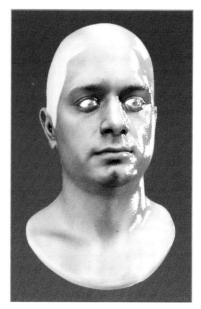

Figure 9.43 A BPR render at the current stage

Figure 9.44
*Adjust light 2
in the LightCap
system.*

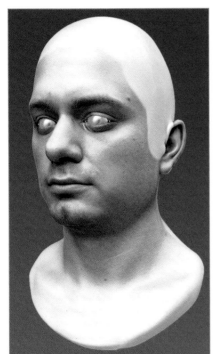

Figure 9.45 *BPR render after
specularity changes*

3. As you remember, you made three lights in LightCap. These will all have an effect on the specularity. Select light 2 now and make the following adjustments, as shown in Figure 9.44:
   - Strength = 0.681
   - Opacity = 0.758
   - Select a blue color for this light.

4. Select light 3 in the LightCap system. Make the following adjustments to this light:
   - Strength = 1
   - HTile = 2
   - VTile = 2
   - Scale Width = 0.4881
   - Scale Height = 0.5576

5. The S3 shader in the material is driving the specularity, so you want to adjust it. Select the S3 shader.

6. Open the Material → Mixer subpalette and turn By Cavity to -58 and the Cavity Exp to 0.4. This adjusts the specularity so it does not penetrate into the cavities of the sculpt, and also breaks up the specularity of the model.

   Figure 9.45 shows the current state of our BPR render.

7. Let's keep making some adjustments here. Turn on the AOcclusion button in the Render → Render Properties subpalette so you can start to use AO in the render.

   With this button on, you need to make adjustments to all the render settings in the BPR Render subpalettes. Figure 9.46 shows all of the changes I made to each subpalette, but let's break them down one at a time.

8. In the Render → Render Properties subpalette, set Global Ambient to -10.

9. In BPR Transparency, set ByColor to 1, Strength to 0.2, and NFactor to 0.2.

10. In the Render → BPR Shadow subpalette, make the following adjustments:
    - Rays = 11
    - Angle = 23
    - Blur = 3
    - Gamma = 1.9

11. Adjust the Render → BPR Ao subpalette to the following:
    - Rays = 20
    - Angle = 180
    - Res = 1942
    - Blur = 8
    - Gamma = 1.75

12. In the Render → BPR SSS subpalette, make the following adjustments:
    - Rays = 10
    - Angle = 360
    - Blur = 10

13. In the Tool → Display Properties subpalette, you need to adjust the transparency of the two spheres that are called Left Reflect and Right Reflect. Move the Tool → Display Properties → BPR Visibility slider to 50 for each of these, as shown in Figure 9.46.

14. I also changed the color for both of these spheres to a blue; go ahead and do the same.

15. Pick a color from the skin tones and paint the back of the head where there is white so it looks a little more like a skin blend.

    Let's see what we have in a BPR render. Figure 9.47 shows what render I get with the changes.

    You have a pretty good render here, but you can do a few more things to make it even more believable. If you duplicate this QuadShader material twice, you can use one of the duplicates to paint specularity where you want it and the other one to give a little more shine to the lips.

16. Select the QuadShaders material you created for this head and click the CopyMat button at the bottom left of the Material palette (see Figure 9.48).

17. Now select a Standard material that you are not using in the scene. I selected the ReflectedFoil material. Click the PasteMat button at the bottom right of the Material palette.

    In the preceding two steps, you have another QuadShader material in the palette with all the settings adjusted to what you have already done. However, you are going to change one thing for the lips, and this new material will be called QuadShaders1.

18. Select S1 (Shader1), turn the Specular slider to **50**, and turn up the Gel Shading slider to **3**. This will help give the lips a wet look.

19. Select the Standard brush and turn on only the M (for *material*) at the top of the interface.

20. Now just paint on the lips with this material, as shown in Figure 9.49.

    You may notice when you start to paint that the materials do not have a smooth transition between them. You can take care of this with one setting.

21. In the Render palette, turn the Materials Blend-Radius to **15**. This slider blends all materials by pixels at render time, in this case by 15 pixels. Be careful, because the higher you go, the longer the render will take. Go ahead and complete a render to see what you have. Figure 9.50 shows what the new material does to the lips.

Figure 9.46
BPR Render subpalette settings that were adjusted

Figure 9.48
Click the CopyMat button to copy the QuadShaders material. Click the PasteMat button to paste this material into another Standard material.

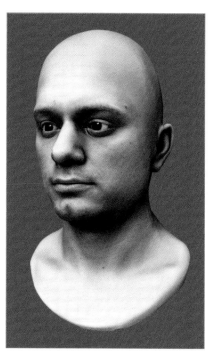

Figure 9.47 Final render before using the filter system

22. Select the QuadShaders material again.

23. Click the CopyMat button again.

24. Select a Standard material that is not being used in the scene. In my case, I selected the Chrome material.

25. Click the PasteMat button to paste another version of this QuadShader material. By default, it is named QuadShaders2.

26. In S3 (Shader3) of this material, play with your SpecularCurve to make a wider specular range for this material. I have exaggerated my curve in Figure 9.51 so you can see my results when I render.

27. Now just paint where you want more specularity. I put more on the forehead and along the jaw, but you can have some fun with this (see Figure 9.52).

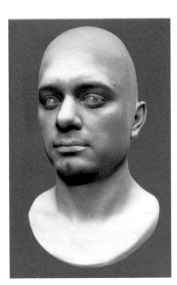

Figure 9.49 *Paint on the lips with the QuadShaders1 material.*

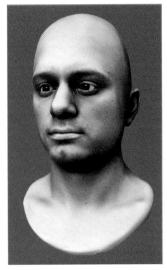

Figure 9.50 *BPR render of face with both materials applied and Materials Blend-Radius turned to 5*

Figure 9.51 *Adjust the SpecularCurve of S3.*

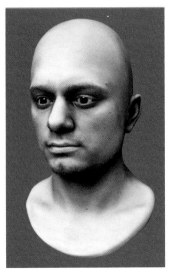

Figure 9.52 *Paint this material where you want more specularity.*

Have some fun with these last steps to get some really cool results. Let's finish up this render by using the BPR Filter system in ZBrush.

Using the Filter System with BPR

Even after all of these changes, you can still add some big adjustments to the final render with the BPR Filter system. The great thing about these filters is that they will update in real time. This allows us some really great freedom to manipulate the render on the fly.

The sliders that I adjust the most are Strength, Radius, and Mask. All the other sliders will tell ZBrush how the filter should be blended with the render. Think of this as similar to how you blended the material shaders together with the Mixer subpalette.

1. Let's start by clicking the closed circle in F1 to activate a filter: select the Blur filter. I am going to exaggerate this so you can see what it will do. Make the following adjustments (also see Figure 9.53):

   - Strength = 1
   - Radius = 7
   - Depth = 1. This tells ZBrush to blur based on the depth of the model.
   - Depth A = -0.0492. This is the starting point for where the blur will gradually begin. You can click this slider and drag out to the model to actually select a point of interest.
   - Depth B = 0.25. This will be the starting point where everything is 100 pecent blurry. You can also click and drag to the model, so you can select the starting point of the 100 percent blur.

2. For the F2 slot, select the Sharpen filter. Make the following adjustments, as shown in Figure 9.54:

   - Strength = 0.8
   - Radius = 1
   - Mask = 1. This tells ZBrush to apply this filter to only the model and not the background.

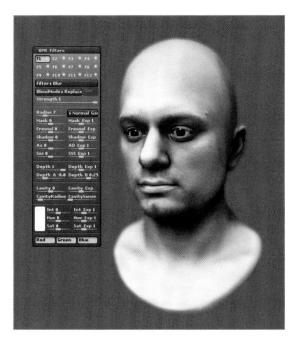

Figure 9.53 *Render with Blur filter applied*

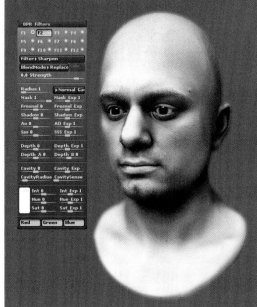

Figure 9.54 *Render with the Blur and Sharpen filters on*

3. In F3, select the Red filter. Make the following adjustments to get what you see in Figure 9.55:
   - Strength = 0.2
   - Mask = 1. Remember, this tells ZBrush to apply this filter to only the model.
   - Fresnel = 1. This tells ZBrush to apply this adjustment to only the faces that are not facing the camera along the edge of the model.

4. For F4, I want to add some very subtle blue to the render. Select the Blue filter for this and make the following adjustments (see Figure 9.56):
   - Strength = 1
   - Mask = 1
   - Fresnel = -1. This tells ZBrush to apply the blue only to the surface faces that are facing the camera.

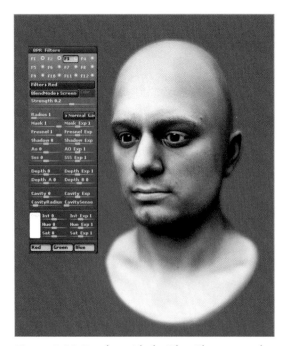 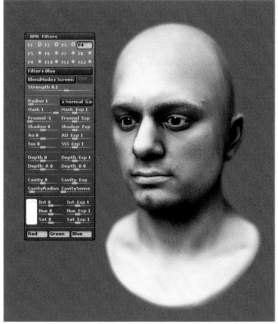

Figure 9.55 Render with the Blur, Sharpen, and Red filters activated

Figure 9.56 Adding a Blue filter to bring that color a little more into the render

5. This will be the last filter. In the F5 slot, add another Sharpen filter. Make the following adjustments, as shown in Figure 9.57:
   - Strength = 1
   - Mask = 1

6. The last thing you can do is turn on the Material → Wax Modifiers to add a little more red under the skin. Turn the Strength of the Wax Modifier to 55 and the Fresnel to **100**. See Figure 9.58 for the final result.

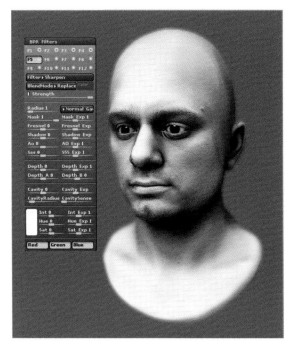

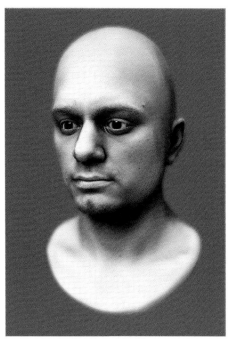

Figure 9.57 Add another Sharpen filter.

Figure 9.58 *Turn on the Material → Wax Modifiers to add a little bit more red under the skin.*

What a journey you have had with this render. I have saved this final file as SSS_ Project.ZPR on the DVD in the Chapter 9 Assets folder. You can see how much filters can change the look of a render. There are so many options here that you could keep making your model look completely different. I encourage you to keep turning on filters and playing around to discover more interesting results. Don't be scared to experiment. Often I discover my best workflows and results during the experimenting phase.

ARTIST SPOTLIGHT: MARK DEDECKER
A DYNAMESH ZSPHERE WORKFLOW

THIS TUTORIAL COVERS the use of ZSpheres and DynaMesh in unison for developing a character.

The amazing freedom of DynaMesh lets us quickly flesh out a character, while ZSpheres let us get back all of our lowest subdivision levels on the fly to create a really fun workflow.

Initially I like to start out with a nicely poly-modeled head with topology that can be animated. Then I sculpt the subtle features of the character. This method enables me to hit the character's likeness while not going too high in polycount. The following image is a great example of a model at level 3, or 20,000 polygons.

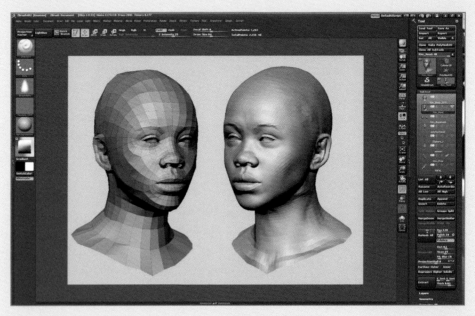

With the head fleshed out, we can now use body references to line it up. I prefer to line everything up by using the Image Plane plug-in in the Texture palette.

Follow these steps:

1. With your model in Edit mode, import your reference into the Texture palette.

2. From the Image Plane menu, choose Load Image.

   If you open the Reference Views menu within the Image Plane menu, you may want to lower the model's Opacity slider so that you can better line up the model to your reference.

3. Line up your model and store the various positions in the Reference Views menu.

A DYNAMESH ZSPHERE WORKFLOW

4. Now for some DynaMesh fun! In the Tool → SubTool subpalette, duplicate your head by clicking the Duplicate button. DynaMesh changes your topology, so you need to save it for later.

5. Rename the head **Dynamesh_head**.

6. In the Tool → Geometry subpalette, click Freeze SubDivision Levels. This drops your head to the lowest level for DynaMeshing and will preserve the higher levels when you exit DynaMesh.

7. Now click the DynaMesh button to enter DynaMesh. You will see in this image that DynaMesh closed any holes in the model. The resolution of the DynaMesh will vary depending on the size of the model. For this model, I put the resolution at 128.

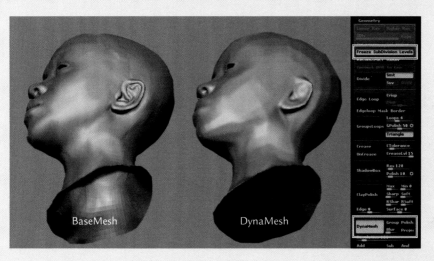

Now we are going to start fleshing out the body.

8. With the reference stored from previous steps, take the Snake Hook, Move, and ClayBuildup brushes and rough out the main form of the torso, as shown in the following image.

When the topology starts to get too distorted or unmanageable, Ctrl+drag in any open space of the document. DynaMesh will automatically add more topology and retopologize the regions you adjusted, as shown in the following image.

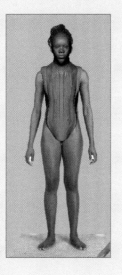

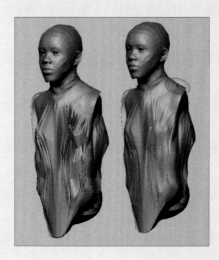

A DYNAMESH ZSPHERE WORKFLOW

Now that the torso is roughed out, it's time to create your ZSphere armature. Pulling out limbs in DynaMesh can be tricky, so let's use ZSpheres.

9. Append a ZSphere as a new subtool. Scale down the ZSphere so it's inside the torso and create an armature that matches the reference, as shown in the following image.

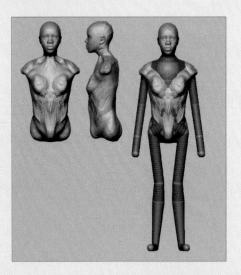

10. In the Tool → Adaptive Skin subpalette, select Use Classic Skinning. Create an adaptive skin by clicking the Make Adaptive Skin button so you have results similar to the following image.

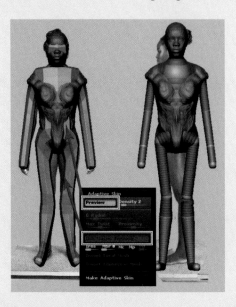

Now let's combine the adaptive skin with our DynaMesh for further sculpting.

11. Append the adaptive skin as a new subtool and duplicate.

12. Use the Move brush to push the adaptive skin back into the model, where it overlaps the original sculpture, as shown in the following image.

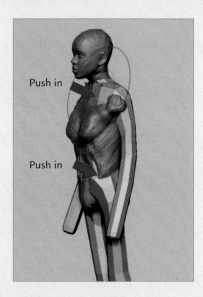

13. In the Tool → SubTool subpalette, make sure your torso tool is above the adaptive skin. Click the Merge Down button and re-enter DynaMesh, as shown in the following image. The adaptive skin and the torso are now one piece. Finish up your base sculpture at this point. Remember, DynaMesh isn't for high details.

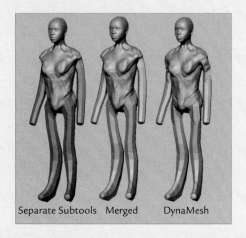

Separate Subtools   Merged   DynaMesh

A DYNAMESH ZSPHERE WORKFLOW

With your sculpture roughed out, it's time to get your levels back into your ZTool by using the previous duplication of your initial adaptive skin.

14. In Transparency Ghost mode, using the Move brush, make sure the adaptive skin is over the top of your sculpture, as shown in the following image. You will want to project it to your DynaMesh model, so you need to make sure it is outside of that.

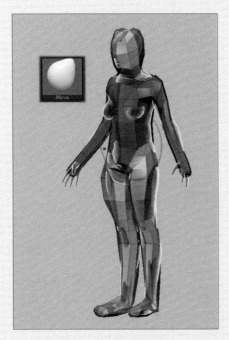

15. With your adaptive skin in position, divide the positioned skin to the level of detail that you want and click the Project All button in the Tool → SubTool subpalette. Make sure that only the adaptive skin and the DynaMesh models are visible

when doing the Project All. Otherwise, ZBrush will try to project all subtools into the mesh.

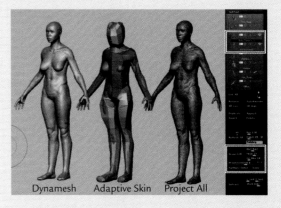

Dynamesh   Adaptive Skin   Project All

After the skin is projected, you have a model with five subdivisions, just like the following image.

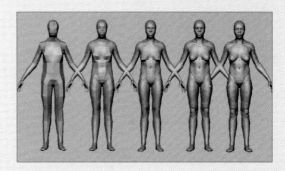

The power of this technique is that you can always DynaMesh new parts (a third arm, for example) and add them to your ZSphere, creating a new adaptive skin. You can then repeat the process of projecting the new adaptive skin.

MARK DEDECKER *has worked as the lead character artist at Gentle Giant Studios and Ignition Entertainment, specializing in high- and low-resolution modeling and texturing for film and game characters. Currently a freelance character artist and Gnomon School instructor, Mark has worked on numerous films, games, and collectibles. Some of Mark's work can be seen in* Golden Axe, Iron Man, *and* Species—The Awakening. *His digital-double work has been in films such as* The Hulk, 10,000 BC, *and* Watchmen. *Mark's bust of* Spiderman 3's *Venom was featured on the June 2007 cover of* ToyFare *magazine. Mark graduated from the Gnomon School of Visual Effects in 2006.*

http://monkeymuscle.blogspot.com/

ARTIST SPOTLIGHT: JULIAN KENNING
CREATING AND RENDERING A TOON SHADER MATERIAL

MORE THAN JUST a tip, this mini tutorial is meant to kick-start your discovery of the power of ZBrush shader editing. It should encourage you to start making your own custom materials and, with the right lighting, get exactly the render you imagine for your sculpt. The toon shader we are creating here is just an example of what can be done and how you can use one material in different ways. But let's start with a few basics.

I am going to use the QuadShaders to build the toon shader. Normally I use only three or four slots of the QuadShaders. I like to build my material on the base of QuadShaders so I have the fourth slot as an option for an additional shader I might want later, such as an SSS shader. Follow these steps:

1. Pick the SkinShade4 material in the Material palette. Copy and paste the shader into the first and second shader of QuadShaders by clicking the CopySH button in the Material → Modifiers subpalette and then selecting each shader and clicking PasteSH.

2. Deactivate the other two shaders for now, by clicking the tiny circles next to S3 and S4.

3. Your settings of the first shader should match the following settings and the following image:

   - Ambient slider = 10
   - Diffuse slider = 63
   - Specular slider = 11

4. Select the second shader and make the Diffuse Curve similar to the following image for Shader 2. Also make the adjustments to the following sliders:

   - Ambient slider = 3
   - Diffuse slider = 35
   - Specular slider = 27

5. From the Light menu, adjust the light position and Intensity Curve of the first light to match the settings you see in the following image. Also set the Intensity itself to **1.4533**.

6. Create a second light by clicking the second light icon, shown in the following image, and set the following options:

   - Set the Intensity to **2**.
   - Turn the Shadow button on.
   - Match the Intensity Curve to what you see in the image.
   - Move the light position to match what you see in the image.

CREATING AND RENDERING A TOON SHADER MATERIAL

For now we need just one main light from the front as the key light, and one light as a backlight. Light 1 is the key light, and light 2 is the backlight.

You change a front light into a backlight by clicking (without dragging) the little light dot once to "send it to the back." If you click it again, it comes back to the front. When the light is located in the back, the light sphere front turns dark, as shown in the image on the left side.

7. In the Render palette, activate only Shadows and Flatten under Render Properties.

8. In the Render → BPR Shadows subpalette, set the following options, as shown in the next image:
   - FStrength = 0.7
   - Rays = 6
   - Angle = 0
   - Blur = 0

The FStrength influences only the strength of the shadow on the floor. You may set that to whatever you prefer.

9. If you want your object to cast a shadow on the floor, don't forget to activate the floor grid in the Draw menu, which serves as an orientation grid and basically turns on "invisible" floor for the render.

10. Finally—hit the BPR render button beside the top-right corner of your viewport or use the shortcut Shift+R. You should get similar results to the render of my bald little guy here.

All right—so far, so good. We got an overall decent diffuse shading, and some not-too-drastic specular. Maybe it's a little flat still, but for a quick first render, it's not too bad. Now, what if we want the shading to be a bit deeper with some more defined highlights on top of what we already have? No problem—that is where the second shader comes into play.

The second shader literally doubles the diffuse and specular level options, which means we can layer a more focused diffuse channel on top of a very wide one, and a sharp glossy specularity on a more subtle and slightly wider channel, which gives four layers and levels of light reflection.

11. Activate Shader 2, and match the specular curve to the following image, because we want the specularity to be sharper and less wide. As a general rule, the more concave your curve, the wider the light reflection on your object. The more convex your curve, the sharper and more narrow the light reflection.

CREATING AND RENDERING A TOON SHADER MATERIAL

To get a very sharp and glossy/wet specularity, as on an eyeball, you drag the curve inward so much that it almost disappears in the lower-right corner.

12. Render again and you should see an appearance similar to my second render.

13. I can't go into the details of each and every option for the shaders here, but three have a strong impact on your diffuse and specular reflection, apart from the obvious Strength sliders and Curve adjustments:

   AnisotropicDiffuse: the higher you push the slider, the wider the diffuse reflection will be spread away from the center to a point where it appears to be wrapping around the object's sides.

   AnisotropicSpecular does the same as AnisotropicDiffuse, but for the specular reflection.

   PhongBlinn Specular can spread/blur your specular reflection to be more like a Phong or Blinn material. Move the slider all the way to the right to make the material a Blinn.

Before you get to the next part, play around with all the settings mentioned so far and observe the effects. Nothing beats learning by doing!

Getting More Advanced with the Toon Shader

To start, take a look at this character I am working on in a normal render, to highlight the difference you should look for in the final product.

1. Before you start working on the shader in ZBrush, create an image of a flat, filled circle with an outline in Photoshop or any other 2D application. This image can also be found in the `Julian Kenning Asset` folder on the DVD and is called `TOONsphere.PSD`.

It's important that the image is of a fixed ratio such as 512×512 and that the sphere fills the image to the edges. The thickness and appearance of the circle stroke depends on how strong you want the outline to be in your shader. Feel free to experiment with a few variations. Also, fill the background with black to make sure no white appears in your cartoon shader outline. I kept it white in the example so you can see the shape of the circle.

CREATING AND RENDERING A TOON SHADER MATERIAL

This image will add to the flat appearance of the shader, ensuring that the character always has a bit of an outline. We want this outline because we are aiming for a cartoon shader.

2. In ZBrush, load TOONsphere.PSD or your image into your Texture palette.

3. From the Material palette, select Framer03, copy its first shader (ignore the second), and paste it into the Shader 3 of a Tri shader material.

4. Select the first shader (S1) and make the following adjustments to the sliders:

- Ambient = 46
- Diffuse = 100
- Specular = 3
- Colorize Specular = 10
- AnisotropicDiffuse = 0.21
- AnisotropicSpecular = 0.25
- CavityIntensity = 1000
- Cavity Radius = 1
- Cavity Diffuse = 1
- Occluded Ambient = -0.15
- PhongBlinn Specular = 0.32

5. Match the DiffuseCurve in Shader 1 (S1) to the following image.

6. Match the SpecularCurve for Shader 1 to the following image.

7. Select the second shader (S2) and make the following adjustments. Also adjust the DiffuseCurve similar to Shader 1's DiffuseCurve.

- Ambient = 0
- Diffuse = 63
- Specular = 8

- HighDynamicRange = 2.35
- Colorize Ambient = 21
- PhongBlinn Specular = 0.09

8. Open the Material → Mixer subpalette and adjust the Fresnel to **-100** and the F Exp to **3.5**. This tells ZBrush how to mix this second shader with the first shader.

9. Select Shader 3 (S3) now (this is the Frame03). Make the following adjustments:

- Intensity A = 5
- Depth A = 0.59
- OverwriteColor = 0.27

10. In the bottom-left corner of the Material → Modifiers subpalette, click the texture icon. The Texture palette pops up. As you remember, in step 2 we loaded the TOONsphere.PSD file. Select this file.

A tip for tweaking individual shaders: start out by activating only the one you are adjusting, and then alternate between that and seeing it work together with the others.

CREATING AND RENDERING A TOON SHADER MATERIAL

11. Take your time to match the settings. When you are finished, activate only Shaders 1 and 3. Select BPR Render or press Shift+R and you should get results similar to my masked fellow in the following image (top).

12. Activate Shader 2 and render again. You should have something similar to the following image (bottom).

On a side note, depending on whether your object is textured or not, you might want to adjust the intensity of your lights. Textured objects tend to need quite a bit more light than plain white sculpts.

If you want the shadow and light transitions even sharper and more harsh, you can adjust the light curves just the same way we adjusted the shader curves, by making them rectangular, as shown in the following image.

The following image shows the resulting render after the lights have been adjusted.

CREATING AND RENDERING A TOON SHADER MATERIAL

13. A quick way to get a slightly softer look is to activate the Tool → Material → Wax Modifier with settings similar to those in the image on the left.

With smooth light curves and Wax Modifier on, the whole thing looks more like the image on the right—a subtle difference, but a difference after all.

I hope you will start creating your own custom materials. Keep in mind that I have only scratched the surface. With powerful options such as LightCaps, which you can also combine in multishaders, you can go crazy lighting and shading your very own ZBrush world.

The materials setup in this tutorial is available on the DVD in the Julian Kenning Asset folder. The materials are free to use, but if you use them for anything public, please do give proper credit.

Enjoy the power of shading and rendering in ZBrush!

There's More

Julian was kind enough to create another tip that you can find on the DVD in the Julian Kenning Asset folder. Take a look at his tip on Creating Holes and Tears to Reveal a Continuous Structure.

COMING FROM *a background as a traditional painter, I slipped into the gaming industry over 10 years ago. In the PC game mod scene of the late '90s I started texturing as sort of a hobby, which eventually turned into a first job as a texture artist. From there, it naturally evolved into complete character modeling and texturing, and finally into art direction. While being familiar with the rather technological aspects of digital art, I'm still a painter at the core, and ZBrush gave me back the direct and intuitive artist's approach to creation that I was missing in most other applications I worked with.*

www.juliankenning.com

APPENDIX

About the Companion DVD

- What you'll find on the DVD
- System requirements
- Using the DVD
- Troubleshooting

This appendix summarizes the content you'll find on the DVD. If you need help with copying the items provided on the DVD, refer to the installation instructions in the "Using the DVD" section of this appendix.

What You'll Find on the DVD

The following sections are arranged by category and provide a summary of the content you'll find on the DVD. If you need help with installing the items provided on the DVD, refer to the installation instructions in the "Using the DVD" section of this appendix.

Chapter Files

In the Chapters directory you will find all the sample files for completing the tutorials and understanding concepts in this book.

Some of the chapters have accompanying video files, which are stored in a Movies folder of the corresponding chapter. The movies show how I use some of the techniques throughout the book.

Some of the Artist Spotlight features have corresponding videos, or they cover techniques that require support files. You can find the files in a folder with the artist's name inside the chapter folder where the feature appears.

Please check the book's website at www.sybex.com/go/zbrushtipsandtechniques, where we'll post additional content and updates that supplement this book, should the need arise.

System Requirements

This DVD does not include the ZBrush software. You will need to have ZBrush 4R2b installed on your computer to complete the exercises in the book.

To complete the core exercises of this book, you need ZBrush version 4R2b or higher.

Hardware requirements are a PC or Mac running ZBrush with a gigabyte or more of RAM. The more RAM you have the better results you can get with ZBrush.

Make sure that your computer meets the minimum system requirements shown in the following list. If your computer doesn't match up to most of these requirements, you may have problems using the files on the companion DVD.

- A PC running Microsoft Windows XP, Windows Vista, or Windows 7 or an Intel based Macintosh running OSX 10.5 or higher. The files on the DVD should be compatible with either operating system. The book was created using ZBrush 4R2b on an Apple Macintosh.
  - Your computer's processor should be a fast, Pentium 4 or newer (or equivalent such as AMD) with optional multithreading or hyperthreading capabilities. ZBrush requires at least a Pentium 3 processor.
  - 2048 MB of RAM (4096 MB for working with multi-million-poly meshes)
  - Monitor: 1280 × 1024 monitor resolution or higher (32 bits)
- A Mac running Mac OSX 10.5 or newer
  - 1024 MB of RAM (2048 MB recommended for working with multi-million-polys)
  - Monitor: 1024 × 768 monitor resolution set to millions of colors (recommended: 1280 × 1024 or higher)
- An Internet connection
- A DVD-ROM drive
- Apple QuickTime 7.0 or later (download from www.quicktime.com)

For the most up-to-date information, check www.pixologic.com/zbrush/system.

While it is possible to use a mouse with ZBrush, a Wacom or other digital tablet will enable you to paint and sculpt naturally. It is essential to use some form of Wacom tablet, be it a Cintiq or a standard Intuos with ZBrush.

Using the DVD

For best results, you'll want to copy the files from your DVD to your computer. To copy the items from the DVD to your hard drive, follow these steps:

1. Insert the DVD into your computer's DVD-ROM drive. The license agreement appears.

2. Read through the license agreement, and then click the Accept button if you want to use the DVD.

The DVD interface appears. The interface allows you to access the content with just one or two clicks. Alternately, you can access the files at the root directory of your hard drive.

Windows users: The interface won't launch if Autorun is disabled. In that case, choose Start → Run (for Windows Vista, choose Start → All Programs → Accessories → Run). In the dialog box that appears, type **D:\Start.exe**. (Replace D with the proper letter if your DVD drive uses a different letter. If you don't know the letter, see how your DVD drive is listed under My Computer.) Click OK.

Mac users: The DVD icon will appear on your desktop; double-click the icon to open the DVD, and then navigate to the files you want.

Troubleshooting

Wiley has attempted to provide programs that work on most computers with the minimum system requirements. Alas, your computer may differ, and some programs may not work properly for some reason.

The two likeliest problems are that you don't have enough memory (RAM) for the programs you want to use or that you have other programs running that are affecting the installation or running of a program. If you get an error message such as "Not enough memory" or "Setup cannot continue," try one or more of the following suggestions and then try using the software again:

Turn off any antivirus software running on your computer. Installation programs sometimes mimic virus activity and may make your computer incorrectly believe that it's being infected by a virus.

Close all running programs. The more programs you have running, the less memory is available to other programs. Installation programs typically update files and programs; so if you keep other programs running, installation may not work properly.

Add more RAM to your computer. This is, admittedly, a drastic and somewhat expensive step. However, adding more memory can really help the speed of your computer and allow more programs to run at the same time.

Customer Care

If you have trouble with the book's companion DVD, please call the Wiley Product Technical Support phone number at (800) 762-2974. Outside the United States, call +1 (317) 572-3994. You can also contact Wiley Product Technical Support at http://sybex.custhelp.com. John Wiley & Sons will provide technical support only for installation and other general quality control items. For technical support on the applications themselves, consult the program's vendor or author.

To place additional orders or to request information about other Wiley products, please call (877) 762-2974.

Index

Wiley Publishing, Inc. End-User License Agreement

READ THIS. You should carefully read these terms and conditions before opening the software packet(s) included with this book "Book". This is a license agreement "Agreement" between you and Wiley Publishing, Inc. "WPI". By opening the accompanying software packet(s), you acknowledge that you have read and accept the following terms and conditions. If you do not agree and do not want to be bound by such terms and conditions, promptly return the Book and the unopened software packet(s) to the place you obtained them for a full refund.

1. License Grant. WPI grants to you (either an individual or entity) a nonexclusive license to use one copy of the enclosed software program(s) (collectively, the "Software," solely for your own personal or business purposes on a single computer (whether a standard computer or a workstation component of a multi-user network). The Software is in use on a computer when it is loaded into temporary memory (RAM) or installed into permanent memory (hard disk, CD-ROM, or other storage device). WPI reserves all rights not expressly granted herein.

2. Ownership. WPI is the owner of all right, title, and interest, including copyright, in and to the compilation of the Software recorded on the physical packet included with this Book "Software Media". Copyright to the individual programs recorded on the Software Media is owned by the author or other authorized copyright owner of each program. Ownership of the Software and all proprietary rights relating thereto remain with WPI and its licensers.

3. Restrictions On Use and Transfer. (a) You may only (i) make one copy of the Software for backup or archival purposes, or (ii) transfer the Software to a single hard disk, provided that you keep the original for backup or archival purposes. You may not (i) rent or lease the Software, (ii) copy or reproduce the Software through a LAN or other network system or through any computer subscriber system or bulletin-board system, or (iii) modify, adapt, or create derivative works based on the Software. (b) You may not reverse engineer, decompile, or disassemble the Software. You may transfer the Software and user documentation on a permanent basis, provided that the transferee agrees to accept the terms and conditions of this Agreement and you retain no copies. If the Software is an update or has been updated, any transfer must include the most recent update and all prior versions.

4. Restrictions on Use of Individual Programs. You must follow the individual requirements and restrictions detailed for each individual program in the About the CD-ROM appendix of this Book or on the Software Media. These limitations are also contained in the individual license agreements recorded on the Software Media. These limitations may include a requirement that after using the program for a specified period of time, the user must pay a registration fee or discontinue use. By opening the Software packet(s), you will be agreeing to abide by the licenses and restrictions for these individual programs that are detailed in the About the CD-ROM appendix and/or on the Software Media. None of the material on this Software Media or listed in this Book may ever be redistributed, in original or modified form, for commercial purposes.

5. Limited Warranty. (a) WPI warrants that the Software and Software Media are free from defects in materials and workmanship under normal use for a period of sixty (60) days from the date of purchase of this Book. If WPI receives notification within the warranty period of defects in materials or workmanship, WPI will replace the defective Software Media. (b) WPI AND THE AUTHOR(S) OF THE BOOK DISCLAIM ALL OTHER WARRANTIES, EXPRESS OR IMPLIED, INCLUDING WITHOUT LIMITATION IMPLIED WARRANTIES OF MERCHANTABILITY AND FITNESS FOR A PARTICULAR PURPOSE, WITH RESPECT TO THE SOFTWARE, THE PROGRAMS, THE SOURCE CODE CONTAINED THEREIN, AND/OR THE TECHNIQUES DESCRIBED IN THIS BOOK. WPI DOES NOT WARRANT THAT THE FUNCTIONS CONTAINED IN THE SOFTWARE WILL MEET YOUR REQUIREMENTS OR THAT THE OPERATION OF THE SOFTWARE WILL BE ERROR FREE. (c) This limited warranty gives you specific legal rights, and you may have other rights that vary from jurisdiction to jurisdiction.

6. Remedies. (a) WPI's entire liability and your exclusive remedy for defects in materials and workmanship shall be limited to replacement of the Software Media, which may be returned to WPI with a copy of your receipt at the following address: Software Media Fulfillment Department, Attn.: *ZBrush Professional Tips and Techniques*, Wiley Publishing, Inc., 10475 Crosspoint Blvd., Indianapolis, IN 46256, or call 1-800-762-2974. Please allow four to six weeks for delivery. This Limited Warranty is void if failure of the Software Media has resulted from accident, abuse, or misapplication. Any replacement Software Media will be warranted for the remainder of the original warranty period or thirty (30) days, whichever is longer. (b) In no event shall WPI or the author be liable for any damages whatsoever (including without limitation damages for loss of business profits, business interruption, loss of business information, or any other pecuniary loss) arising from the use of or inability to use the Book or the Software, even if WPI has been advised of the possibility of such damages. (c) Because some jurisdictions do not allow the exclusion or limitation of liability for consequential or incidental damages, the above limitation or exclusion may not apply to you.

7. U.S. Government Restricted Rights. Use, duplication, or disclosure of the Software for or on behalf of the United States of America, its agencies and/or instrumentalities "U.S. Government" is subject to restrictions as stated in paragraph (c)(1)(ii) of the Rights in Technical Data and Computer Software clause of DFARS 252.227-7013, or subparagraphs (c) (1) and (2) of the Commercial Computer Software - Restricted Rights clause at FAR 52.227-19, and in similar clauses in the NASA FAR supplement, as applicable.

8. General. This Agreement constitutes the entire understanding of the parties and revokes and supersedes all prior agreements, oral or written, between them and may not be modified or amended except in a writing signed by both parties hereto that specifically refers to this Agreement. This Agreement shall take precedence over any other documents that may be in conflict herewith. If any one or more provisions contained in this Agreement are held by any court or tribunal to be invalid, illegal, or otherwise unenforceable, each and every other provision shall remain in full force and effect.